CAMBRIDGE TEXTBOOKS IN LINGUISTICS

MOOD AND MODALITY

MOOD AND MODALITY

F. R. PALMER

DEPARTMENT OF LINGUISTIC SCIENCE
UNIVERSITY OF READING

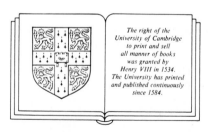

The right of the
University of Cambridge
to print and sell
all manner of books
was granted by
Henry VIII in 1534.
The University has printed
and published continuously
since 1584.

CAMBRIDGE UNIVERSITY PRESS

CAMBRIDGE

NEW YORK   NEW ROCHELLE

MELBOURNE   SYDNEY

Published by the Press Syndicate of the University of Cambridge
The Pitt Building, Trumpington Street, Cambridge CB2 1RP
32 East 57th Street, New York, NY 10022, USA
10 Stamford Road, Oakleigh, Melbourne 3166, Australia

First published 1986
Reprinted 1988

Printed in Great Britain at The Bath Press, Avon

British Library cataloguing in publication data

Palmer, F. R.
Mood and modality. –
(Cambridge textbooks in linguistics)
1. English language – Auxiliary verbs
2. English language – Modality
I. Title
425   PE1315.A8

Library of Congress cataloguing in publication data

Palmer, F. R. (Frank Robert)
Mood and modality.
(Cambridge textbooks in linguistics)
Bibliography
Includes index.
1. Modality (Linguistics)
2. Grammar, Comparative and general – Mood.
I. Title. II. Series
P299.M6P35 1986   415   86-9530

ISBN 0 521 26516 9 hard covers
ISBN 0 521 31930 7 paperback

To
RICHARD
and
CLAIRE

CONTENTS

Contents

Contents

NOTATION

In addition to the usual conventions for the use of italic, quotation marks and asterisks, the following notation is used.

In the text:

Initial Capitals	typological categories
SMALL CAPITALS	verbs, including modals
'single quotation marks'	terms used by authors quoted in the text

In the inset examples:

italic	relevant words in the language material not indicated by the gloss
SMALL CAPITALS	grammatical categories and source language material in the glosses
- hyphen	morphemic boundary in the language material and corresponding division in the gloss
+ plus sign	combined categories in the gloss represented by a single element in the language material

The transcriptions, and to a large extent the glosses and translations, are those of the original authors. Glosses are not usually provided here if they are not given in the original text. Where glosses have been added here, only directly relevant grammatical categories are indicated.

Readers will be familiar with most of the abbreviations used in the glosses. It is generally the case that abbreviations used are those of the original authors (with minor changes for consistency), and these are either explained or are easily deduced from the text.

GREEK AND LATIN WORKS CITED IN THE TEXT

Where no title is given the author wrote only one work or all his works are collected under one title.

Greek

Aeschylus	*Prometheus Vinctus*
Aristophanes	*Aves*
	Plutus
Demosthenes	
Euripides	*Alcestis*
	Hecuba
	Hippolytus
Herodotus	
Homer	*Iliad*
	Odyssey
Plato	*Apologia*
	Leges
	Mercator
	Phaedo
	Respublica
Sophocles	*Ajax*
	Antigone
	Philoctetes
Thucydides	
Xenophon	*Anabasis*
	Institutio Cyri
	Symposium

Latin

Caesar	*de Bello Gallico*
Cato	*de Agri Cultura*
Catullus	
Cicero	*de Lege Agraria*
	Epistulae ad Atticum
	Brutus
	in Catilinam
	de Finibus Bonorum et Malorum
	pro Milone
	pro Murena
	de Deorum Natura
	Philippicae
	pro S, Roscio Amerino
	pro Sestio
	Sermones
	Tusculanae Disputationes
	in Verrem
Horace	*Sermones*
Livy	
Ovid	*Metamorphoses*
Plautus	*Aulularia*
	Bacchides
	Miles Gloriosus
	Mostellaria
	Persa
	Trinummus
Sallust	*Catilina*
	Jugurtha
Tacitus	*Historiae*
Terence	*Andria*
	Eunuchus
	Hecyra
Virgil	*Aeneid*

I
Introduction

1.1 Modality and typology

There are two basic assumptions in this work. The first is that it is possible to recognize a grammatical category, that of modality, which is similar to aspect, tense, number, gender, etc. The second is that this category can be identified, described and compared across a number of different and unrelated languages; it is this that characterizes typology.

1.1.1 Modality

A brief glance at two well-known languages, Latin and English, is sufficient to suggest that the first assumption can be justified. Latin has its system of mood: indicative, subjunctive and imperative; while English has a system of modal verbs: WILL, CAN, MAY, MUST, etc. (see Palmer 1979b). Moreover, there is some translational equivalence between the Latin subjunctive and these verbs of English:

> Ut illum di ... perduint!   (Pl. *Aul.* 785)
> that him gods destroy+3PL+PRES+SUBJ
> 'May the gods destroy him!'

> At tu   dictis,   Albane, maneres   (Virg. *Aen.* 8. 643)
> but thou to words Alban   remain+2SG+IMPERF+SUBJ
> 'But thou, Alban, shouldst have kept thy word'

Classical Greek has an optative, as well as a subjunctive, mood. This, too, may often be translated into English with a modal verb:

> taút' eípois   Akhiléːi   (Hom. *Il.* 11. 791)
> these say+2SG+AOR+OPT to Achilles
> 'You might tell Achilles'

What is less obvious is the characterization of the semantic function of modality. Tense can be defined as the grammatical category related to time, number as the category related to enumeration. There are some problems in the precise definition of aspect (see Comrie 1976), and gender is often extended to include more than sex; but, in practice, there is no difficulty in deciding what should be treated as examples of such categories. The notion of modality, however, is much more vague and leaves open a number of possible definitions, though something along the lines of Lyons' (1977:452) 'opinion or attitude' of the speaker seems promising.

It is generally unwise in linguistic studies to confine oneself to the characteristics of familiar languages. It would be especially wrong to do so in a work such as this. There is, then, good reason to include in the discussion rather different systems, such as the system of five 'modes' that Hockett (1958: 237–8) presents for Menomini (Algonquian, USA):

> pi·w   he comes, is coming, came
> pi·wen   he is said to be coming, it is said that he came
> pi·ʔ   is he coming, did he come?
> piasah   so he *is* coming after all! (despite our expectations to the contrary!)
> piapah   but he was going to come! (and now it turns out that he is not!)

None of the translations suggests modality in exactly the same sense as it seems to be applicable to Latin or English, but the speaker's 'attitudes and opinions' are involved, and there are good grounds here for arguing that, in many languages, there is a mood or modal feature to indicate 'hearsay' or what is reported, and that often questions too belong, as here, to the modal system (see 2.1.1, 2.3.3, 2.5).

There is one further point. The modal system of most familiar languages, whether it is mood in Latin and Greek or modal verbs in English, is formally associated, along with tense, aspect and voice, with the verbal system of the language (and even gender, number and person are marked on the verb). But modality, as will be seen, does not relate semantically to the verb alone or primarily, but to the whole sentence. Not surprisingly, therefore, there are languages in which modality is marked elsewhere than on the verb or within a verbal complex (see 1.5.3).

1.1.2 *Typology*

The typological study of any grammatical category involves two basic steps: first, the identification of some grammatical categories in different languages; and secondly, the identification of these categories as being the same across languages. But the nature of the identification in each step is quite different. In the individual languages the category is identified and defined in terms of the formal characteristics of each of those languages and so is, by definition, language-specific. But the identification across languages (and, in consequence, the use of common terminology) rests upon shared semantic characteristics. It is this that will lead to what Thrane (1983: 155) calls '(cross-linguistic) equivalence classes'. It must be assumed that there will be at least partial correspondence in terms of meaning between one system and another, and that there will, therefore, be some translational equivalence. (The terms 'meaning' and 'semantics' are here used in a wide sense, for much of modal meaning is included in what is sometimes distinguished as 'pragmatics'.)

The ultimate definition of a typological category is, then, in terms of meaning, though it may not always be possible to give a precise definition. Yet in some cases, although there appears to be considerable variation and no one-to-one correspondence across languages, it may be that there is some very basic or 'prototypical' (Hopper and Thompson 1984: 707) feature that is, in essence, the same for all languages, e.g. that of visible or tangible entities for nouns. (But this may be difficult or impossible for modality – see 1.1.3.)

This is not an appropriate place to discuss in detail the arguments for the theoretical status of typological studies, still less for a debate about universality; both issues are well presented by Comrie (1981; see also the subsequent discussion in Smith 1981; Comrie 1983; Smith 1983). But as a general rationale, it may be said that it seems reasonable to assume that the basic functions of language are very similar in different societies, though with different linguistic conventions, in all parts of the world, because all people have similar needs, similar relationships, and, in general, share the same world (cf. Robins 1952). There is, indeed, evidence that different languages have a great deal in common. The contrary view was, of course, presented by Sapir (1929 [1949: 160]) and Whorf (1940) [1956: 207–19]), who argued that language determines the nature of each society's 'world' and that language differences, therefore, imply different 'worlds'. But although this may be true to a small degree, the fact that we can learn languages other than our own and can translate from one language to another with a fair degree of accuracy suggests that different languages have much in common, that we can identify meanings across languages, and that we can properly ask how different languages deal with roughly the same phenomena.

1.1.3 Grammaticalization

Another way of looking at the issue is in terms of grammaticalization, i.e. with the idea that semantic features that are common to many languages may be captured or signalled by the grammatical forms and systems of individual languages (and, indeed, may be captured in some languages but not others).

The first task is to identify the relevant area of meaning; this is not easy in the case of modality. Ideas that have been put forward include such notions as attitudes and opinions, speech acts, subjectivity, non-factivity, non-assertion, possibility and necessity. ('Non-factuality', however, is to be preferred to 'non-factivity' – see 1.3.3.) These are not mutually exclusive: attitudes and opinions can be associated with non-factuality or non-assertion – the idea that we are concerned with sentences that are not used to make statements of fact. But this must also be associated with subjectivity, involving the speaker (1.3.2). There are, however, problems at several levels of description, both with individual languages and typologically.

To begin with, the definitions are, in practice, vague and difficult to apply with any degree of precision, and do not lead to clearly distinct categories. The real problem with modality, moreover, is not just that there is great variation in meaning across languages, but that there is no clear basic feature. The notion of 'prototypicality' is difficult, if not impossible, to apply.

Where precise criteria are given, moreover, the precision may be more apparent than real, and may involve special pleading or a degree of circularity. Thus both Hooper (1975) and Klein (1975) claim that in Spanish the indicative signals assertion and the subjunctive signals non-assertion. Yet the data provided show only that, in certain syntactic structures only, the choice of the indicative or subjunctive depends upon the degree of commitment by the speaker to the truth of what is being said. That is a very different matter from the contrast between assertion and non-assertion and the incidence of the relevant structures is fairly arbitrary, as is shown by the fact that Spanish does not use the subjunctive in direct questions, though they are obviously non-assertive. Where a choice of mood is possible, it is, indeed, reasonable to argue in terms of degree of commitment as in:

> Tal vez venga   mañana
> such time come+3SG+PRES+SUBJ tomorrow
>
> Tal vez vendrá   mañana
> such time come+3SG+FUT+INDIC tomorrow
>
> 'Perhaps he'll come tomorrow'

But to say that one is non-assertive and the other assertive at best is an over-simplification, at worst involves circularity. (See 2.2.5, 4.2.4.)

Secondly, even at the formal grammatical level, grammaticalization is a matter of degree, of 'more or less' rather than 'yes or no'. Inflectional mood is a very clear example of grammatical marking, but the markers of modality may be modal verbs, clitics or particles (see 1.5). Whether these are grammatical or not can only be decided in terms of the degree to which they have syntactic restrictions and the extent to which they can be defined as a limited rather than open-ended system of items. It is by no means clear whether the 'modal' particles of German form a grammatical system (see 1.5.4). Similarly, the 'modal' verbs of French are far less easily distinguished from other verbs than are the modal verbs of English, whose grammatical status is not seriously in doubt (see 1.5.1). This situation is only to be expected if it is assumed that a modal system (or any other grammatical system) will develop gradually over time, and at any one point in time will have reached a particular stage of development and so show a particular degree of grammaticalization. A good example of this is the creation of the modal verbs in English, which involved the gradual recategorization of what were previously main verbs, as portrayed by Plank (1984), who specifically rejects the opposing 'catastrophic' (and 'yes or no') view of the recategorization as presented by Lightfoot (1979).

Thirdly, and as a corollary of the second point, there is a fair degree of arbitrariness in the choice of grammatical form, in the sense that it is not always directly determined by meaning. This is a very familiar point that has been illustrated by the English plural *oats* compared with the singular *wheat*, or the fact that *Mädchen* and *Fräulein* in German, both words used to refer to young women, are neuter in grammatical gender (see Palmer 1984: 34–7). It seems likely that, in general terms, the more clearly grammaticalized a category is, the greater is the degree of arbitrariness.

Fourthly, and again as a corollary of the previous point, even with the more easily definable categories such as tense and number there is a very considerable difference in the extent of grammaticalization in different languages. There are even some languages that do not grammaticalize these familiar categories at all. Some languages have a fairly complex system of number, while others have no grammatical system at all, and the same is true of tense. That is not to say, of course, that such languages have no way of indicating enumeration or time, it is simply that they do not do so within a grammatical system. In a similar way, many of the features associated with modality may not be marked grammatically. It is reasonable, for instance, to include hoping and fearing among such features, but they are marked lexically rather than grammatically in English:

> I hope John has gone
> I am afraid that John will get hurt

The insistence upon grammaticalization, then, means that purely lexical means of expressing modality will not be considered. Yet there are two reasons why lexical items cannot be wholly ignored. First, many of them exhibit a close semantic relationship with modal grammatical forms and alternate with them in a comparative analysis of different languages, or even within the same language (e.g. English *I wish* ..., and *Would that* ...). Secondly, lexical forms are used by the speaker to report modal expressions being used by another, and the use of modal forms in subordinate clauses (which is an essential part of a study of modality – see Chapter 4) depends to some degree on the choice of the lexical items in the main clause. A classic example of this is to be found in the difference between the Latin verbs IUBEO and IMPERO, both meaning 'order'; the first takes the infinitive, the second the subjunctive:

> Eum venire iubet
> him come+PRES+INF he orders
>
> Ei ut veniat imperat
> to him that come+3SG+PRES+SUBJ he orders
>
> He orders him to come

For similar reasons, intonation and other prosodic features must also be excluded even though they often mark what can clearly be regarded as modality in a purely semantic sense. Indeed, doubt and lack of commitment are often expressed by intonation in English (see Coates 1983: 134). Comparisons have been made between intonational and other systems, e.g. Schubiger's (1965) comparison of the German modal particles with English intonation (but see 1.5.3 for the status of these particles). Intonation is a separate study and only rarely interacts in a systematic way with grammatical systems of modality (*pace* Coates 1980: 340–1, 1983: 237; Palmer 1983b: 289); as with lexis, however, it will occasionally be mentioned where it closely parallels grammatically expressed modality.

It follows from all that has been said that it will often be very difficult to decide what to include and what to exclude from a grammatical study of modality. Both semantic considerations and judgments about grammaticality may have to be made simultaneously. For the French 'modal' verbs, for instance, the semantics are clearly relevant; but at the same time there are a few formal criteria to indicate that they have a grammatical status (see 1.5.1). However, some degree of arbitrariness in the choice of items is inevitable.

The insistence upon grammaticalization relates, by definition, to the fact that this is a grammatical study. But it is particularly important with a category for which all semantic definitions seem very vague. By looking for some formal grammatical criteria, it is possible for the investigator to look to the languages themselves, so to speak, and see what is systematized and organized within their grammatical systems.

There is one final terminological point. The terms 'mood' and 'modality' have both been used. It might seem *prima facie* to be very desirable to make a clear distinction between the two terms, exactly parallelling the distinction between tense and time, number and enumeration, gender and sex, the one being grammatical, the other notional or semantic; but there are problems, best discussed when other proposals have been considered (see 1.3.6).

1.1.4 *Differences of system*

It is probable that there are very few languages that do not have some kind of grammatical system of modality, but the systems differ in at least three ways. First, different languages grammaticalize different parts of the overall semantic system: for instance, many languages grammaticalize 'report' or 'hearsay' to indicate that what is said has been told to the speaker (who is, therefore, not committed to its truth). This can be handled in terms of the modal feature Quotative, which is a feature that is not grammaticalized in English. Secondly, they may organize the semantic field in different ways, into different patterns and systems: the complex patterns of Ngiyambaa, for instance (1.5.4), are quite unlike anything found in European languages. Thirdly, they use different grammatical devices: an obvious set of examples is that of mood in Latin and the modal verbs of English. Most of these points are made succinctly by Steele *et al.* (1981: 21): 'the hypothesis is that there is some semantic field which is defined by the notions of possibility, probability, etc. Languages appear to be able to divide up the field in various ways; they are also not obliged to exhaust it.' However, as will be seen in the next section, 'the notions of possibility, probability, etc.' is not a sufficient definition of the relevant semantic field.

There is one corollary. It is often fairly simple to establish that a grammatical system is modal because it is largely concerned with modality in the general sense proposed here. Within that system, however, there may be forms whose meanings seem to be only marginally modal or hardly modal at all. Yet this is both helpful and interesting, for it indicates areas of meaning that are clearly handled by such languages within an overall system of modality, and can justifiably be used both to establish doubtful

7

cases as modal and to include categories that might otherwise not have been considered. For instance, it can be argued that WILL and SHALL in English are markers of modality rather than tense (see 6.2.3), because they are members of a clearly defined system of modal verbs. Similarly, the justification for discussing questions (Interrogatives) and Quotatives lies in the fact that, in a variety of languages, they appear in a grammatically defined system that is clearly modal overall (see 1.4.4, 2.5, 2.1.1, 2.3.3).

There are, however, problems. Sometimes a formal system contains some members that are clearly to be recognized as modal but others that appear to belong to a system of tense or aspect or both. In such cases it is better to deal with them in terms of mixed systems rather than to attempt to argue that they belong to one only. There is, moreover, a danger of using misleading labels – the 'modal' auxiliaries of Gujerati (Indo-Iranian, India), as presented by Cardona (1965: 118ff), include not only 'is necessary' and 'be able', but also 'go', 'come', 'remain', 'give', 'begin', 'place', 'fall', 'miss', 'throw off', all of which seem to have functions that are aspectual.

1.1.5   The data

This is not primarily a theoretical work, except in the sense that it aims to provide a framework within which modality will be discussed. Its main aim is to present, within such a framework, as systematic a statement as possible about what is actually to be found in the languages of the world.

Unfortunately, the language material available is, on the whole, of less than desirable quality and quantity. This results from three main causes:

(i)   Many of the grammars are written in fairly traditional terms and present modal systems that look very similar to those of familiar languages, so that there is a strong suspicion that the traditional categories have merely been imposed upon the language. It is not of much help in a typological study of modality to be presented with examples of the 'subjunctive' or the 'optative' with little further detail beyond a translation.

(ii) Many theoretically oriented studies have little to say about modality because the topic is not central to the theory, and especially because modality cannot be clearly analysed without a detailed statement in terms of meaning. Very little information is to be gleaned from most TG-based works, or even, disappointingly, from the huge amount of material that has been written within a tagmemic framework.

(iii) There is always a danger that the interpretation is highly subjective, so that we are presented more with the views of the investigator than with facts about the language. A good example is that of Hidatsa discussed in 2.6.1.

There is, however, no alternative to accepting the material, or at least most of it, at its face value. Occasionally it is possible to reinterpret it or to ignore what seems highly dubious, but in general we can only accept what we find.

There are some works, however, that provide a good deal of detail, and in recent years there have appeared some articles which describe facets of modality in a particular language very thoroughly. Because of this, some languages may seem to be quoted too frequently, while others are neglected (there is, inevitably, a great deal from the European Classical languages, Latin and Greek). That is not to be taken as evidence that modality is more grammaticalized in such languages, but only as an indication that they have been better described for our purposes.

Inevitably, there are enormous differences in the presentation of the data by different scholars. The terminology varies greatly: e.g. 'report'/ 'hearsay'/'quotative', or 'uncertain'/'indefinite'/'conjective'/'speculative'/ 'possibility' for categories which are semantically very much the same. The transcriptions, too, are often highly idiosyncratic. It would be impossible to standardize either of these with any regularity. In the presentation of the data the author's terminology and transcriptions will be unaltered, but in the typological discussion sets of terms will be used consistently – e.g. Quotative and Speculative for the two types illustrated above. In the text these will be indicated by an initial capital letter, while author's terms will appear (in the text only) with no capitals and within quotation marks (for further details see 1.4.1).

1.2 Some earlier proposals

It may be useful to look briefly at some of the proposals that have been made by earlier scholars.

1.2.1 *Jespersen*

A good starting point is Jespersen's discussion of mood. He says of the indicative, subjunctive and imperative moods:

> they express certain attitudes of mind of the speaker towards
> the contents of the sentence, though in some cases the choice
> of mood is determined not by the attitude of the actual
> speaker, but by the character of the clause itself and its
> relation to the main nexus on which it is dependent. Further,
> it is very important that we speak of 'mood' only if the attitude

9

of mind is shown in the form of the verb: mood thus is a syntactic, not a notional category (Jespersen 1924: 313)

He also offers (1924: 320–1) a list of suggested sub-categories divided into two sets:

1. Containing an element of will

Jussive	go (command)
Compulsive	he has to go
Obligative	he ought to go/we should go
Advisory	you should go
Precative	go, please
Hortative	let us go
Permissive	you may go, if you like
Promissive	I will go/it shall be done
Optative (realizable)	may he still be alive
Desiderative (unrealizable)	would he were still alive
Intentional	in order that he may go

2. Containing no element of will

Apodictive	twice two must be (is necessarily) four
Necessitative	he must be rich (or he could not spend so much)
Assertive	he is rich
Presumptive	he is probably rich/he would (will) know
Dubitative	he may be (is perhaps) rich
Potential	he can speak
Conditional	if he is rich
Hypothetical	if he were rich
Concessional	though he is rich

(But he says that the placing of the 'conditional' and 'concessive' is 'subject to doubt' and suggests that 'subordinate' should, perhaps, be added.)

Jespersen's proposals contain little of theoretical significance except for his recognition of two types, which is of great importance (see 1.3.4). Their merit is that they are based upon what he considered to be the features to be found in language (or at least in English); but they are purely notional, and both his choice of the sub-categories and his criteria for them may be seriously questioned.

1.2.2 *von Wright*

In a pioneering work on modal logic von Wright (1951: 1–2) distinguishes four 'modes':

the alethic modes, or modes of truth
the epistemic modes, or modes of knowing
the deontic modes, or modes of obligation
the existential modes, or modes of existence

He sets out the possibilities in a table:

alethic	epistemic	deontic	existential
necessary	verified	obligatory	universal
possible	—	permitted	existing
contingent	undecided	indifferent	—
impossible	falsified	forbidden	empty

The most important distinction here, for our purposes, is that between Epistemic and Deontic modality (which correspond, very roughly, to Jespersen's two types). It will be considered basic to our whole discussion (see 1.3.4) and may be briefly illustrated here in the comparison of the uses of English MAY and MUST in the pairs of sentences:

John may be there by now
You may come in now

John must be there by now
You must come in now

It could be argued that there is alethic modality (necessity) in:

He is a bachelor, so he must be unmarried

But there is no formal grammatical distinction in English, and, perhaps, in no other language either, between alethic and epistemic modality. It should be noted that we might equally say:

He is a bachelor so he *is* unmarried

There is no distinction between the uses of *is* to state what is logically true and what the speaker believes, as a matter of fact, to be true.

Existential modality is, perhaps, expressed by CAN or MAY in:

Lions can be dangerous   (Leech 1969: 223)
... the lamellae may arise de novo from the middle of the cell and migrate to the periphery   (Huddleston 1971: 297–9)

These can be interpreted as 'some lions are dangerous', 'some lamellae migrate . . .' (or in terms of 'sometimes'). But there is no reason to recognize them as examples of another, distinct, type of modality, at least for English, since they can be handled in terms of epistemic modality with the gloss 'It may be that . . .', and the same verbs as for epistemic modality, MAY and CAN, are used.

In a footnote von Wright (1951: 28) also mentions 'dynamic' modality which is concerned with ability and disposition, as in:

John can speak German

Although something similar appears in Jespersen's analysis, it is doubtful whether this should be included within modality at all. It will not merit separate consideration in this book, except for the discussion of its status and relation to other modalities (1.3.2, 3.2.3).

1.2.3 *Rescher*

A more extended system, within a logical framework, is proposed by Rescher (1968: 24–6). His remarks about modalities begin: 'A proposition is presented by a complete, self-contained statement which, taken as a whole, will be true or false: *The cat is on the mat*, for example.' He then continues: 'When such a proposition is itself made subject to some further qualification of such a kind that the entire resulting complex is itself once again a proposition, then this qualification is said to represent a *modality* to which the original proposition is subjected.'

Taken as a definition of modality, this raises serious theoretical problems, and would define modality too widely; but Rescher's list of modalities is of some interest. In addition to 'alethic', 'epistemic' and 'deontic' modalities, he mentions 'temporal' modalities, 'boulomaic' modalities, 'evaluative' modalities and 'causal' modalities. He further argues for three types of 'conditional' modality. Some of these may be of interest to us.

'Temporal' modalities ('It is sometimes/mostly/always, etc., the case that *p*') need not concern us for long. Many philosophers have wished to deal with tense as a modality (see Lyons 1977: 809–23). But most languages distinguish tense from modality and tense is, therefore, best treated as a separate typological category. There is, however, some interchange and overlap and that is something that will have to be discussed (6.1).

'Boulomaic' modalities are glossed: 'It is hoped/feared/regretted/desired (or: X hopes/fears/regrets/desires) that *p*'. Unfortunately, the term 'boulomaic' betrays a sad ignorance of etymology: the etymologically correct form, which is actually found in Modern Greek, would be 'bouletic'. In this book, however, Latin-based terms are generally used for consistency and the appropriate term is Volitive. The only volitive modality that is extensively grammaticalized is that of wishing.

'Evaluative' modalities are glossed 'It is a good/perfectly wonderful/bad thing that *p'*, and 'causal' modalities 'The state of affairs will bring it about/prevent (or merely: will impede) its coming about that *p'*. Neither of these are obvious candidates for modality in language, mainly because they relate to actual states of affairs that 'can be true or false', as Rescher says; but there are some interesting examples of both types that will be considered (3.4.3, 5.2.4).

1.2.4   Searle

The relevance of the theory of speech acts, which derives from Austin (1962), is noted by Lyons (1977: 725) as a general framework for the discussion of mood and modality. The theory is further developed by Searle (1979: 1–29), and the results are summarized in a later work (Searle 1983: 166). He argues that there are five basic categories of illocutionary acts:

assertives:	where we tell our hearers (truly or falsely) how things are
directives:	where we get them to do things
commissives:	where we commit ourselves to doing things
declarations:	where we bring about changes in the world with our utterances
expressives:	where we express our feelings and attitudes

Searle's approach to the problem is different from those already discussed, but it provides a useful semantic framework for the discussion of modality (and it should be noted that Searle refers to the issues in terms of 'meaning'). For speech act theory is concerned with a relation between the speaker and what he says. Some comments, however, are called for.

'Assertives' are described in terms of the speaker's 'belief' or 'commitment', but these 'mark dimensions' so that 'the degree of belief or commitment may approach or even reach zero'. They must be concerned, that is to say, with the whole of epistemic modality, though they also include statements of fact (my Declaratives), which are excluded by Rescher's definition of modality. This is a point of view that must be taken seriously (see 1.3.3, 1.4.2, 2.6).

Directives correspond very largely to deontic modality and are the main topic of Chapter 3. Indeed, what Searle calls 'assertives' and 'directives' are central to any discussion of modality.

Searle has some doubts about the clear distinction between 'directives' and 'commissives' since both are concerned with 'fitting the world to the word' – with making things correspond to what is said; but one clearly gets others to act, one gets the speaker to act. 'Commissives' will be treated here under deontic modality.

'Expressives' are a little more doubtful, but correspond roughly to Rescher's 'evaluatives'. Searle (1979: 15) argues that there are six 'paradigm' verbs in English: THANK, CONGRATULATE, APOLOGISE, CONDOLE, DEPLORE, WELCOME.

The term 'declaration' is a little unfortunate because of its similarity to 'declarative' which belongs with 'assertives'. It relates to what Austin (1962: 32) calls 'explicit performatives', but Searle cannot use 'performative' because, as Austin saw, even assertion is a kind of performative. These are usually indicated in language by a particular formula – *I* with the simple form of the verb:

> I name this ship 'The Queen Elizabeth'
> I declare this meeting closed

They are seldom, if ever, expressed by any distinct grammatical feature (but see 4.7).

1.3   The definition of modality

A number of criteria have been proposed, implicitly or explicitly, for the definition of modality. Many of the ideas to be discussed here are to be found in Lyons (1977). It is for that reason alone that the previous section did not contain a sub-section on Lyons' views.

1.3.1   *Proposition and modality*

Jespersen (1924: 313; see this volume, section 1.2.1) talked about the 'contents of the sentence' and Lyons (1977: 452) about 'the proposition that the sentence expresses', both wishing to distinguish them from the speaker's attitude or opinion. This assumes that a distinction can be made in a sentence between the modal and the propositional elements, between modality and proposition.

The distinction between proposition and modality is very close to that of locutionary act and illocutionary act as proposed by Austin (1962: 98). In the locutionary act we are 'saying something', while in the illocutionary act we are 'doing something' – answering a question, announcing a verdict, giving a warning or making a promise. These ideas are at the basis of speech act theory (see 1.2.4).

The dichotomy is a familiar and traditional one. There are plenty of definitions along the lines of Lewis (1946: 49): 'The proposition is assertable; the contents of the assertion ... can be questioned, denied or merely supposed, and can be entertained in other moods as well.' But 'modality' in this sense, referring to all the non-propositional elements of a sentence, is much wider than in the sense in which it will be used here. It would include such matters as tense and aspect, which can be regarded as distinct grammatical categories, and also, as the quotation from Lewis suggests, question and negation. Fillmore (1968: 23) similarly includes negation, tense, mood and aspect. Yet Interrogative (question) is, indeed, a category that must be discussed within a study of modality (1.4.4, 2.5), and there are some relationships between modality and both tense and negation (6.1, 6.2).

Rescher, too, talks about propositions and argues that where a proposition (which may be true or false) is subject to further qualification, this qualification represents modality. But some of his examples, e.g. 'X believes *p*', 'X hopes that *p*', rather imply that any kind of subordination that involves complement clauses (see Chapter 4) can be regarded as a matter of modality. Now it is reasonable enough, in a study of modality, to consider not only the ways speakers express their attitudes and opinions, but also the ways in which others may report their expressions of them, for example:

> He may be there
> John thought he was there

But there are many other kinds of complement clauses, involving many different lexical items (See 4.1.2), that should be excluded on semantic grounds, for example:

> John liked/tried/condescended to come
> It is fortunate/curious/reasonable that he came

These go well beyond the general notions that are plausibly called modal.

The strategy here, therefore, is to treat grammatical main clause modality, in which speakers express opinions and attitudes, as basic, and consider only those complement clauses that are clearly related to them, and indeed, generally, report such expressions. For this reason, there is little to say about Volitive because wishes are not often expressed grammatically in a main clause. On the other hand, it is essential to find a place for 'X says that ...' (Quotative), although it does not appear among Rescher's examples.

Main clause modality, if it is expressed grammatically, is almost by definition marked by a fairly simple element within the sentence. The presence of a modal marker or the change of one for another does not usually greatly alter the structure of a sentence. As Langacker (1974: 631)

15

says, the auxiliary verbs of English 'typically represent non-objective content' and an auxiliary verb is 'one that does not define a separate clause in surface structure' because its function is to ensure that the objective content 'will not be too deeply embedded'. It is for this reason no doubt that Akmajian, Steele and Wasow (1979) argued for a universal category of AUX, which is not necessarily an auxiliary verb but is nevertheless highly restricted in syntax and associated semantically with modality. Some scholars have argued that auxiliaries should be treated as main verbs taking sentential complements, but this argument ignores their essentially different functions (see Palmer 1979a, 1979b: 178–85), and is contrary to the whole spirit of this book. These considerations apply not only to modal auxiliaries, but to others such as those of aspect (1.1.4).

1.3.2 *Subjectivity*

Although a distinction can be made between subjective and objective modality, the traditional logic has been more concerned with objective modality, which excludes speakers. Modality in language, especially when marked grammatically, seems to be essentially subjective; this has already been shown in the discussion of speech acts, and in reference to the speaker's 'opinion or attitude'. (However, it must be conceded that the quotation from Lyons (1977: 452) which uses these terms refers to the use of adverbs such as *frankly*, *fortunately*, *possibly*, *wisely*, which Lyons says express his opinion or attitude towards 'the proposition that the sentence expresses or the situation that the proposition describes'. But he adds that 'many of them express what we will later discuss under modality' and he also comments (1977: 739) that 'subjectivity is of the greatest importance . . . for the understanding of . . . modality'.) Modality in language is, then, concerned with subjective characteristics of an utterance, and it could even be further argued that subjectivity is an essential criterion for modality. Modality could, that is to say, be defined as the grammaticalization of speakers' (subjective) attitudes and opinions.

Difficulties arise, however, when the English modal verbs are considered. First, some of them are used for what von Wright calls 'dynamic' modality, e.g. CAN for the expression of the subject's ability (1.2.2). This could, of course, simply be excluded on semantic grounds, though it should be remembered that it is included in Jespersen's types (1.2.1).

More serious is the observation that often modals are used where it is not possible to make a clear decision whether they are subjective or not, as in:

You must leave at once

This might indicate either the speaker's insistence or a general (objective) necessity for leaving, or it could well be indeterminate between the two readings. It is in principle not possible to justify the one interpretation rather than the other. Nevertheless, if modality is concerned with the attitudes and opinions of the speaker, subjectivity is clearly basic. Only grammatical systems in which a great deal of subjectivity is involved can therefore be considered modal – and that is a characteristic of the English modal verbs. There is further detailed discussion in 3.2.3.

1.3.3   *Factuality*

Lyons (1977: 794) introduces into the discussion of modality the notion of 'factivity' with its opposite 'non-factivity' (as well as 'contra-factivity' which raises more difficult issues – see 5.4). He uses the terms to talk about 'non-factive utterances' of which examples are (1977: 796):

> He may have gone to Paris
> Perhaps he went to Paris
> It is possible that he went to Paris

He further indicates that these are to be discussed in terms of modality, and notes that they contain a modal verb, a modal adverb and a modal adjective respectively. By contrast, 'straightforward statements of fact' (i.e. categorical assertions) may be described as 'epistemically non-modal', because the speaker then commits himself to the truth of what he asserts. In a similar way Lavandera (1983: 211), with specific reference to the subjunctive in Spanish, distinguishes [+assertive] and [−assertive] utterances, and says that utterances in the subjunctive 'do not refer to states or events whose occurrence is questionable, or just feared, wished, doubted, etc., but to "states of affairs" whose occurrence could easily be denied or affirmed, but is instead left unasserted'.

The use of the term 'factive' and its derivates here is unfortunate for two reasons. First, dictionary definitions relate it to the notion of 'making' rather than of 'fact', and the more natural, or even correct, term is 'factual', together with 'factuality', etc. This is the terminology that will be used here. Secondly, the terms 'factive' and 'non-factive' were used by Kiparsky and Kiparsky (1971: 345) to refer to the status of subordinate clauses in sentences such as:

> John regrets that she is leaving
> John believes that she is leaving

The first is 'factive' in that the speaker is committed to the truth of the proposition, the second 'non-factive' in that he is not so committed. This is again an idiosyncratic use of the terms, but it is different from that of Lyons. It is not concerned with statements of fact, but with presupposition, which is actually contrasted with assertion. Moreover, it will be found that in some languages, e.g. Spanish, 'factives' in the Kiparsky sense are often indicated by the essentially modal subjunctive and not by the form used for 'statements of fact', the indicative (see 4.2.2, 4.2.3).

It would, moreover, be a mistake to confine a study of modality to non-factuality, for there are good reasons for handling factual statements together with opinions and judgments. It can be argued that both are subjective, representing the speaker's point of view. Indeed, they too must be handled with speech acts. As Lyons (1977: 736) says, 'the illocutionary force of a statement is not exhausted by its propositional content: it must be associated with the illocutionary act of assertion'.

Nevertheless, there are problems about the status of utterances used to make factual statements (see 1.4.2, 2.6) and, in particular, whether they belong to the modal systems of languages or not. Often they belong to the same formal system, e.g. the mood systems of indicative, subjunctive and imperative in Latin and other languages. But when Lyons argues that 'straightforward statements of fact are non-modal' (see above), it is easy to understand why. What seems clear, however, is that the study of modality cannot ignore such utterances, and that it is not concerned only with non-factuality but with factuality in the wide sense that includes (positive) factuality, non-factuality and perhaps even contra-factuality.

1.3.4 *Epistemic and deontic*

The distinction that Jespersen draws between his two sets ('containing an element of will' and 'not containing an element of will') is closely parallelled in Lyons' (1977: 452) reference to 'the speaker's opinion or attitude towards the proposition that the sentence expresses or the situation that the proposition describes'. Lyons (in conjunction with other scholars) then recognizes two kinds of modality, using von Wright's terms: 'Epistemic modality which is concerned with matters of knowledge, belief' (1977: 793) or 'opinion rather than fact' (1977: 681–2) and 'Deontic modality which is concerned with the necessity or possibility of acts performed by morally responsible agents' (1977: 823).

Steele *et al.* (1981: 21) implicitly make the same distinction: 'Elements expressing modality will mark any of the following: possibility or the related notion of permission, probability or the related notion of obligation, certainty or the related notion of requirement.' The remarks in Steele *et al.* can be illustrated from English; the following sentences can be interpreted either in terms of possibility, probability, and necessity, or in terms of permission, obligation and requirement (the glosses are rough paraphrases):

> He may come tomorrow
> (Perhaps he will/He is permitted)
>
> The book should be on the shelf
> (It probably is/Its proper place is)
>
> He must be in his office
> (I am certain that he is/He is obliged to be)

There is no doubt that not only the English modals, but also the modal verbs of other languages (e.g. German, Modern Greek – see below), have both epistemic and deontic interpretations, and it would appear from the glosses that in quite different languages both interpretations are available for a single form (see 3.5).

However, although the same forms are used, there are often quite clear formal distinctions between the epistemic and deontic use. In English, for example, the negative form *mustn't* is generally used only deontically, as in:

> He mustn't be in his office

The only way of expressing the negative of epistemic MUST is to use *can't*:

> He can't be in his office

There is, similarly, a distinction in Modern Greek. Here the same verb (BORO) is used in both senses, but in the epistemic sense the 'impersonal' (3rd person singular) form is found, with no agreement with the subject, while in the deontic and dynamic senses fully inflected forms, with agreement, are used:

> ta peðjá borí   na
> the children BORO+3SG+PRES+IMPERFECTIVE that
>   fíɣun   ávrio
>   leave+3PL+PRES+PERFECTIVE tomorrow
> 'The children may leave tomorrow'
>
> ta peðjá borún   na
> the children BORO+3PL+PRES+IMPERFECTIVE that

fíɣun   ávrio
leave+3PL+PRES+PERFECTIVE tomorrow
'The children can leave tomorrow'

(Further details and a discussion of German and French are found in 1.5.1; see also 2.2.1 and 2.3.1.)

It is not immediately obvious why two such different notions should be handled in many languages with the same devices. The remarks in Steele *et al.* (1981) about 'related notions' begs the question. In what sense is probability, for instance, 'related to' obligation? Yet the distinction between epistemic and deontic modality is essentially part of the wider distinction between the use of language to inform and the use of language to act, between language as a 'mode of action' and language as a 'countersign of thought' (Malinowski (1923 [1949: 300–1]). There will be a detailed discussion of this problem when a full exposition of both epistemic and deontic modality has been given (3.5).

1.3.5 *Possibility and necessity*

Where epistemic and deontic modality are so clearly linked, the link depends upon possibility and necessity, which are, as Lyons (1977: 787) says, 'the central notions of traditional modal logic'. These are logically related in terms of negation, and this accounts for the fact that *can't* as an expression of negative possibility appears to function as the negative of epistemic *must* (see above and 2.2.1; also Palmer 1979b: 53, 64–5).

Yet it is probable that the epistemic/deontic *cum* possibility/necessity systems of modality are by no means universal, and it may be argued that the logicians' preoccupation with them is a reflection of the linguistic systems of only some of the languages of the world, especially those of Europe. For there are other languages in which the speaker may indicate the strength of his commitment to what he is saying, not in terms of possibility and necessity but in terms of what kind of evidence he has. There is a detailed discussion of such Evidential systems in 2.3. It is worth noting here, however, that even European languages may use these modal markers as evidentials. German, for instance, uses the modal verbs SOLLEN and WOLLEN to express what everyone says and what the subject of the sentence says or claims, respectively (Hammer 1983: 231, 232):

Der Geschäftsführer sollte   schon   nach Hause
the manager   SOLLEN+3SG+PAST already to   house
gegangen sein
gone   to be
'The manager was said to have gone home already'

Er wollte   mich nicht erkennen
he WOLLEN+3SG+PAST me   not   to recognize
'He pretended not to recognize me'

This is not a matter of judgment, still less of possibility and necessity, but relates to the commitment of the speaker to the truth of what he is saying. He indicates that his responsibility is limited by the fact that some one else said it. With the evidential systems mentioned above, such matters as the kind of observation (visual or non-visual) are also included. It would be foolish to deny the name of 'epistemic' to such features, for not only are they clearly concerned with speakers' knowledge and belief, though a little more indirectly, but also they often occur in the same formal system as Judgments.

1.3.6   Mood and modality

It was suggested in 1.1.3 that it might be useful to draw a clear distinction between 'mood' and 'modality'. In languages such as Latin and many modern European languages, with their indicative and subjunctive moods, the distinction can indeed be handled in terms of the formal features versus the typologically relevant semantic categories of which they are the exponents. The distinction between mood and modality is then similar to that between tense and time, gender and sex. There are, however, some problems concerning both the terminology and the nature of mood and the way it relates,or is seen to relate, to modality.

First, the term 'mood' is traditionally restricted to a category expressed in verbal morphology. It is formally a morphosyntactic category of the verb like tense and aspect, even though its semantic function relates to the contents of the whole sentence. But traditionally its verbal nature is not in doubt. Jespersen (1924: 373) insists that it is a 'syntactic not a notional category, which is shown in the form of the verb', and dictionary definitions usually refer to verbal inflection. Yet modality is not expressed in all languages within the verbal morphology. It may be expressed by modal verbs (which are at least still within the verbal element of the sentence) or by particles which may well be quite separate from the verb. It is because of the restriction of the term 'mood' to verbal morphology that Lyons can remark (1977: 848) 'mood is a grammatical category that is found in some, but not all, languages'. For it is probably the case that formal markers of modality are found within the grammars of all languages, though not always within the verb. But if 'mood' is restricted in this way and not applied to grammatical systems that are not marked on the verb, there will be no general term for all the grammatical systems that are exponents of (semantic) modality, no term precisely parallel to 'tense', 'number' or 'gender'.

Huddleston (1984: 164) talks of 'an analytic mood system' when auxiliaries, rather than inflection, are the exponents of the grammatical system. This is an attractive solution but will not be adopted here, because the alternative terminology is now well established. But if the term 'mood' is used solely to refer to inflectional categories, it will be necessary to refer to 'modal' systems or 'modal' categories that are no less grammatical, while restricting the term 'modality' to the typological category.

There is a second point that may, in some degree, justify the restricted use of the term 'mood'. It is that the moods of the familiar languages (or the subjunctive at least) have a whole variety of semantic functions, and that the choice between them is determined grammatically more than by modal meanings. This is illustrated in sections 1.5.2, 2.2.4, 3.2.4, 4.1.5 and elsewhere. Of particular relevance is the fact that, as Jespersen noted (1924: 314), one of the functions of the subjunctive is that of being 'subordinate', in that it is typically the mood used in subordinate sentences. It is no coincidence that the term 'subjunctive' is a translation of the Greek *hypotaktikē* which means 'subordinate'. Thus, in indirect commands (reported commands) the subjunctive is used:

> His   uti conquirerent   et
> to them that search+3PL+IMPERF+SUBJ and
> reducerent ...   imperavit   (Caes. *B.G.*1.28)
> bring back+3PL+IMPERF+SUBJ he ordered
> 'He ordered them to search and bring back'

For a direct command the imperative would be used (though a negative command is also expressed by the subjunctive).

What all of this shows is the extent to which mood has become grammaticalized and fairly removed from the semantics (though the same is largely true of gender in modern European languages). The subjunctive, in particular, is little more than a generalized marker of modality.

A third problem with analysis in terms of traditional moods is that these are generally restricted to indicate subjunctive, imperative and optative. But in many of the languages of the world there are categories, some even wholly marked in the verbal morphology, that cannot be easily designated by any of these terms (though the term 'subjunctive' is perhaps reasonably applied to languages other than the familiar European ones). One such commonly found category is the Quotative, the form used to indicate what was said by someone, and a whole set of new terms is needed to label the categories within evidential systems (2.3.1). In general, an attempt will be made to provide typologically valid labels with a Latin-type derivation, such as Quotative, Volitive, etc., though individual scholars use a whole variety of names in their analyses and these are, naturally, repeated when their material is quoted. This may be confusing at first but in fact it helps by distinguishing between the typologically valid term used here, such as Quotative, and the actual language category, which may be labelled 'hearsay' or 'report'. Often, however, there will not be two terms and the same term will be used for both (see 1.4.1).

Considerations such as these explain why the title of this book is not simply *Mood* but *Mood and modality*.

1.4   Declaratives, Imperatives, Interrogatives

There are some problems concerning the status of such notions as declarative, statement, indicative, as well as the terminology itself.

1.4.1   *Sentence types*

Lyons (1977: 745) argues that there are three basic sentence types to be found in languages: 'declaratives', 'interrogatives' and 'imperatives' (or 'jussives'). The three types can be illustrated from English:

> John shut the door
> Did John shut the door?
> Shut the door, John!

There is no doubt that the ways in which languages make statements, ask questions and give commands are important and, indeed, relevant to a typological study of modality. The next three sections are, for that reason, entitled 'Declaratives', 'Interrogatives' and 'Imperatives', in accordance with Lyons' terminology. But the suggestion that there are three basic sentence types raises two issues, one concerning the notion of sentence type, the other questioning whether these three types are basic or form any kind of linguistic (let alone modal) system.

To take the first point, Lyons insists that these are types of sentence not types of utterance. For utterances we may make a related, but not identical, distinction between 'statements', 'questions' and 'commands'. The need for the distinction is based on the fact that not all declarative sentences may be statements – they may equally be questions or even commands (see 1.4.5 on 'indirect' speech acts). Since the term 'command' is often used rather confusingly to refer to requests and entreaties as well as commands or orders in the narrow sense, he further suggests that the term 'mand' rather than 'command' be used as a more general one.

Furthermore, he distinguishes these sentence types (as well as the utterance types) from the notion of mood as expressed formally in the verbal systems of many languages, e.g. French, German, Latin, Greek, which have indicative, subjunctive and imperative moods (and Greek also the optative). Indeed, he goes on to suggest that the term 'imperative' should be used only for the imperative mood, an inflectional category in many languages; he proposes the term 'jussive' to refer to the sentence type. (This is a slightly unfortunate choice of terminology, since 'jussive' is often used as a term within the mood system of many languages (see 3.3.2) parallel to, and in contrast with, 'imperative'.)

This results in the following set of distinctions:

Utterances:	statements	questions	mands
Sentences:	declaratives	interrogatives	jussives
Mood:	indicative	—	imperative (subjunctive)

There is, however, a problem here, related to, but not wholly identical with, that of 'mood' and 'modality' (1.3.6). Where a language has an indicative and an imperative mood, these are the formal grammatical markers associated with the notions of statement and mand, though there is no exact one-to-one correspondence. But this takes care of the form–meaning relation and it is difficult to see why there is further need for the sentence types declaratives and jussives. If defined formally they are identical with the moods. If defined semantically they are identical with the utterance types. Only with questions and interrogatives is there still a problem, because such languages do not have an interrogative mood; but that is partly the terminological issue discussed in 1.3.6, partly an indication of the fact that if there is a formal category of interrogative it is not marked in the mood system. (But is there a formal grammatical category in these languages?)

In practice, the notion of sentence type seems clear enough in English, as has already been illustrated and can easily be illustrated further in terms of the indirect speech acts discussed in 1.4.5: there it is clearly shown that there is no one-to-one correspondence between the three sentence types and their utterance meanings and that a command (utterance) can be expressed by a declarative, an interrogative or an imperative sentence. English, however, does not in addition have different moods, as many other languages have, and moreover, the imperative mood in these languages is clearly the marker of command or mand and the indicative of statement. If, then, the three levels are distinguished, including both sentence types and mood, there are several anomalies. First, English has only two. Second, where sentence type and mood are both to be recognized, they are formally identical for statements and mands (but not for questions, since the familiar languages have no mood to correspond to interrogative sentences). Obviously, both the syntactic structure of sentences and mood can be markers of modality and other semantic features, but to establish three distinct levels raises problems.

The second question raised by Lyons' argument that there are three basic sentence types is whether the distinction declarative/interrogative/ imperative is of particular significance typologically or in the formal description of any particular language.

It is certainly true of English that there is a very striking formal relationship between declarative and interrogative sentences, for the latter typically require inversion of the auxiliary verb and subject and insertion of DO if there is no auxiliary verb. But in this respect the interrogative functions like the negative (as well as the emphatic affirmative), involving the so-called NICE properties (see Palmer 1974: 15; Huddleston 1976: 333; and this volume, section 2.7.1):

> John came
> *Did* John come?
> John *didn't* come
> John *did* come

Moreover, if interrogative is important because of its utterance function (question), is not emphatic affirmation, which has in part the function of answer, also important and in the same theoretical system?

In Latin and Greek the three-term system is traditionally used for the analysis of indirect statements, indirect questions and indirect commands, all having their own syntactic characteristics (see 4.1.4). But there are also specific syntactic features associated with reported expressions of wishes and of fear – and these alone would suggest two extra sentence types. Indeed, even in main clauses, expressions of wish (and fear, in Greek at least) are clearly different from those used to express statements, questions and commands. It is also very significant that the mood system does not correspond at all to the three types. In particular there is no interrogative mood.

In other languages (e.g. Menomini, see 1.1.1) the Interrogative actually belongs to the same formal system as the Declarative (or indicative), but in such languages there are other formally defined categories such as Quotative, and clearly not a simple three-term system (see e.g. 2.3). Neither, then, as a general typological category nor as a language-specific category does the three-term system seem to have any clear justification.

Yet Lyons' terminology can be useful and may help to tidy up the use of the terms 'mood' and 'modality', if it is adapted to a typological framework where three sets of terms are needed. The conventions indicated in (i), (ii) and (iii) below will be followed in this book from now onwards:

(i) Terms such as 'statement', 'question', 'answer', usually without quotation marks, are used for the semantic functions. All are common English words except where 'mand' is used instead of 'command'.

(ii) Terms such as 'Declarative', 'Interrogative', 'Imperative', 'Quotative', 'Speculative', 'Deductive' (with initial capitals when first introduced in the discussion, but subsequently only to avoid misunderstanding) are used for the typological categories. Most of these are Latin-based forms though the term 'Judgment' will also be used and 'Epistemic' and 'Deontic' are based on Greek. It should be noted that there are hierarchical systemic relations between the categories: thus it will be argued that the Imperative is a member of the Directive system, and that Judgment includes Speculative and Deductive (i.e. 'Speculative' and 'Deductive' are terms in the Judgment system), while all the categories are subsumed under either Epistemic or Deontic.

(iii) Traditional terms such as 'subjunctive', 'indicative' and 'imperative' and any terms introduced by individual authors for specific languages (e.g. 'irrealis') will be used for language-specific categories. As noted earlier (1.1.4), some will be identical with the typological terms (e.g. 'imperative'), and where this is the case, the language-specific terms will be presented in quotation marks, except when they are very familiar terms such as 'subjunctive', or where there is extended discussion of them and no danger of confusion.

1.4.2 *Declaratives*

It is undoubtedly the case that most, perhaps all, languages have a clear way of indicating that the speaker is making a statement that he believes to be true. This is what may be called the Declarative – the grammatical form that is typically used for such statements.

Following his discussion of factivity (factuality), Lyons (1977: 797) says 'straightforward statements of fact ... may be regarded as epistemically non-modal'. However, this does not preclude the possibility that they may be treated as the 'negative', 'unmarked' or 'neutral' terms within a modal system. In a similar way, it was argued earlier that factuality, as a definition of modality, could include non-factuality (1.3.1). It will be recalled, too, that Searle (1.2.4) includes both epistemic modal judgments and declaratives within his 'assertion'. For such reasons, a study of modality must have a place for declaratives, probably within the Epistemic system. There are several general arguments to support this.

First, it is reasonable to assume that in uttering a declarative sentence the speaker is expressing his opinion, that he is making the modal judgment that what he says is true.

Secondly, there are objections in theory to according a very special status to declarative sentences. There has been a tendency in linguistics and philosophy to do this, treating them as grammatically or logically simple, while all others are seen as more complex and even derivable from them. Lyons (1982: 103) is highly critical of the 'intellectual prejudice' in linguistics, logic and philosophy of language that 'language is, essentially, if not solely, the instrument for the expression of propositional thought'.

It is worth noting that even within speech act theory a similar problem has arisen. In his pioneering work Austin (1962) began by clearly distinguishing performatives in which the uttering of a sentence is, or is part of, an action, from constatives (i.e. declaratives) and introduced the notions of illocutionary force and speech act to deal with performatives. But at the end of the work he came round to the view that constatives, too, involved one type of speech act.

Thirdly, in languages that have systems of mood, the indicative, which typically indicates a declarative, is as clearly marked by the verbal morphology as the subjunctive or imperative and is rightly treated in traditional works as one of the moods. Moreover, there are some languages in which a speaker cannot utter 'a subjectively unmodalized declarative sentence' (Lyons 1982: 110), in the sense that the form typically used for declaratives belongs semantically, as well as formally, to a modal system. One of the best examples of this is Tuyuca (Brazil and Columbia – Barnes 1984; see this volume, section 2.3.1), which has a system of Evidentials. All sentences indicate the kind of evidence the speaker has for what he says by an evidential suffix on the verb. The 'strongest' kind of evidence is that of visual observation (Barnes 1984: 257):

> díiga apé-wi
> soccer play+3MSG+PAST+VIS
> 'He played soccer' (I saw him play)

This is the closest to a declarative, but -*wi* is one of an obligatory set of endings and so is formally (and perhaps semantically) modal. There is good reason for arguing that Tuyuca has no unmodalized declarative sentences.

In many languages, however, declaratives are completely unmarked in terms of modality and may, therefore, be said to be unmodalized. That does not preclude their being incorporated into the modal system as the unmarked term, but there are here two different, though often related, senses of 'marking'. A term may be said to be formally unmarked within a particular system if it is associated with absence of any of the morphological or other formal markers associated with the other terms in the system. Thus in English the declarative is associated with absence of any modal verb and in other languages with absence of certain particles or suffixes. A term may also be said to be semantically unmarked if it has no specific semantic function within the general range that is signalled by the other terms in the system. Whether the declarative is unmarked in this sense is a little more problematic.

Lyons (1977: 809) argues that 'there is no epistemically stronger statement than a categorical assertion' and that the 'fact of introducing *must, necessarily, certainly*, etc., into the utterance has the effect of making our commitment to the factuality of the proposition explicitly dependent upon our perhaps limited knowledge'. Intuitively, this seems not to be wholly true – *certainly* is often used to emphasize the commitment over and above what would be indicated by a simple declarative in English. There are two further problems of a formal kind.

First, there are languages that have forms to contrast knowledge with belief (see 2.2.4, 2.6.2). It would appear reasonable to treat belief as the essential characteristic of the declarative, as Searle (1979: 12) suggests. A statement of knowledge is, surely, epistemically stronger.

Secondly, the form typically used for the declarative is used in many languages in clauses where it does not indicate any kind of commitment by the speaker. It is used, for instance, in subordinate sentences where the main verb clearly indicates that the speaker does not accept the proposition:

> I don't think that John is coming
> I wonder if John is coming

This is also true of real conditions (see 5.4.2), where the speaker is not committed to the truth of either clause:

> If John is here, Mary will come too

This is not just a feature of English: it is equally found with languages with mood, where the indicative is used.

These arguments suggest that the declarative is not the strongest epistemically, but may, perhaps, be epistemically unmarked or neutral, the expression of a proposition with no direct indication of its epistemic status. Rather, it simply 'presents' the proposition to the hearer, generally for acceptance. This suggestion will be discussed in more detail later (2.6.4), after detailed discussion of epistemic modality.

1.4.3 *Imperatives*

Most languages have a form that is typically used to express mands. The obvious term for this is the Imperative.

In several respects the imperative holds a relation to the deontic system similar to that of the declarative to the epistemic, though it seems not to have been argued (as it might be) that the imperative is 'deontically non-modal'. It would be included among Searle's 'directives' in exactly the same way as the indicative is included in the 'assertives', but the question is whether it should be treated as the unmarked term in the deontic system.

It usually differs from other Directives in being formally unmarked. This is clearly true of English, where it requires no modal verb and is thus as unmarked modally as the declarative. But it is also often unmarked or minimally marked even in inflected languages, where the declarative (the indicative) has a full set of inflections. In Latin, for example, there are only two forms of the imperative, singular and plural, and the singular consists of the bare stem (and is the only form that does so):

> Dic! Speak! (sg)
> Dicite! Speak! (pl)

There is, moreover, a good case for arguing that the imperative is unmarked semantically as well. It is often portrayed as the strongest type of directive, the most confident and direct. But this is questionable, rather in the way that the notion of the declarative as the 'strongest' epistemically can be questioned. This becomes clearer from a comparison of the imperative with a form with MUST. On the one hand, the imperative seems much stronger because it will be used by a person in full authority, e.g. a superior in the army, to ensure that an order is obeyed; MUST would not be used in such circumstances. On the other hand, it seems to be much weaker when used in, for instance, *Come in!*, in reply to a knock at the door. This surely gives permission and the use of MUST would be quite inappropriate; the hearer might well retort 'Who are you to give me orders?' Even MAY or CAN, the modals for permission, might be less polite than the imperative; the hearer might similarly retort 'Who are you to give me permission?' The imperative seems to do no more than express, in the most neutral way, the notion that the speaker is favourably disposed towards the action. He merely 'presents' a proposition, just as with the declarative, but for action, not merely for acceptance as true, by the hearer. This is not belied by the use of the imperative by a superior in the army; on the contrary, his rank ensures that what he presents deontically will be carried out. For, in a similar manner the army uses WILL for written instructions, as in:

> Private Jones will report at 18.00 hrs

Merely saying that this 'will' happen, ensures that it does. People in position of power can use the mildest of indications to get things done. It can be argued, then, that the imperative is the unmarked or neutral term within the deontic system, or at least within the sub-system of directives.

1.4.4 *Interrogatives*

Although all languages probably have devices for asking questions, and although there is certainly a need to recognize the typological category of Interrogative, the ways in which questions may be expressed vary greatly.

First, some languages have a syntactic device that does not belong to any modal system. In English it is the inversion of subject and auxiliary verb; there is a similar device in French and German, though involving verbs other than auxiliaries. In English the device belongs, with others, to a formal system which is characteristic of the auxiliary verbs, of which the modals are a sub-set (see 1.5.1 for the NICE properties). The interrogative in English belongs, then, to a formal system that is not part of the modal system, but interacts with it.

Secondly, questions are often introduced by particles, clitics, etc.; for example, *-ne, nonne* and *num* in Latin:

> Venitne?   Has he come?   (venit 'he has come')
> Nonne venit? Hasn't he come?
> Num venit?   Surely he's come?

Other languages have interrogative particles, e.g. *-do* in Tigrinya (Ethiopia – personal observation):

> John näti mägbi bäli'uwo do?
> John the food   he ate it INT
> 'Did John eat the food?'

This is only of marginal interest, since such particles seldom seem to belong to a system that is clearly modal.

Thirdly, questions are often indicated by intonation. This is perfectly possible in English, and is the only regular device in many languages. But it has already been argued (in 1.1.3) that the insistence on grammaticalization excludes intonation from this study. It might be supposed that a rising intonation could be identified as a formal marker of the interrogative, but this is unacceptable for (at least) two reasons. First, there is no one-to-one correspondence between such an intonation and questions. Secondly, there are many other intonation tunes that would then have to be considered and possibly given similar status, e.g. the fall–rise:

> John's coming (rise)   'Is he coming?'
> John's coming (fall–rise) 'He's coming but ...'

There would be yet other intonation patterns that might similarly be included. Unless, then, there is an attempt to write a complete 'grammar' of intonation, it is unreasonable to treat just one intonation pattern as the formal mark of interrogation.

Finally, and of greatest interest in a study of modality, is the situation where questions are asked by a formal device that is within the modal system, as in Menomini (1.1.1). Often, however, this device is represented by investigators as essentially an expression of the speaker's ignorance of the facts, with merely the implication that it is hoped that the hearer will supply them. This is clearly what is suggested by Donaldson (1980: 260, 262) for Ngiyambaa (1.5.4), when she calls the forms used the 'ignorative':

> guya-gaɪ-   ndu dha-yi
> fish- IGNOR-you eat-PAST
> 'Did you eat a fish?' /'You ate a fish, I don't know'

In Serrano (Uto-Aztecan, California – Hill 1967; and see 2.1.2), the 'dubitative' particle, which has extensive use, is often the only indication of a question. A similar point is made by Matthews (1965: 99–100) for Hidatsa (2.3.3), when he glosses 'question' as 'the speaker does not know whether or not the sentence is true ... the speaker thinks that the listener does know' (though Matthews' presentation is suspect – see 2.5, 2.6.1). Whether this should be treated as an example of the interrogative (rather than the semantically related Dubitative) is not easy to decide (see 2.5).

Yet it must be admitted that formally the interrogative is unrelated to the modal systems of many languages and that semantically it seems to belong to discourse rather than modality, to matters of asking questions, giving replies, etc. Nevertheless, there are connections between modality and discourse, and the latter is discussed in some detail in 2.7.

1.4.5 *Indirect speech acts*

It has been suggested that in English, for example, declaratives, interrogatives and imperatives are typically used for statements, questions and mands. But there are problems with the use of the term 'typically', for there is no one-to-one correspondence between these sets. A declarative may be used as a statement, question or mand. All three interpretations are possible for:

>You are coming tomorrow

Conversely, a mand may be expressed by an interrogative or a declarative as well as an imperative, as in:

>Can you open the door?
>You can open the door
>Open the door!

(There are yet other ways of expressing mands, e.g. *I want you to open the door*, but the use of the lexical item *want* takes this outside our discussion.) Within speech act theory this problem is dealt with by distinguishing 'direct' and 'indirect' speech acts, an interrogative being used as a direct speech act for a question but as an indirect speech act for a statement or mand. There are, however, some difficulties about this apparently simple solution.

To begin with, a sentence like *Can you open the door?* is not formally exactly like a normal interrogative. It is often accompanied by *please*, which is a marker of a request, and it is clearly highly conventionalized in that CAN is not here replaceable by BE ABLE TO. The request is not conveyed by:

>Are you able to open the door?

Such expressions, then, have been partly fossilized (become fixed phrases) and partly grammaticalized, as requests rather than questions. Even formally they are not wholly identifiable as interrogatives.

The issue becomes of significance in the discussion of modality when an attempt is made to provide a clear statement of the function of declaratives, interrogatives and imperatives. Consider briefly the issues raised in the last section concerning interrogatives and dubitatives. It might be necessary to decide, in a given language, whether the category is an interrogative as a direct speech act but used as an indirect speech act to express doubt, or directly a dubitative indirectly used to pose questions. Clearly the definition of what is 'indirect' depends on the status of what is 'direct'.

There is a curious situation in Huichol (Mexico – Grimes 1964: 27) where the form used as a question is often the unmarked form, though Huichol also has a marker for the 'assertive' mood. It might be argued that in this language the interrogative is the unmarked form. Alternatively, it may be that the unmarked form is basically a kind of simple declarative, merely presenting propositions (sometimes for acceptance, sometimes for questioning), as contrasted with the more positive assertive, and that the question use of this form is, in a sense, indirect.

By a similar argument, it could even be proposed that declaratives and imperatives are indirect speech acts: they merely 'present' propositions which are indirectly interpreted as assertions or mands. The distinction between direct and indirect is not as simple as it first appears (see 1.4.2, 1.4.3, 2.6, 3.3).

1.5   Grammatical types

Modality is marked in various ways – by modal verbs, by mood and by particles and clitics. Languages may employ one or many of these; some have very complex systems.

1.5.1   *Modal verbs*

There is no doubt that English has a set of modal verbs that can be formally defined. They are MAY, CAN, MUST, OUGHT (TO), WILL and SHALL, and marginally, NEED and DARE (including *might, could, would* and *should*). The facts have been stated many times (e.g. Palmer 1979b) and will only be briefly summarized here.

First, they are members of a larger set of auxiliary verbs which exhibit what Huddleston (1976: 333) has called the NICE properties – their occurrence with negation, inversion, 'code' and emphatic affirmation as in:

> Must I come?
> I can't go
> He can swim and so can she
> He will be there

These properties the modal verbs share with the other auxiliary verbs BE and HAVE, but in addition have formal features of their own:

(i)   They do not co-occur: there is no *will can come*, *may shall be*, etc. (though in a few dialects there are some very restricted possibilities of co-occurrence such as *might could*).

(ii)   They have no –*s* forms for their 3rd person singular: e.g. *He oughts to come*. The form *wills* exists, but as a form of the lexical verb, as does

33

cans, in entirely different senses. (DARE has forms both with and without *–s*: *He dares to come*, *Dare he come?* This suggests that it functions both as a lexical verb and as a modal.)

(iii) They have no non-finite forms: e.g. no **to can* or **canning*; there is no **I hope to can come tomorrow.*

(iv) They have no imperatives: **Can be here! *Must come now!*

(v) MUST has no morphologically past tense form, although the others do (*could, should, might*, etc.); of those forms, only *could* is used to refer to past time (though all may occur in reported speech).

(vi) There are suppletive negative forms (see 2.2.1 and 3.2.1):

He may be there   →   He can't be there

He must be there   →   He needn't be there

(vii) There are formal differences between the modal verbs, in their epistemic and deontic senses, in terms of negation and tense (see below and 1.3.4, 2.2.2 and 3.2.1).

It is instructive to compare these verbs with similar verbs in German and French. German certainly has six potential candidates for the title of modal verb: KÖNNEN, DÜRFEN, MÖGEN, MÜSSEN, SOLLEN and WOLLEN, obvious cognates of the English ones. These are also used both epistemically and deontically, epistemic MAY being translated by either KÖNNEN or MÖGEN, and deontic MAY by either KÖNNEN or DÜRFEN, while both epistemic and deontic MUST is translated by MÜSSEN (see Hammer 1983: 223ff for examples):

Er kann/mag   krank sein

he KÖNNEN/MÖGEN+3SG+PRES+INDIC ill   be

'He may be ill'

Du   kannst/darfst   den   Bleistift behalten

thou KÖNNEN/DÜRFEN+2SG+PRES+INDIC the   pencil   keep

'You can keep the pencil'

These are less clearly identified as members of a grammatical system than the English modals, but they have some idiosyncrasies, notably:

(i) There is no final *–t* in the 3rd person singular of the present indicative: e.g. *kann, mag* (cf. *gibt* 'gives').

(ii) In subordinate clauses the order of the elements of the verbal complex is changed if one of them is a modal verb in the infinitive occurring with the finite form of another auxiliary verb (as it cannot occur in English). The usual rule is that the finite form occurs last, but in these circumstances it occurs at the beginning of the verbal complex (Hammer 1983: 224):

Es war klar, dass er sich   würde   anstrengen
It was clear, that he himself be+3SG+IMPERF+SUBJ exert
  müssen
  must+INF
(n.b. the order is not *anstrengen müssen würde)
'It was clear that he will have to exert himself'

There are similar modal auxiliaries in the Scandinavian languages, but they 'differ in complex ways from language to language, making translation difficult' (Haugen 1976: 80).

French has verbs such as POUVOIR, DEVOIR and VOULOIR, which again look reasonable candidates. The first two can be used epistemically or deontically, e.g.:

Il peut   venir demain
he POUVOIR+3SG+PRES come tomorrow
'He may come tomorrow' ('perhaps')
'He can come tomorrow' ('is able to')

Il doit   parler Anglais
he DEVOIR+3SG+PRES speak English
'He must speak English' ('it is necessary'/'it must be true')

Moreover, DEVOIR in the negative, like the negative form *mustn't*, has the meaning of 'necessary not' rather than 'not necessary' (which is *can't* in English and the negative of POUVOIR in French). Also, with following AVOIR it has the meaning 'must have', not 'had to' (cf. Huot 1974; and for English, Palmer 1979b: 50, 97–8).

Yet these verbs are not as clearly distinguished from other verbs as are the modal verbs of English. The NICE properties do not apply to them (or not exclusively – any verb can take inversion and negation), and they can co-occur:

Il veut   pouvoir . . .
he VOULOIR+3SG+PRES POUVOIR+INF
'He wants to be able . . .

Il peut   vouloir . . .
he POUVOIR+3SG+PRES VOULOIR+INF
'He may wish . . .'

35

They all have past tense forms and there are no other severe syntactic restrictions (see Schogt 1968). The fact that DEVOIR and POUVOIR may be either epistemic or deontic is of some interest, but not a criterion of modal status, since the distinction is not confined to modal verbs even in English (3.5).

We might then conclude with Ruwet (1967: 185ff) that the modal verbs cannot be clearly established in French. There is, however, at least one characteristic that suggests that they are more closely linked syntactically to the verb that follows than other verbs. This relates to the positioning of objects *tout* 'all' and *rien* 'nothing' (Kayne 1975: 1–27); where there is more than one verbal element, such elements may occur in several positions:

> Elle a   voulu   lire   tout
> She has wanted to read all
> Elle a   voulu   tout lire
> She has wanted all   to read
> Elle a   tout voulu   lire
> She has all   wanted to read
>
> 'She wanted to read everything'

However, the third type above is possible only with VOULOIR 'wish', POUVOIR 'be able', DEVOIR 'must', FAILLIR 'miss' and OSER 'dare'. It is not possible with, e.g., AVOUER 'confess' or DÉCLARER 'declare':

> Elle va   avouer   tout mépriser
> She goes to confess all   to despise
> *Elle va   tout avouer   mépriser
> She goes all   to confess to despise
>
> 'She is going to confess to despising everything'

Since *tout* in the examples is the object of *lire* and *mépriser*, the fact that it can precede *voulu*, but not *avouer* suggests that the former, but not the latter, is an auxiliary verb.

Although the same modal verbs may be used in English for both epistemic and deontic modality (1.3.4), and although it is an interesting question why they have both uses (3.5), in general the distinction is quite clear; so sentences with MAY, MUST, etc. may be ambiguous in terms of the distinction, but they are not vague (whereas this is not so of deontic versus 'dynamic' modality – 1.3.2). There are also some positive formal distinctions between the modals in their two uses (for details and examples see 2.2.1 and 3.2.1):

(i) Deontic MUST has negative *mustn't* and a suppletive *needn't*, but epistemic MUST has no morphologically related negative.

(ii) *May not* negates the modal when deontic (no permission), but the following verb when epistemic ('It may be that it is not so').

(iii) MAY and MUST followed by *have* are always epistemic, never deontic.

(iv) MAY is replaceable by CAN only in the deontic use, though *can't* may be epistemic.

Furthermore, when it refers to the future, MUST is almost always deontic; the epistemic sense is provided by BE BOUND TO (see Palmer 1979b: 45–6 and, for discussion, Coates 1983: 42–3 and Palmer 1983b: 291), while *might* is closely related in its meaning to present tense *may* only in its epistemic sense.

There is a similar position in German, in that KÖNNEN and MÜSSEN are used both epistemically and deontically. Again, however, there are differences (see 2.2.1, 2.3.1):

(i) KÖNNEN is equivalent to MÖGEN epistemically, but to DÜRFEN deontically.

(ii) MÜSSEN plus *nicht* negates either modality or proposition when deontic, but only the modality when epistemic.

In French, POUVOIR and DEVOIR are also used both epistemically and deontically (though we may doubt whether French has a clear modal system). Again, when followed by *avoir* they are equivalent to English *may/must have*, i.e. only with the epistemic sense (and a similar point is true of German).

In Modern Greek, similarly, although the same form is used for deontic and epistemic modality, the syntax associated with each is different: PREPI plus *na* and a finite verb is used for 'should' in both senses, so that the following is ambiguous (all examples provided by Dr. Irene Philippaki-Warburton):

o jánis prépi na fíɣi ávrio
the John PREPI that leave+3SG+PRES+PERFECTIVE tomorrow
'John should leave tomorrow'

With a past tense verb, however, only the epistemic sense is possible:

o jánis prépi na éfiɣe
the John PREPI that leave+3SG+PAST
'John probably left'

For 'may/'can', forms of the verb BORO are used, as was noted in 1.3.4, but in the epistemic use an 'impersonal' (3rd person singular) form is found,

similar to PREPI, though in other uses it is a fully inflected form that agrees
with the subject:

```
ta peðjá    borí                              na
the children BORO+3SG+PRES+IMPERFECTIVE that
    fíɣun                        ávrio
    leave+3PL+PRES+PERFECTIVE tomorrow
'The children may leave tomorrow'

ta peðjá    borún                             na
the children BORO+3PL+PRES+IMPERFECTIVE that
    fíɣun                        ávrio
    leave+3PL+PRES+PERFECTIVE tomorrow
'The children can leave tomorrow'
```

As with PREPI, a past tense verb in the subordinate clause will entail the
epistemic meaning. So, too, will negation of that verb:

```
(borí                          na vréksi
BORO+3SG+PRES+PERFECTIVE that rain+3SG+PRES PERFECTIVE
    alá) borí                      ke   na mi
    but BORO+3SG+PRES+PERFECTIVE also that not
    vréksi
    rain+3SG+PRES+PERFECTIVE
'(It may rain but) it may not rain'
```

The use of auxiliary verbs to express modality is very characteristic of
European languages, but not exclusive to them. Thus Mandarin Chinese
(Li and Thompson 1981: 173–88) has a set of auxiliary verbs that can be
formally defined, in that:

(i)   they must co-occur with a lexical verb (or, at least, one must be
       understood from the context)
(ii)   they have no aspect markers or intensifiers
(iii) they cannot precede the subject
(iv)   they cannot have objects

All of these are semantically modal; the list is:

yīnggāi, yīngdang, gāi	'ought to, should'
néng, nénggòu, huì, kěyi	'be able to'
néng, kěyi	'have permission'
gǎn	'dare'
kěn	'be willing to'

děi, bìxū, bìyào, bíděi	'must, ought to'
huì	'will, know how'

It will be noted that some verbs appear twice – clearly for semantic reasons – but there is no reason for thinking that they are different verbs, rather than single verbs with several meanings. *Huì*, for instance (Hockett 1968) has the general meaning of 'know how' even though it can be used of inanimate objects. What Hockett says is:

> If a person knows how to speak Swahili, he *hwèi* speak Swahili; if he smokes he *hwèi* smoke; even of inanimate objects, one can say that a high wind *hwèi* (here perhaps 'is apt to') blow down a tent or that an electron *hwèi* behave in accordance with the equations of wave mechanics [Hockett's *hwèi=huì*]   (Hockett 1968: 62)

Although the verbs of Chinese have no inflections, these auxiliaries appear to be essentially verbal. There is also a set of verbs in Cashibo (Peru – Shell 1975: 178–91) which are inflectional and marked for person–number (though the stems may combine), but which may, perhaps, belong more to a discourse system than a modal system (see 2.7.1).

1.5.2 Mood

Many of the European languages, both Classical and modern, have a subjunctive mood. Classical Greek has an optative mood as well.

It has already been noted that the subjunctive in Latin is a generalized marker of modality (1.3.6); some distinct meanings appear to be associated with it. Following Lakoff (1968: 172ff), but not accepting her theoretical arguments (see 4.4.4), we can see at least six meanings of the subjunctive:

Imperative:

Naviget!	haec summa est, hic nostri nuntius
sail+3SG+PRES+SUBJ	this point is, this of us message
esto	(Virg. *Aen*.4.237)
let it be	

'Let him sail, this is the point, let this be our message'

Optative:

Ut illum di ... perduint	(Pl. *Aul*.785)
that him gods destroy+3PL+PRES+SUBJ	

'May the gods destroy him!'

Jussive:

Sed maneam   etiam, opinor   (Pl.*Trin.*1136)
but remain+1SG+PRES+SUBJ still,   I think
'But I should still stay, I think'

Concessive:

Sit   fur, sit   sacrilegus ...
be+3SG+PRES+SUBJ thief be+3SG+PRES+SUBJ temple robber
    at est   bonus imperator   (Cic. *Verr.* 5.4)
    yet he is good   general
'Though he is a thief, though he is a temple-robber ...
    he is a good general'

Potential:

Iam apsolutos censeas   quom incedunt infectores
                                         (Pl. *Aul.* 520)
now paid off   think+2SG+PRES+SUBJ when come in dyers
'You may think they are already paid off, when in come the dyers'

Deliberative:

Quid agam   iudices?   (Cic. *Verr.* 5.2)
what do+1SG+PRES+SUBJ jurymen
'What am I to do, gentlemen of the jury?'

(Lakoff gives two others, 'purpose' and 'relative purpose', but these are in subordinate clauses and involve rather different issues.)

There is a close parallelism between the subjunctive in an independent (main) clause and the subjunctive in a subordinate clause where the semantics of the modality are carried by lexical elements in the main clause. (It is this parallelism that is crucial for Lakoff for her theory of 'abstract performatives' – see 4.4.4.) Thus for 'ought', either the subjunctive alone or *oportet* in the main clause followed by the subjunctive in the subordinate clause is used:

Sed maneam   etiam, opinor   (Pl. *Trin.* 1136)
but remain+1SG+PRES+SUBJ still,   I think
'But I should still stay, I think'

Me igitur   ipsum ames   oportet,
me therefore self   love+2SG+PRES+SUBJ it is necessary,
    non mea   (Cic. *Fin.* 2.26)
    not my things
'So you should love me myself, not my possessions'

This emphasizes the need to investigate the use of modal forms in subordinate clauses, and to discuss the relation between modal in such clauses and modal in main clauses.

There is a little more to be said about Classical Greek. First, it has both a subjunctive and an optative mood. In some respects the optative functions as the past tense of the subjunctive: in subordinate clauses its occurrence is often determined by a sequence of tenses rule (stated traditionally in terms of 'primary' versus 'historic' clauses). However, it can also be more tentative, as in:

> humín d' en pántessi periklutá dó:r' onomé:no: (Hom. *Il.* 9.121)
> you   but in all   excellent gifts   name+1SG+AOR+SUBJ
> 'In the midst of you I may mention the excellent gifts'

> autár toi   kái keino:i egó: paramuthe:saíme:n (Hom. *Il.* 15.45)
> but   surely even to him I   counsel+1SG+AOR+OPT
> 'But I might even counsel him'

This can be compared with the 'tentative' use of the past tense of MAY (*might*) in English (see 2.2.3); but it also has some specific uses, for example, that of *wish*:

> ó: paí, génoio   patrós   eutukhésteros
>   (Soph. *Aj.* 550)
> o child, become+2SG+AOR+OPT of father luckier
> 'My child, may you be luckier than your father'

Secondly, Greek has two negative particles, *ou(k)* and *mé:*. To some extent these are associated with the indicative versus the subjunctive, optative and imperative, *mé:* being thus essentially the modal negator. Yet they have some independence, as shown by:

> ouk ésth' hoútosané:r oud' éssetai oudé
> not is   this   man nor will be nor
> géne:tai   (Hom. *Od.* 16.437)
> become+3SG+AOR+SUBJ
> 'This man is not, will not be, may never be' (*ou* with subjunctive)

> ísto: nún tode gaía ...   mé: di'   éme:n ióte:ta
> know now this earth ... not through my   will
> Poseidáo:n enosíkhto:n pe:maínei   (Hom. *Il.* 15.36, 41)
> Poseidon earth-shaker hurt+3SG+PRES+INDIC
> 'Earth is my witness ... not by my will does Earth-shaking
> Poseidon hurt me' (*mé:* with indicative)

This is usually explained in a way that suggests that *mé:* is somehow modal (particularly, deontic). In the first case the use of *ou(k)* shows clearly that 'may' is not to be taken deontically (as a wish). In the second, the use of *mé:*

is associated with the clearly indicated nature of the sentence as an oath. But the relations between *ou(k)* and *mé:* are very complex and not always directly indicative of modal differences. In questions, for instance, *ou(k)* expects the answer 'Yes', while *mé:* expects the answer 'No' (see Moore 1934: 165):

> ou toúto aristón estí?
> not this best is
> 'This is best, isn't it?'/'Isn't this best?'

> mé: toúto aristón estí?
> not this best is
> 'This isn't best, is it?'/'Surely this isn't best?'

It is also reasonable to recognize a subjunctive mood in non-European languages, even in non-Indo-European languages. In, for instance, the West African language Fula (Arnott 1970: 299ff) there is a paradigm of the verb that has functions very similar to those of the Latin subjunctive (though it lacks tense distinctions); some of these are illustrated by:

(i) *Injunction*
ŋgaraa
come+2SG+SUBJ
'Come on!'

(ii) *Wish or prayer*
njuutaa   balɗe
be long+2SG+SUBJ in days
'May you live long!'

(iii) *Report for instruction or permission*
minasta-na?
come in+1SG+SUBJ-INTERROG
'May I come in?'

(iv) *Expostulation or rhetorical question*
njooɗoɗaa
sit+2SG+SUBJ
'What? You sit down!'

(v) *Offer or request for permission or invitations with* HAA
haa njahen
HAA go+1PL+SUBJ
'Let's go'

(vi) *Obligation with* SEY
sey ŋgurtoɗaa
SEY come out+2SG+SUBJ
'You ought to come out'

(The difference between the 2nd person forms is accounted for in terms of voice: (i) and (ii) being active, (iv) and (vi) being middle voice. There are other uses, especially in subordinate clauses, that resemble those of Latin but which are not illustrated here.)

There is no need to be much concerned with the subjunctive in English. The only possible candidate for this is the simple form (identical with the infinitive) that is used in formal language after verbs of ordering, requiring, etc. This has largely disappeared from English, and it can well be argued that it has been replaced by the modal verbs, though traditional scholars may still argue for its use. A very curious place, for instance, to find a defence of the English subjunctive is in a footnote in a Turkish grammar:

> It is a pity that the subjunctive is dying in England, though it seems more healthy in America. It will be a sad day when we forget the distinction between 'I insist that the claimant is adequately compensated' and 'I insist that the claimant be adequately compensated'. (Lewis 1967: 133)

But the writer has failed to note that the ambiguity he fears can be, and normally would be, avoided by using *should* or *must* in the second example.

There are also languages which have a multiple set of verbal paradigms for what can be described as mood, tense and aspect. Thus Bilin (Cushitic, Ethiopia – Palmer 1957) has separate paradigms (all with at least five different forms for number-person-gender) of the following kind:

jəbäkʷ	'he buys'	jəbét	'(says) that he bought'
jəbíxʷ	'he bought'	jəbék	'he bought and . . .'
jəbäxʷ	'which he buys'	jəbú	'while he bought'
jəbéxʷ	'which he bought'	jəbíra	'he will buy'
jəbín	'let him buy'	jəbírəd	'he would buy'
jəbän	'if he buys'	jəbíro	'(begins) to buy'
jəbinädik	'if he bought'	jəbíror	'in order to buy'
jəbät	'(says) that he buys'		

No fewer than fifty such paradigms were recorded. Most of them indicate various types of subordinate clauses (with no subordinator present).

1.5.3 Clitics and particles

Two kinds of expression of modality have been considered: modal verbs and verbal inflection. The term 'inflection', however, should be used in a wide sense to include the features of agglutinative languages,

43

where by definition there will be a one-to-one correspondence between the modal marker and its semantic function, and possibly also to include what may have been described by authors as 'particles', if they have a fixed place in the verbal complex. This would include, for instance, the markers of modality in Luiseño (Uto-Aztecan, California). According to Akmajian, Steele and Wasow (1979: 3; see also Steele *et al*. 1981), the first element in a Luiseño sentence is followed by one or more particles. For three types of such particles the sequence is modal–clitic pronoun–tense:

> noo xu n   po heyi
> I   modal 1+SG+CP FUT dig
> 'I should dig'

(Four tense clitics are mentioned and three modal particles: *xu* (with future clitic *po*) 'should', *su* 'question and somewhat weak expectation' and *kun* 'quotative'.)

Some modal particles, however, are quite clearly not part of the verbal complex at all, but occur at various positions, according to the language, in the relevant clause. A very clear example of this is the set of 'topic' particles found in Ngiyambaa (N.S. Wales, Australia – Donaldson 1980), which are illustrated in some detail in 1.5.4. These all occur on the initial word, irrespective of its class. Similarly, in Inga (Levinsohn 1975) there are clitics that occur with the verb in 'unmarked' sentences, but with the most 'thematic element' in thematically marked sentences. The clitic *mi* (action witnessed, affirmative – see 2.1.1) may occur in:

> nispaca   Santiagoma-mi rini
> After that to Santiago-AFF I went
> 'After that I went (rheme) to Santiago'
>
> nispaca   rini-mi   Santiagoma
> After that I went-AFF to Santiago
> 'After that I went to Santiago (rheme)'.

In Jacaltec (Guatemala – Craig 1977: 70–2, 93–6) the irrealis suffix *-oj*, which occurs with other particles, may occur:

> (i) with an adverbial (plus the exhortative) in the sense of 'even if':
> c'ul-uj   ab chu cu cañalwi matzet x̌jicanl-oj yiñ
> well-IRR EXH do we dance   nothing we get-IRR in
> 'Even if we dance well, we do not get anything out of it'
>
> (ii) with a verb (plus the exhortative) for wishes:
> chura-oj   ab s-c'ul   anma tu'
> get angry-IRR EXH stomach people that
> 'Let them get angry!'

(iii)   with a non-specific noun (see 5.2.3) after verbs such as 'look for':
x'-'oc   heb ix   say-a'   hun-uj munlabal
ASP-start PL   woman look for-FUT a-IRR   pot
'The women started looking for a pot'

Modality is not, then, necessarily marked in the verbal element, nor is there any obvious reason why it should be, apart from the fact that the verb is the most central part of the sentence. There is no reason why tense should be marked there either, though modality is, perhaps, more independent semantically; aspect, on the other hand, is semantically more closely related to the verb, in that it indicates types of actions rather than when they occurred or the speaker's beliefs and attitudes.

Since modality is not confined to verbal features, quite independent 'modal' particles can also be considered. It has already been noted that Classical Greek has two distinct negative particles (1.5.2); these differ in several ways, some of which are clearly modal, though there is no exact one-to-one correspondence between the particles and the moods of Greek.

For Japanese, Kuno (1973: 5) notes four particles in final position:

Kore wa   hon desu yo
book THEME this is   YO
'I am telling you this is a book'

Kore wa   hon desu ne
book THEME this is   NE
'I hope you agree that this is a book'

Kore wa   hon desu ka?
book THEME this is   KA
'Is this a book?'

John wa   baka sa
John THEME fool SA
'It goes without saying that John is a fool'

However, *ka* is also used for 'or', and may not be primarily a question marker, and the others do not appear to belong to a very clearly defined modal system.

This is even more true of the modal particles of German. Curme (1905: 368 [1960: 350–2]) talks of 'modal adverbs which denote in what manner a thought is conceived by the speaker'. The most important ones (with Curme's glosses) are:

ja   'truly, why, don't you see, you know'
doch   'after all, though, just, truly, surely . . .'
denn   'evidently, as is well known, as I learn . . .'

> schon   'never fear, no doubt, surely, as a matter of course'
> wohl   'indeed, certainly'

However, these all seem to be essentially comments on the proposition rather than opinions about it, and so not very obviously modal.

A set of particles is also reported for Huichol (Mexico – Grimes 1964: 60–1):

> tietʌ   'perhaps, it must be that'
> kauka   'possibly, it seems that'
> zʌkaa tʌma   'oh that, would that'
> kauka zʌari   'most definitely not'

But it is not clear whether it can be shown that these belong to a grammatical system rather than that they are merely a set of lexical adverbs such as English *perhaps*, *certainly*, *probably*, etc.

1.5.4   *A complex system*

One of the most complex systems of modality to be found is that of Ngiyambaa (N.S. Wales, Australia – Donaldson 1980). Since it is particularly interesting and will be discussed in a number of different places in this book, it will, perhaps, be helpful and instructive to set out the entire system in detail.

To begin with, there are verbal inflections which provide a system of 'imperative', 'past', 'present', 'purposive' and 'irrealis'. Then there are some particles or clitics that always occur on the first word in the sentence (somewhat misleadingly referred to as the 'topic'). Apart from the clitics that relate topics to discourse (which are not of interest here), there are (i) the counterfactual clitic, (ii) modal clitics of two kinds, i.e. 'belief' clitics and 'knowledge' clitics, and (iii) 'evidence' clitics. These all belong to separate systems, the membership of each set being mutually exclusive. Members from different sets, however, may co-occur, except perhaps for 'evidence' clitics and the 'counterfactual' (no examples are given and these may be semantically incompatible), the modal clitics always occurring before the others (and there is an example both of a 'belief' clitic preceding a 'knowledge' clitic and of the opposite sequence). Finally, there is a set of free particles in 'topic' position, many of which have modal meanings.

There are, then, six systems as illustrated below (page numbers in Donaldson are given in parenthesis).

(1) Verbal inflections:

    (i)   *Imperative*
        ŋindu   bawuŋ-ga yuwa-dha   (159)
        you+NOM middle-LOC lie-IMP
        'You lie in the middle!'

    (ii) *Past*
        yuruŋ-gu ŋidjiyi   (160)
        rain-ERG   rain+PAST
        'It rained'

    (iii) *Present*
        yuruŋ-gu ŋidja-ṛa   (160)
        rain-ERG   rain-PRES
        'It is raining'

    (iv) *Purposive*
        ŋadhu   bawuŋ-ga yuwa-giri   (162)
        I+NOM middle-LOC lie-PURP
        'I must lie in the middle'

        yuruŋ-gu ŋidja-l-i   (162)
        rain-ERG   rain-CM-PURP
        [CM=conjugation Marker)
        'It is bound to rain'

    (v)   *Irrealis*
        yuruŋ-gu ŋidja-l-aga   (160)
        rain-ERG   rain-CM-IRR
        'It might/will rain'

(2) Counterfactual:
        ŋinuː-ma-ni   buraːy   giyi
        you+OBL-CNTRFACT-3ABS+VIS child+ABS be+PAST
        ŋindu-ma-ni   yada gurawiyi   (251)
        you+NOM-CNTRFACT-3ABS+VIS well   look after+PAST
        (VIS=VIsual)
        'If this child had been yours, you would have looked after it
        well'

(3) 'Belief' clitics:
    (i)   *Assertion*
        waŋaːy-baː-na   yana-nhi   (254)
        NEG-ASSERT-3ABS   walk-PAST
        'He didn't walk (again)'

    (ii) *Categorical assertion*
        guniːm-baṛa-nuː   balu-y-aga   (254)
        mother+ABS-CATEG ASSERT-2OBL die-CM-IRR
        'Your mother is bound to die'

(iii) *Counter-assertion*

guyan-baga:-dhu   gaṯa   (255)
shy+ABS-CNTR ASSERT-1NOM be+PRES
'But I'm shy!'

(iv) *Hypothesis*

gali:-ŋinda-gila   ŋiyanu   balu-y-aga   (256)
water-CARIT-HYPOTH we+PL+NOM die-CM-IRR
(CARIT=CARITative)
'We'll probably die for lack of water'

(4) 'Knowledge' clitics:

    (i) *Exclamative*

minja-wa:-ndu   dha-yi   (260, 262)
what+ABS-EXCLAM-2NOM eat-PAST
'What did you eat?/You ate what?'

guya-wa:-ndu   dha-yi   (260, 263)
fish+ABS-EXCLAM-2NOM eat-PAST
'So you ate a fish!'/'What? You ate a *fish*?'

    (ii) *Ignorative*

minjaŋ-ga:-dhu   dha-yi   (260, 262)
what+ABS-IGNOR-1NOM eat-PAST
'You ate something, I don't know what'/
'I don't know what you ate'

guya-ga:-ndu   dha-yi   (260, 265)
fish+ABS-IGNOR-2NOM eat-PAST
'Did you eat a fish'/
'You ate a fish, I don't know'

(5) 'Evidence' clitics:

    (i) *Sensory evidence*

ŋindu-gara   girambiyi   (275)
you+NOM-SENS EVID sick+PAST
'One can see you were sick'

gabuga:-gara-lu   ŋamumiyi
egg+ABS-SENS EVID-3ERG lay+PAST
'It's laid an egg by the sound of it'
(Donaldson gives further examples for smell,
taste and feeling.)

    (ii) *Linguistic evidence*

ŋindu-dhan   girambiyi   (276)
you+NOM-LING EVID sick+PAST
'You are said to have been sick'

(6) Free particles in 'topic' position:
  (i) *Prohibitive*
      garaː yanaː   (239)
      PROHIB go+IMP
      'Don't go'
  (ii) *Negative*
      waŋaːy winar   manabi-nji   (239)
      NEG   woman+ABS hunt-PAST
      'The woman didn't go hunting'
  (iii) *'Believed true'*
      ŋadhangaː-lu   guya   mamiyi   (240)
      BELIEVED TRUE-3ERG fish+ABS catch+PAST
      'I think she caught a fish'
  (iv) *Dubitative*
      yama-gaː   dhuru   miŋga-dhi   guɽuga-nha-ba   (242)
      DUBIT-IGNOR snake+ABS burrow-CIRC be in-PRES-SUBJ
      'I wonder whether there is a snake in the burrow'
  (v) *'Good job'*
      mandaŋgul dhiː ndu   waŋaːy   ŋiyiyi   (242)
      GOOD JOB   1OBL 2NOM NEG   say+PAST
      'Good job you didn't tell me!'
  (vi) *'Bad job'*
      gaːmbada yana-nhi   (242)
      BAD JOB go-PAST
      'Bad job (she) came!'/'She shouldn't have come'

These examples have been presented in some detail because they suggest a number of points that must be taken into account in this study of modality. Chief among these are the following:

(i)   The purposive, irrealis and imperative all appear in the same system as past and present. This illustrates both the relation between epistemic and deontic modality and a possible relation between modality and tense (see 6.1).
(ii) Only this one system is marked in the verbal elements. All other systems are marked by 'topic' clitics, i.e. by clitics appearing with the first word, irrespective of its class (see 1.5.3).
(iii) The ignorative can be used to express ignorance, or with hypothesis probability or a question. This may both explain and confirm the idea that questions should be treated as a kind of modality.
(iv) The marker for what is 'said to be so' is paired with the marker for what 'appears to be so from the senses' and both are treated as 'evidential' (2.3.4).

49

(v) The free particles include: (i) prohibitive and negative; (ii) 'believed true' and dubitative, which are clearly semantically modal; (iii) 'good job' and 'bad job' which do not affect the truth of the proposition, but comment upon it in a modal kind of way (and one of them is translated by a modal verb in English – *shouldn't have*). These might seem to be examples of Rescher's 'evaluative modalities' (1.2.3). There is, perhaps, something similar (a comment on a fact) in the forms of Menomini that are translated 'So he *is* going to come' and 'But he *was* going to come' (see 1.1.1).

2
Epistemic modality

2.1 Definition of the term 'epistemic'

It was suggested in 1.3.5 that the term 'epistemic' should apply not simply to modal systems that basically involve the notions of possibility and necessity, but to any modal system that indicates the degree of commitment by the speaker to what he says. In particular, it should include evidentials such as 'hearsay' or 'report' (the Quotative) or the evidence of the senses. The Declarative, moreover, can be regarded as the unmarked ('unmodalized') member of an epistemic system, though by this definition some languages have no 'unmodalized' declaratives (1.4.2).

This use of the term may be wider than usual, but it seems completely justified etymologically since it is derived from the Greek word meaning 'understanding' or 'knowledge' (rather than 'belief'), and so is to be interpreted as showing the status of the speaker's understanding or knowledge; this clearly includes both his own judgments and the kind of warrant he has for what he says.

2.1.1 *Judgments and Evidentials*

There are at least four ways in which a speaker may indicate that he is not presenting what he is saying as a fact, but rather:

(i) that he is speculating about it
(ii) that he is presenting it as a deduction
(iii) that he has been told about it
(iv) that it is a matter only of appearance, based on the evidence of (possibly fallible) senses.

All of these seem to be expressed in some language or other, though there may be no language which distinguishes all four.

All four types are concerned with the indication by the speaker of his (lack of) commitment to the truth of the proposition being expressed. It will be possible, therefore, to find paraphrases with a subordinate sentence introduced by *that*, with the modality indicated by a lexical item in the main clause, e.g.:

   (i)   It is possible that .../ I think that ...
   (ii) It is to be concluded that .../ I conclude that ...
  (iii) It is said that .../ X said that ...
  (iv) It appears that ...

A language that has ways of indicating three of these – opinion, conclusion and report, which may be termed Speculative, Deductive and Quotative – is Inga (a Quechuan language of Colombia). Levinsohn (1975: 14–15) records five particles in Inga:

   mi   action witnessed – affirmative (AFF)
   chu   action witnessed – negative
   si   action reported to the speaker (REP)
   cha   action deduced by the speaker as having occurred (DED)
         (char – probability reinforced)
   sica action speculated as possible by the speaker

Examples of three are given (Levinsohn's page numbers in parenthesis)

   nis   puñuncuna-mi   (15)
   there they slept-AFF
   'There they slept'

   chipica diablo-char ca
   there   devil-DED   it was
   'A devil was presumably there'

   chacapi-si   yallinacú   (22)
   on bridge-REP they were crossing
   'They were crossing on the bridge'

The same three possibilities are found in the German modals MÖGEN, MÜSSEN and SOLLEN (Hammer 1983· 228–30):

   Er mag   krank sein
   he MÖGEN+3SG+PRES+INDIC ill   be
   'He may be ill'

   Er spielt heute Tennis, also muss   es
   He plays today tennis, so   MÜSSEN+3SG+PRES+INDIC it
      ihm   besser gehen
      to him better go
   'He is playing tennis today so he must be better'

Bei den Unruhen soll   es bisher vier
at the disturbances SOLLEN+3SG+PRES+INDIC it until now four
 Tote gegeben haben
 dead given have
'So far four are reported killed in the disturbances'

It can be argued that these three types belong to two different systems of epistemic modality. Opinions and conclusions involve judgments by the speaker, but reports indicate the kind of evidence he has for what he is saying. There are thus two sub-systems, one of Judgments, involving Speculative and Deductive, the other that of Evidentials, of which Quotative is a member.

The idea that there are two basic types of epistemic modality is to be found in the suggestion of Givón (1982: 24) that three types of proposition can be recognized:

(i) Propositions which are taken for granted, via the force of diverse conventions, as unchallengeable by the hearer and thus requiring no evidentiary justifications by the speaker

(ii) Propositions that are asserted with relative confidence, are open to challenge by the hearer and thus require – or admit – evidentiary justification

(iii) Propositions that are asserted with doubt as hypotheses and are thus beneath both challenge and evidentiary substantiation

Type (i) refers to declaratives, (ii) and (iii) to evidentials and judgments respectively.

Some languages have grammatical systems of one type of epistemic modality only: English has only judgments, while Tuyuca (see sections 1.4.2, 2.3.1), it appears, has only evidentials. Other languages, e.g. Inga and German, combine the two in a single grammatical system.

The question was raised earlier (1.3.2) whether modality is essentially subjective. In general, or perhaps by definition, the answer might seem to be that it is. But there is a difference in this respect between judgments and evidentials. There can be little doubt that a judgment, expressed by e.g. MAY and MUST in English, usually reflects the judgment of the speaker. Although Lyons (1977: 798) offers a theoretically possible, but rather contrived, example of objective epistemic modality, he admits that the 'epistemological justification' for the distinction 'is, to say the least, uncertain' (p. 797). The position with evidentials is clearly different. The Quotative, at least, looks *prima facie* to be wholly objective, indicating not what the speaker believes, but what has been said by others. But if this is

53

taken together with other evidentials, e.g. those that indicate the kind of observation (e.g. visual versus non-visual) on which the statement is based, it becomes clear that their whole purpose is to provide an indication of the degree of commitment of the speaker: he offers a piece of information, but qualifies its validity for him in terms of the type of evidence he has. In this sense evidentials are not indications of some objective modality, but are subjective in that they indicate the status of the proposition in terms of the speaker's commitment to it.

2.1.2 *Specific epistemic markers*

There are some languages that have a specific marker for epistemic modality. For instance, in Hixkaryana (Carib, N. Brazil – Derbyshire 1979: 143–5) there is a 'non-past uncertain' form of the verb, which, when occurring without any particle, marks an interrogative:

> (i) nomokyaha   nomokyano
> he come+NONPAST   he come+NONPAST UNCERT
> 'He is coming'   'Will he come?'

With other particles (occurring usually with the 'intensifier' *ha–*), it may also express:

> (ii) 'hearsay' with *-tɨ*
>
> nomokyan   ha-tɨ
> he come+NONPAST UNCERT INT-HSY
> 'He's coming (they say)'
>
> (iii) 'uncertainty' with *-na*
> nomokyan   ha-na
> he come+NONPAST UNCERT INT-UNC
> 'Maybe he'll come'
>
> (iv) 'deduction' with *–mɨ*
> nomokyan   ha-mɨ
> he come+NONPAST UNCERT INT-DED
> 'He is evidently coming' (on hearing the sound of an outboard motor)
>
> (v) 'Positive doubt, scepticism' with *-mpe*
> nomokyatxow   ha-mpe
> they come+NONPAST UNCERT INT-SCEP
> 'They are coming! I don't believe it'

Here there is a general marker of epistemic modality which is interpreted as a question when it occurs alone. When it is combined with particles, 'hearsay', 'deduction', 'uncertainty' and 'positive doubt' are expressed.

Similarly, for Serrano (Uto-Aztecan, California), Hill (1967 and personal communication) presents a set of evidential particles which 'specify the validity of the statement'. These seem rather a miscellaneous set, some deontic, some epistemic, plus the negative; some may co-occur. They are:

ha	inferential	(88–9)
kʷə'ə	potential 'can'	
kʷənə	quotative	
may	'may'	
na'a	volitative	
pata	intensive	
qáy	'not'	
ta	dubitative	

The particle that is relevant here is the 'dubitative' for which four points may be noted:

(i) It occurs alone only with the future or in questions:

'iːp t   wahi' pinkiv   (21)
here DUBIT coyote pass+FUT
'The coyote will pass here'

haiːŋkʷa   ta-bɨ   mi
to where   DUBIT-he+PAST go
'Where did he go?'

(ii) Except for the 'quotative', the 'dubitative' is the only evidential that may occur alone with the future, all other evidentials requiring its presence also. An example of the 'quotative' is:

pɨmia' kʷɨnɨ-č quçib   (89)
with him QUOT-we dwell+FUT
'We would live with him (so we were told)'

(iii) It is obligatory in questions, even though questions are also marked by intonation (shown as '?' in the examples), unless the potential is present:

kʷa'i ta-m   ç   ?   kihʷuːçi   (20)
eat DUBIT-PL you QUES fish+ACC
'Are you (pl.) eating fish?'

kʷi?-ç   pɨ   yɨː?ɨ?   (Hill, personal communication)
POT-you   you+them dry
'Can you dry them?'
It is often the only mark of question, as in the example in (i) above, where the word glossed 'to where' is an indefinite so that a more appropriate gloss would be 'somewhere'.

(iv) It is obligatory with the 'inferential':

'ama' t   X   ma:mç   (22)
He   DUBIT INFER hear
'He must hear it'

Steele (1975: 299) comments on Hill's material: '*ta* is apparently basic to any Serrano sentence that contains a shred of doubt. The hypothesis is that *ta* indicates the basic unreal nature of the situation the sentence describes.' In other words, it is a generalized marker of epistemic modality.

A further question is whether there are languages which have just one marker of epistemic modality but make no further distinction, and so include several types of epistemic modality within the function of that marker. A possible example is an Iranian language of the USSR, Tajik. Rastorgueva (1963: 59–65) distinguishes between 'evident' and 'non-evident' (or 'narrative') forms, the latter being glossed as referring to 'an occurrence or action known to the speaker, not on the basis of personal experience, but from collateral sources, i.e. from someone else's words or from logical inference'. The non-evident verb forms are compounds including a form of the copula, but they are clearly idiomatic in the sense of not being semantically transparent, and originally had a resultative function. An example given is:

aka ʃodi: *meomadaast*, rost-mi   (64)
'(they say that) Mr. Shodi is coming. Is that true?'

Rastorgueva also gives an example of the form used to indicate non-immediate awareness:

man avval u:ro naʃinoxtam, dik̦k̦at karpa binam, Ax̣mad *budaast*(64)
'At first I didn't recognize him; then when I looked carefully, I saw it was Ahmed'

In a sense, presumably, this is to be interpreted as not being direct observation; but the point is that Tajik distinguishes just two types.

Similarly for Turkish, Lewis (1967: 101) speaks of the 'inferential', which is glossed as both 'is/was said to be' and 'I infer', though only examples of the former are given, e.g.:

Orhan hasta imis
Orhan ill   is said to be
'Orhan is said to be ill'

A further possible example is Abkhaz (N.W. Caucasus – Hewitt 1979: 196), where there is a suffix on the verb in certain tense forms to 'indicate that the assertion is made as a result of inference or hear-say', e.g.:

də-r-s-x̌à-zaap'
him-they-kill-PERF-INFER/HSY
'Apparently they have already killed him'

2.1.3 *Other systems*

Both judgments and evidentials can be seen as devices for the speaker to indicate that he wishes to modify his commitment to the truth of what is being said. Some languages exhibit only one of these systems, others combine the two. The next two sections, 2.2 and 2.3, will look at each of these in detail.

There are, however, other ways in which there may be some indication of the status of the proposition, which are marginally matters of epistemic modality or at least overlap it. All are discussed in detail later. One concerns the knowledge of the hearer as well as the speaker. Systems of this kind are found in Kogi (Colombia) and Nambiquara (Brazil), where various combinations of speaker's and hearer's knowledge are indicated (2.4).

Further problems concern the status of the interrogative and the declarative in relation to these systems. These are the topics of 2.5 and 2.6.

More marginally related to epistemic systems are systems that mark discourse functions and place the proposition within the concepts of assertion, counter-assertion, question, answer, etc. A good example of this is to be found in Cashibo (Peru), though other quite different languages, including English, have some grammatical devices that relate to discourse. Within discourse, however, expressions of doubt, deduction, possibility, etc. are essential, and the primarily discourse features inevitably mingle with other types of epistemic modality (2.7).

2.2 Judgments

In many languages it is possible to make at least two kinds of epistemic judgment, a 'weak' one and a 'strong' one. A typical example is English with its modal verbs MAY and MUST, and this will be considered first.

2.2.1 *MAY and MUST*

English appears to have a fairly simple epistemic system involving primarily the modal verbs MAY and MUST, though there are others to be considered. In *Modality and the English modals* (Palmer 1979b), these were distinguished in terms of 'degrees' of modality, the term 'kinds' of modality being reserved for epistemic, deontic, dynamic. There are similar pairs of verbs in other languages, especially the Germanic ones, e.g.

57

MÖGEN and MÜSSEN in German, although in the Romance languages the corresponding verbs are less grammaticalized (1.5.1). The issue to be discussed here is the nature of the semantic distinctions that are made by these verbs. There are two possible approaches.

First, the relation between them can be clearly stated in terms of possibility and necessity. They express what is epistemically possible and what is epistemically 'necessary', although the word *necessary* itself is not used in an epistemic sense in ordinary language (*It is necessary that ...* is not a possible paraphrase of *must*). This is clearly illustrated in von Wright's schema (1.2.2).

The possibility/necessity notions are also clearly illustrated in the relationships that hold between the modals in terms of negation. Positive judgments can be made about negative propositions and negative judgments about positive ones. For MAY, English uses *may not* for the first of these, *can't* for the second:

> He may be there
> He may not be there
> He can't be there

The second of these expresses 'It is possible that he is not there', the third 'It is not possible that he is there'. Yet there is no similar set for MUST. Instead, for a positive judgment about a negative proposition ('It is "necessary" that it is not so') *can't* may be used, while for a negative judgment about a positive proposition *may not* can be used ('It is not "necessary" that it is so'):

> He must be there
> He can't be there
> He may not be there

The same forms are used, but in reverse order. This is easily explained in terms of logical relations between possibility and necessity, since 'not possible' is equivalent to 'necessary not' and 'not necessary' to 'possible not'. But English uses only the CAN and MAY forms and this may be significant. Lyons (1977: 802) remarks: 'in English at least, possibility rather than necessity should be taken as primitive in the analysis of epistemic modality'. But it is not only in English that this phenomenon is found. The same is partly true of German, where KÖNNEN supplies at least one of the negative forms corresponding to MÜSSEN:

> Er muss   krank gewesen sein
> he MÜSSEN+3SG+PRES+INDIC ill   been   be
> 'He must have been ill'

Er kann   nicht krank gewesen sein
he KÖNNEN+3SG+PRES+INDIC not   ill   been   be
'He can't have been ill'

In terms of necessity, this is a denial of the proposition 'necessary that not'; for the denial of the modality 'not necessary that' MÜSSEN is still possible, or KÖNNEN plus a word such as *auch* ('also'), but a third verb BRAUCHEN is more likely than either (Bouma 1975: 333):

Er kann   auch nicht krank gewesen sein
he KÖNNEN+3SG+PRES+INDIC also   not   ill   been   be

Er muss/braucht   nicht krank gewesen sein
he MÜSSEN/BRAUCHEN+3SG+PRES+INDIC not   ill   been   be
'He may not have been ill'

See also 3.2.1 and, for Chinese, 6.2.

A second way of approaching the meaning of MAY and MUST is simply in terms of the kind of judgment being made, and in particular between speculation and deduction. This is clearly suggested in the comments of Coates:

In its most normal usage, Epistemic MUST conveys the speaker's confidence in the truth of what he is saying, based on a deduction from facts known to him (which may or may not be specified).   (1983: 41)

MAY and MIGHT are the modals of Epistemic Possibility, expressing the speaker's lack of confidence in the proposition expressed.   (1983: 131)

It could be argued that possibility and necessity are more basic, because they are to be found in the deontic system too and expressed by the same modals MAY and MUST (3.2.1), and that it is the parallelism between these that makes it possible to account for the inclusion of epistemic and deontic modality within a single overall system (3.5). There are two arguments against this however. First, the epistemic/deontic argument is not as strong as it might seem, because the patterns of relationship between MAY and MUST in terms of negation are different in the two systems, which shows that the meanings of the modals cannot be wholly predicted by the logical notions and relationships, and are not directly dependent upon them. Secondly, it is only analysis in terms of judgments, degrees of commitment, etc., that brings out the subjective nature of epistemic modality; notions of possibility and necessity are more applicable to objective statements. The subjective (and performative) nature of epistemic judgments is emphasized by the fact that epistemic MAY and MUST have no past tense forms that are used to refer to past time (for the formally past tense forms see 2.2.3). *May have* and *must have* occur, but make present time judgments about past events. It is the proposition, not the modality, that is past. A 'performative' expression of subjective modality can be made only at the moment of speaking.

Yet there is not necessarily a conflict between necessity/possibility and the notion of judgment. A speaker can indicate what he believes to be 'necessarily' so or 'possibly' so, and such notions seem particularly appropriate to judgments that are essentially inferences from known facts.

For the moment, it can be suggested that there are two basic types of judgment, which may be called Deductive and Speculative. There are many other languages for which a similar system may be established. For Inga (Quechua, Guatemala), for instance, Levinsohn (1975; see 2.1.1) notes:

cha 'action deduced by the speaker as having probably occurred'
sica 'action speculated as possible by the speaker'

It will noted that the glosses contain both the notions of deduction and speculation and the notions of possibility and necessity.

Similarly, in the related language Imbabura (both are varieties of Quechua), Cole (1982: 164) notes 'conjecture' and 'doubt':

kaya-shi   kanpaj churi shamu-nga
tomorrow-CONJ you-of son   come-FUT+3
'I suppose your son will come tomorrow'

Juzi-ka   Kitu-man chaya-shka-chá
Jose-TOP Quito-to arrive-PERF-DOU
'Perhaps Jose has arrived in Quito'

However, these belong to a more extensive system of modality, which includes other evidentials. At best, it can be said that there is a sub-system of two (see 2.3.2).

A basic system of Speculative and Deductive is found in the proposals of Gary and Gamal-Eldin (1982: 99) for Egyptian colloquial Arabic:

jimkin   jikuun hinaak
probable/possible he be there
'It is probable/possible that he is there'

laazim jikuun hinaak
must   he be   there
'He must be there'

Literary Arabic uses different forms (Zayed 1984):

> rubbama yabtasima Zeidun (92)
> RUBBAMA smile+3MSG+IMPERF Zeid
> 'Zeid may smile'

> labudda ʔan yaku:na filbayti (114)
> LABUDDA that be+3MSG+IMPERF in the house
> 'He must be at home'

Not only do these belong together formally in a variety of ways, but they are curiously linked in meaning. For the form used to mean 'may' with the imperfect tense (as above) can mean 'must' with the perfect:

> rubbama ʔibtasama Zeidun (134)
> RUBBAMA smile+3MSG+PERF Zeid
> 'Zeid must have smiled'

This may also mean, however, 'Zeid may still smile', while the negative (with the imperfect only) has the possibility meaning:

> rubbama lam yagida Zeidun nuqu:dahu wa
> RUBBAMA not find+3MSG+IMPERF Zeid his money and
> lam yarhala (179)
> not leave+3MSG+IMPERF
> 'It is possible that Zeid didn't find his money and didn't leave'

In Tamil (Dravidian, S. India and Sri Lanka – Thiagarayan 1982; Asher 1982) there are a number of potential modal forms, but only two are in the form of a verbal suffix. These Asher (1982: 167–72) calls 'debitive' and 'permission', though they are used epistemically as well as deontically (see 3.5). (The 'debitive' also has a full independent form.) Relevant epistemic examples are:

> Kantacaami vantaalum varalaam
> Kandaswami come+CONCESS come+PERM
> 'Kandaswami may perhaps come'

> Ganeecan ippa Mannaarkuṭiyile irukkaṇum
> Ganesan now Mannargudi+LOC be+DEB
> 'Ganesan must be in Mannargudi now'

2.2.2 WILL

Strictly, English does not have only two 'degrees' (2.2.1) of epistemic modality. To begin with, there is also the modal WILL, used in such sentences as:

> They'll be on holiday at the moment
> That'll be the postman

It could well be argued that *may* indicates a possible judgment, WILL a reasonable judgment and MUST the only possible judgment. If this is so, WILL falls between weak MAY and strong MUST.

It is tempting to identify this with the notion of 'probability', but although 'probable' appears in von Wright's system (1.2.2), it does not have equivalence relations with the other items in the system like those that hold for 'possible' and 'necessary' in terms of negation. Moreover, WILL often seems, like MUST, to indicate that the judgment is based on known facts, and in particular, on what is usually the case, as in the first example above. It is for this reason that it is not equivalent to 'probable'. It seems, then, that a third term should be introduced into the Judgment system that contains Deductive and Speculative. An appropriate label would be Assumptive.

WILL is also used to refer to future time. This is not particularly surprising: the future is not fully known, but it is a reasonable assumption that it will ensue. Conversely, it is often possible to paraphrase the epistemic use of WILL as 'You will find that . . .'; but that is less appropriate in the first sentence above than in the second. In any case, it is clear that there is a difference between epistemic WILL and 'future' WILL, though the relations between them will have to be discussed in some detail (6.1.3).

It is relevant to this issue that even the morphologically marked future tenses of the Romance languages, French, Spanish and Italian, express the same meaning. The following examples are from Italian (Lepschy and Lepschy 1977: 139, with modification of the translations):

> Suonano   sarà   Ugo
> they are ringing be+3SG+FUT+INDIC Ugo
> 'The bell's gone; it'll be Ugo'

> Hai   idea dove siano? Saranno   tornati
> have you idea where they are be+3PL+FUT+INDIC returned
>   a   casa
>   to house
> 'Have you any idea where they are? They'll have gone home'

In colloquial Spanish, moreover, the 'future tense' is not normally used to express future time but only this 'degree' of epistemic modality. For future time the verb *ir* 'to go' is used with the infinitive.

2.2.3 *Modifications*

English has ways of modifying the basic system of three types of judgments. First, it has what might be called 'tentative' forms (Palmer 1979b: 48–50) that are formally past tense forms, i.e. *might* and *would* (*'d*):

> He might be there by now
> They'd be on holiday now

The form that most closely corresponds to MUST is *ought to*, or *should* (although this is formally the past tense of a different modal verb, SHALL):

> He ought to/should be there by now

But this carries with it some notion of conditionality – 'provided things are as I expect them to be' etc., and is not just a weaker or more tentative form of MUST (Palmer 1979b: 49, cf. 100–2).

Similarly in German, although the present form of MÖGEN is most typically used to express a weak epistemic judgment, the past tense forms (but subjunctive) of MÖGEN, KÖNNEN and DÜRFEN are also used to express greater tentativeness (Hammer 1983: 227ff):

> Er mag krank sein (229)
> he MÖGEN+3SG+PRES+INDIC ill be
> 'He may be ill'

> Man möchte meinen, dass ... (229)
> one MÖGEN+3SG+IMPERF+SUBJ think that
> 'One might think that ...'

> Er könnte krank sein (227)
> he KÖNNEN+3SG+IMPERF+SUBJ ill be
> 'He might be ill'

> Er dürfte krank gewesen sein (228)
> he DÜRFEN+3SG+IMPERF+SUBJ ill been be
> 'He might well have been ill'

(According to Hammer, '*möchte* often denotes possibility or probability or conveys a hesitant or polite doubt', while '*dürfte* implies greater probability than *könnte*, but is at the same time more tentative and polite'.)

It is also possible for the speaker to modify his commitment still further by the addition of 'harmonic combinations' (Halliday 1970: 331), which reinforce the modality, or by 'hedges'. Coates (1983: 46, 138) notes for epistemic MUST the occurrence of harmonic *I'm sure*, *surely*, and *certainly*, and of the hedges, *I think* (the most common), *I mean*, *I suppose*, *I fancy*, *I take it* and *I would guess*; and for MAY, harmonic *perhaps*, *possibly*, and

63

hedges *I suppose*, *I think*, *I don't know*, *I wouldn't know*, *I'm not sure*, *I mean* and *It seems to me*. An analysis of these is beyond the scope of this work, but they show that there is potentially great variation in the degree of speaker commitment.

2.2.4 *Inference and confidence*

In her comments on MUST Coates (1983: 41) writes of 'the speaker's confidence in the truth of what he is saying, based on a deduction from facts known'; on MAY she writes (p. 131) of 'the speaker's lack of confidence in the proposition expressed' (see 2.2.1).

There are, however, two issues here, one a matter of 'confidence' or degree of commitment by the speaker, the other a matter of making inference from other available information ('known facts'). With MUST there is often some indication of the facts on which the inference is based. An example from Coates (1983: 41) is:

> His teeth were still chattering but his forehead, when I felt it, was hot and clammy. He said 'I must have a temperature.'

A similar example is found in Palmer (1979b: 44):

> All the X-rays showed absolutely negative. There was nothing wrong, so it must just be tension, I suppose.

Moreover, it is the notion of deduction or inference from known facts that is the essential feature of MUST, not just the strength of commitment by the speaker. For MUST does not have the same kind of meaning as the adverbs *certainly*, *definitely*, etc., which are, indeed, indications simply of the speaker's confidence or commitment. With MAY, in contrast, there is little sense of inference or reference to known facts, and no very clear distinction between the meanings of MAY and that of adverbs such as *perhaps*, which again indicate degree of confidence.

There are, then, two different, though closely related, types of epistemic modality, one concerned with inference, the other with confidence. In one the speaker indicates that he is inferring from available information, in the other he indicates the degree of confidence he has in what he is saying. With the stronger type of judgment, there is a clear difference between MUST and adverbs such as *certainly*, the modal expressing inference and the adverb confidence. The same is true of WILL, which is different from *probably*. With the weaker judgment, there may, in theory, be a difference between MAY and *perhaps*, *possibly*, etc., but in practice it is difficult to distinguish them.

An obvious question is whether the inference/confidence distinction is marked grammatically in any languages, The evidence is sparse and not very clear, but there are some indications of grammatically different forms for the stronger types of inference and confidence in Hixkaryana (Brazil) and Ngiyambaa (Australia).

In Hixkaryana (Derbyshire 1979) the 'non-past uncertain' form of the verb appears to be used as a general marker of epistemic modality (see 2.1.2), but fits into two formal systems. With the intensifier *ha* it contrasts with the 'non-past' in terms, apparently, of degree of confidence:

nomokyaha   ha   (144)
he come+NONPAST INT
'He must certainly come'

nomokyan   ha
he come+NONPAST UNCERT INT
'He may come'

With the addition of further particles (in addition to *ha*) the 'non-past uncertain' provides what seems to be a system that includes 'deduction'. The example quoted was:

nomokyan   ha-mɨ
he come+NONPAST UNCERT INT-DED
'He is evidently coming'

In Ngiyambaa (Donaldson 1980) there are two forms glossed 'bound to', one formed with the inflectional 'purposive', the other with 'irrealis' plus 'categorical assertion' (see 1.5.4):

yuruŋ-gu ŋidja-l-i   (162)
rain-ERG   rain-CM-PURP
'It is bound to rain'

guni:m-baṯa-nuː   balu-y-aga
mother+ABS-CATEG ASSERT-2OBL die-CM-IRR
'Your mother is bound to die'

But Donaldson glosses 'categorical assertion' as 'absolute truth', and one may assume that with the 'irrealis' it indicates a slightly lower level of confidence. The purposive, however, is often used deontically to express what must be, and this together with Donaldson's example suggests that its epistemic meaning is that of positive inference from what is known.

2.2.5 *Mood*

The European languages that have mood seldom mark epistemic modality clearly by it. The subjunctive is sometimes used in Greek to express 'may', e.g.:

ouk ésth'   houtos anéːr oud' éssetai
not be+3SG+PRES+INDIC this   man   nor be+3SG+FUT+INDIC
  oudé géneːtai   (Hom. *Od.* 16. 437)
  nor become+3SG+AOR+SUBJ
'This man is not, will not be, may not be'

The subjunctive here actually contrasts with both the present and the future indicative, and there are other examples of the Homeric subjunctive being used to refer to a possible future event. There is a similar use in Latin:

Iam apsolutos censeas,   quom incedunt infectores
                                    (Pl. *Aul.* 520)
now paid off   think+2SG+PRES+SUBJ when come in dyers
'You may think they are already paid off, when in come the dyers'

However, not only is there no corresponding 'must' form, but also this is only one use of the subjunctive among many, including deontic uses. There is no formal distinction – only the context can decide. We may contrast with the examples above:

heːmeís dé phrazóːmeth',   hópoːs okh' árista
we   but think+1PL+PRES+SUBJ how   best
  géneːtai   (Hom. *Od.* 23.117)
  become+3SG+AOR+SUBJ
'Let us consider how this may be best'

Sed maneam   etiam, opinor   (Pl. *Trin.* 1136)
but remain+1SG+PRES+SUBJ still   I think
'But I should still stay, I think'

In modern Spanish, however, which has the verbs PODER and DEBER which can be used for epistemic (as well as deontic) modality, the subjunctive is often used to express epistemic doubt, especially with adverbs, in contrast with the indicative which expresses greater confidence (see 4.2.4):

Tal vez venga   mañana
perhaps come+3SG+PRES+SUBJ tomorrow

Tal vez vendrá   mañana
perhaps come+3SG+FUT+INDIC tomorrow
'Perhaps he'll come tomorrow'

2.3 Evidentials

There are many languages in which the epistemic system appears to consist of both evidentials and judgments. 'Pure' evidential systems are much rarer, though at least one seems to have been attested.

2.3.1   *'Pure' systems*
One clear example of an evidential system is found in Tuyuca
(Brazil and Colombia – Barnes 1984). A system of five evidentials is there
illustrated (p. 257) with five different sentences, all of which have the same
English translation 'He played soccer', and all with 3rd person masculine
singular endings:

   (i)   díiga apé-wi
         (I saw him play)
  (ii)   díiga apé-ti
         (I heard the game and him, but I didn't see it or him)
 (iii)   díiga apé-yi
         (I have seen evidence that he played: his distinctive shoe print on the
         playing fields. But I did not see him play)
  (iv)   díiga apé-yigi
         (I obtained the information from someone else)
   (v)   díiga apé-hĩyi
         (It is reasonable to assume that he did)

Barnes proposes five names for these:

   (i)   visual
  (ii)   non-visual ('to indicate any of the senses other than visual')
 (iii)   apparent
  (iv)   secondhand
   (v)   assumed

The evidential nature of the system is most clearly suggested by the first
two, where the distinction is between the kind of sensory evidence, but
'secondhand', which is clearly Quotative, is no less a matter of evidence.

One important point about the Tuyuca system is that there is a
hierarchical relation between the terms. At the bottom is 'assumed', which
is used when the speaker has prior knowledge about the state of things or
about habitual or general 'behaviour patterns', but 'only when no information about the state or event is being or has been received'. In that sense
it is the negative member of the evidential system, used when no ready
evidence is available.

In contrast, the 'visuals' are the 'preferred evidentials'. They are
according to Barnes (1984: 12ff) used whenever a speaker has seen, or is
looking at, a state or event. Even if he has or has had another type of
evidence, he will still use the visual evidential rather than that appropriate
to the other types. She stresses the importance of giving visual information
whenever possible. Thus if a person is asked, on leaving his mother's

house, whether she is in, he will reply 'She was', with the visual evidential, rather than 'She is', which would require the assumed evidential. The status of the visual evidential is important for the discussion of declaratives (1.4.1) and will be considered again later in this chapter (2.6).

Rather different is the situation in Ngiyambaa (see 1.5.4) where there is an evidential system that is independent of several other modal systems in the language. There is here a system of two terms, 'sensory evidence' and 'linguistic evidence':

> ŋindu gara   garambiyi
> you+NOM-SENS EVID sick+PAST
> 'One can see you were sick'

> ŋindu-dhan   garambiyi
> you+NOM-LING EVID sick+PAST
> 'You are said to have been sick'

The independence of the system from other systems is shown by an example in which a clitic from each of the 'belief', 'knowledge' and 'evidence' systems occur:

> ŋindu-gila-gaː-dhan   guɾuŋa-y-aga
> you+NOM-HYPOTH-IGNOR-LING EVID swim-CM-IRR
> 'I gather that perhaps you are going to swim'

The Declarative, in particular, is in no sense a member of the evidential system (as it might be said to be in Tuyuca). It is, indeed, not a member of any of the epistemic systems that are marked by clitics, but belongs to the distinct inflectional system. Moreover, not only is the evidence of sight not distinguished in Ngiyambaa from the evidence of other senses, but sensory evidence in general is not presented as the strongest or preferred type, but rather suggests the possible fallibility of the senses.

2.3.2 *Judgments and Evidentials again*

There are several languages that have a modal system that contains more than one Evidential, but also what seems to be Deductive and, in some cases, Speculative. A simple three-term system is proposed for Nambiquara (unclassified Brazil – Lowe 1972: 361):

> observation: I report what I saw
> deduction: I tell my deduction
> narration: I was told

(But this represents only one parameter in the overall system; another is in terms of who saw, deduced or was told – see 2.4.)

Five possibilities were noted for Inga (2.1.1): 'witnessed positive', 'witnessed negative', 'reported', 'deduced' and 'speculative'. (Positive/ negative is thus a sub-system within 'visual' or 'witnessed'.) There is a similar system in the closely related language Imbabura (Cole 1982: 164), where the full system is:

ma(rí)	emphatic firsthand information
mi	firsthand information
shi	conjecture
cha(ri)	doubt
chu	Yes–No question
chu	negation

e.g.

ñuka-ta miku-naya-n-mari
I-ACC   eat-DESID-3-EF INF
'I want to eat'

kan-paj ushi-wan   Agatu-pi-mi
you-of daughter-with Ageto-in-F INF
'I met your daughter in Ageto'

kaya-shi   kan-paj churi shamu-nga
tomorrow-CONJ you-of son   come-FUT+3
'I suppose your son will come tomorrow'

Juzi-ka   kitu-man chaya-shka-chá
Jose-TOP Quito-to arrive-PERF-DOU
'Perhaps Jose has arrived in Quito'

mayistru-chu ka-ngui
teacher-QUES be-2SG
'Are you a teacher?'

ñuka-ka mana chay llama-ta   shuwa-shka-ni-chu
I-TOP   not   that sheep-ACC steal-PERF-2SG-NEG
'I didn't steal that sheep'

(Here it would appear that there are two sub-systems within 'firsthand' – emphatic/non-emphatic and, presumably, positive/negative.)

It would be perfectly reasonable to argue that these languages have mixed evidential and judgment systems. But the same argument could apply to Tuyuca. Among the evidentials of Tuyuca were 'apparent' and 'assumed', and since these can often be translated by English MUST and

WILL, it could be said that they too involve judgments. (Barnes glosses 'apparent' by 'I have seen evidence', but clearly there is an implication of an inference with both evidentials.)

Arguments of this type would also lead to the suggestion that what was called 'inference' in the previous section, as contrasted with 'confidence', is a matter of evidential modality. MUST in English infers or deduces from available information, i.e. from evidence.

It would be a futile exercise to try to decide whether a particular system (or even a term in a system in some cases) is evidential rather than a judgment. There is often no very clear distinction because speakers' judgments are naturally often related to the evidence they have. But it is still reasonable to argue that some systems, e.g. that of Tuyuca, are predominantly evidential, while others, e.g. that of English, are predominantly judgments.

Some modal systems may be even more mixed. One system that will be discussed in several places later is that of Hidatsa (Siouan, USA). Matthews (1965: 99–100) suggests that the final clause of each sentence ends in a mood morpheme; six such morphemes are established and are glossed as follows:

Emphatic:	'indicates that the speaker knows the sentence to be true; if a sentence that ends with the Emphatic is false, the speaker is considered a liar'
Period:	'indicates that the speaker believes the sentence to be true; if it should turn out otherwise, it would mean that he was mistaken, but by no means a liar'
Quotative:	'indicates that the speaker regards what he has said to be something that everyone knows'
Report:	'indicates that the speaker was told the information given in the sentence by someone else, but has no evidence of its truth value'
Indefinite/question:	'both indicate that the speaker does not know whether or not the sentence is true. The Indefinite also means that the speaker thinks the listener does not know; whereas the Question indicates that the speaker thinks that the listener does know.'

But there are serious problems about Matthews' interpretation, which will be discussed in 2.5 and 2.6.1.

2.3.3 *Quotatives*

A number of examples have been given of languages with formal markers for what has been said to be true, for 'reports', 'hearsay', e.g. Menomini (1.1.1), Hidatsa (2.3.2), Ngiyambaa (1.5.4), Hixkaryana (2.1.2) and Serrano (2.1.2). Examples from Ngiyambaa (Donaldson 1980: 276), Hixkaryana (Derbyshire 1979: 144) and Serrano (Hill 1967: 23), respectively, are:

ŋindu-dhan　　　girambiyi
you+NOM-LING EVID sick+PAST
'You are said to have been sick'

yawaxa yariy　　hati　waraxa
axe　　he took it HSY　Waraxa
'They say Waraxa took the axe'

'iːp kʷini'-bi　　wahi'　pinq
here QUOT-he+PAST coyote pass
'The coyote passed here (so I am told)'

It was also noted that in some languages, e.g. Tajik and Turkish (2.1.2), it may be that there is a single marker for epistemic modality which at least includes report among its meanings.

There is a rather special situation with Quotative, in that some languages that have a predominantly judgment system include quotative within that system, although quotative seems to be clearly evidential – the evidence being what others have said. The Germanic languages, e.g. German and Danish, are examples of such languages, though not, of course, English. German has no fewer than three devices to indicate what is said (examples from Hammer 1983).

First, the subjunctive may be used in main clauses to indicate that it is what is said or was said and not part of the writer's or speaker's own statement:

Bei seiner Vernehmung berief sich H. auf Notwehr.　Er
in　his　examination appealed　H. to　self-defence he
sei　　　　　　　　mit S. in Streit　geraten und
be+3SG+PRES+SUBJ with S. in quarrel fallen　and
habe　　　　　　　sich von diesem bedroht　gefühlt　(269)
have+3SG+PRES+SUBJ self　by　him　　threatened felt

'In the course of his cross examination, H. pleaded self-defence. He had become involved in a quarrel with S, and had felt himself to be threatened by him'

The second sentence here is what H. claimed, not part of the writer's own report.

Secondly, the modal verb SOLLEN can be used to mean 'it is said that . . .':

> Er soll   steinreich sein   (231)
> he SOLLEN+3SG+PRES+INDIC very rich be
> 'He is said to be extremely rich'

Thirdly, another modal WOLLEN can be used to indicate what the subject of the sentence claims or says:

> Er will   eine Mosquito abgeschossen haben
>   (232)
> he WOLLEN+3SG+PRES+INDIC a   Mosquito shot down   have
> 'He claims to have shot down a Mosquito (plane)'

Similarly, in Danish SKAL is used for 'report' (Davidsen-Nielsen 1986):

> Peter skal   være en dårlig forsker
> Peter SKAL+PRES be   a   poor researcher
> 'Peter is said to be a poor researcher'

With the examples of the subjunctive it might be argued that this is to be accounted for by saying that there is a verb of reporting in the context or that such a verb is understood. For the subjunctive is used in subordinate clauses after indirect speech (see 4.2.2) and the use of 'He had become' to report 'I became' in the English translation can be accounted for in the same way (see 4.6.2). To do so is to account for modal markers in the main clauses in terms of subordinate modality. But this is essentially a chicken-and-egg problem. Should there be an account of main clause modality in terms of subordinate clause modality or vice versa?

There are undoubtedly some languages in which the quotative is used only in main clauses, and so cannot be explained in terms of verbs being understood. Hidatsa (Siouan, USA) appears to be one: Matthews (1965: 98 fn. 1) has examples of reported speech where a verb of saying is present, but the subordinate clause is marked not with the 'report' morpheme, but with 'period' (=Declarative).

In other languages the quotative is used in both main and subordinate clauses, and often, with main clauses, there is no verb of saying that can in any way be retrieved from the context. This is so in Ngiyambaa (Donaldson 1980: 276):

> buraːy-dja-lu   gaː-y-aga
> child+ABS-LING EVID-3ABS bring-CM-IRR
> 'It's said she's going to bring the children'

```
ŋadhu-dhan        wiri-nji
I+NOM-LING EVID cook-PAST
```
'I am supposed to have cooked'

It is also true of Cashibo (Shell 1975: 178–82), except that in main clauses the form used consists of both 'declarative' and 'report'. (Shell distinguishes 'report in independent clause' and 'report in dependent clause', but the former is clearly two elements):

```
Jorgenïn ka          aín lápiz   ćasiaşa                         (178)
George   DECL+3 his pencil break+PAST+3
```
'George broke his pencil'

```
Jorgenïn kaísa       aín lápiz   ćasiaşa                         (181)
George   REP IND+3 his pencil break+PAST+3
```
'George broke his pencil, it is said'

```
aín lápiz   isa           ćasiaşa kišon              ka
his pencil REP DEP+3 break+PAST+3 CLOSE OF QUOTE DECL+3
   Jorgenïn ʔï kaaşa                                             (182)
   George   me say+PAST+3
```
'George told me that he broke his pencil'

In modern societies one important use of a report form is in journalism, where it is important for the writer to report what has been said in criminal cases without being caught by the laws of libel. English has the clumsy device of the use of the verb ALLEGE (*the alleged attacker* etc.), but German can use the subjunctive. French has the device of the conditional tense, which belongs to modality only if conditionals do (see 5.4):

```
Il l'   aurait           tué
he him have+3SG+COND killed
```
'He is alleged to have killed him'

If the quotative is used where there is a verb of reporting in the context, or at least understood from the context, it is clear who is responsible for what is said. If it is not, there is a possible distinction between 'Someone told me ...' and 'People say ...'. The translations offered by Lowe (1972) for Nambiquara suggest the former ('I was told by someone ...'), whereas German SOLLEN almost certainly has the second meaning. In other languages it may be that no distinction is made.

There are other possibilities. German WOLLEN indicates what the subject of the sentence says – usually it indicates a boastful claim. But at least it is clear that there is a contrast between the function of WOLLEN and SOLLEN, the former indicating what is said by the subject, the latter what is said by

other people (generally). In both cases the speaker disclaims responsibility
for the validity of what is said.

Another possibility is that there is a form to indicate that what is being
said is part of a myth or story – that it is what everyone in the society knows.
Thus in Hidatsa there is, in addition to the morpheme for 'report', another
one for 'quotative' in the restricted sense of what everyone knows (see 2.6.1
for details). Even where there are not two distinct forms, as in Hidatsa, the
quotative may be used for such myths and stories. In Hixkaryana the
particle for 'hearsay' is obligatory and has to be repeated continually
throughout the story (Derbyshire 1979: 145). Similarly, in the quite
unrelated language Sherpa (Tibeto-Burman – Givón 1982) the 'indirect/
hearsay marker' is used in passages from religious texts.

This raises problems concerning the nature of declaratives and factivity,
which will be discussed in 2.6.

Finally, it may be briefly noted that the subjunctive is sometimes used in
subordinate clauses in Latin, and some other languages, simply to indicate
what is 'reported'. This will be discussed in 4.1.5.

2.3.4 *Sensation*

There has already been some discussion about the place of
sensation in evidential systems, and it was noted in particular that Tuyuca
distinguishes visual and non-visual evidence (2.3.1), while Ngiyambaa
indicates all sensory evidence with a single clitic (2.3.4), though visual
evidence also has a different status in the two languages.

In both languages all five traditional senses may be involved. Thus in
Tuyuca the non-visual evidential may be 'used to report how someone,
something or some event smelled, sounded, tasted or felt (smells, sounds,
tastes or feels)' (Barnes 1984: 260). Examples are:

> yoáro   susúhã-ta   (*ta* =3PL+PAST)
> 'They smelled (of liquor) a long way off'

> mũtúru   bisí-ti   (*tí* = 'other'+PAST)
> 'The motor roared'

It is also used to refer to the speaker's own emotion, pain or knowledge:

> paága   pũní-ga   (*ga*='other'+PRES)
> 'My stomach hurts'

> tisá-ga
> 'I like it'

> mãsíri-ga
> 'I don't know'

In Ngiyambaa (Donaldson 1980: 275–6) the clitic that is used for sensory evidence may involve all five senses:

ŋindu-gara girambiyi
you+NOM-SENS EVID sick+PAST
'One can see you were sick'

gabugaːgara-lu ŋamumiyi
egg+ABS-SENS EVID-3ERG lay+PAST
'It's laid an egg by the sound of it'
(The chicken concerned was out of sight.)

yuraːbad-gara ŋidji guṟuga-nha
rabbit+ABS-SENS EVID here+CIRC be inside-PRES
ŋama-ṟa-baṟa-dhu-na
feel-PRES-CATEG ASSERT-INOM-3ABS
'I can tell there's a rabbit in here. I (can) feel it for sure'
(The speaker had her hand in a burrow.)

dhagun-gir-gara ŋina dhiŋaː ga-ṟa
earth-nasty with-SENS EVID this+ABS meat+ABS be-PRES
'This meat tastes nasty with earth'
(Said while attempting to eat it.)

waraːy-gara-dhu-na bungiyamiyi
bad+ABS-SENS EVID-INOM-3ABS change with fire+PAST
dhiŋaː-dhiː
meat+ABS-IOBL
'I have burnt my meat so it's no good, to judge by the smell'
(Said outside the house where the meat was cooking.)

Even in English there is some connection between sensation and modality. The most common way of expressing what one sees, hears, smells, tastes or feels is with the modal verb CAN:

I can see the moon
I can hear a funny noise
I can smell something burning
I can taste salt in this
I can feel something hard here

All of these indicate that the speaker has the sensation, not that he has the ability to have it. There is in fact a potential ambiguity in:

I can hear high frequencies

This could mean either that I do now hear them, or that my hearing is good enough to hear them. CAN is a dynamic modal in this sense and not strictly within the topic of this book. But it is relevant that English does not normally present information about sensation with simple declarative statements, but chooses instead to use a form that is much less categorical, just as Ngiyambaa indicates sensory evidence with a clitic that distinguishes it from declaratives.

2.4 **Speakers and hearers**

In Kogi (Chibchan, N. Colombia) there is, Hensarling (1982) tentatively suggests, an 'evidential' system indicating 'who knows what about the situation being discussed'. She suggests (p. 52) a matrix for five particles, as shown in table 1.

Table 1. *Kogi 'evidential' system*

	Speaker	Hearer	Gloss
ni	+	+	remind
na	+	−	inform
shi	−	+	ask
skaN	−	−	doubt
ne	−	?	speculate

Examples are:

> ni-gu-ku-á   (21)
> REM-do-I-NEAR PAST
> 'I did it just a while ago, as you know'

> na-gu-ŋgú   (21)
> INFORM-do-INTERMEDIATE PAST
> 'I tell you he did it some time ago'

> shi-ná   (22)
> ASK-be PROXIMATE
> 'Is that the way it is?'

> skaŋ-gú   (22)
> DOU-do PROXIMATE
> 'Who knows if it did just now?'

> näbbi nóŋgutse né   haŋgna   (23)
> lion little   SPEC think PUNCTILIAR
> '"I wonder if it is a small lion", he thought'

(*né* is different in that it appears in sentence-final position here, but it can occur in the same place as the others.)

'Remind' relates what both speaker and hearer know, 'inform' what the speaker knows but the hearer does not, 'ask' what the hearer knows but the speaker does not, 'doubt' what neither know and 'speculate' what the speaker does not know (the hearer's knowledge not being considered). The term 'evidential' does not seem strictly appropriate, but is in fairly general use for modal systems for languages of the Americas. (The term 'hearer' is not strictly accurate since the person concerned is the one that is being spoken to, and not anyone who might, quite accidentally, hear. The term 'addressee' is clearly better and is used by some scholars, but the majority use 'hearer' and that is the term adopted here.)

A more complex system is proposed by Lowe (1972) for Nambiquara (Brazil; see also 6.4). He suggests that there is a two-dimensional system involving:

> event verification: individual, collective
> speaker orientation: observation, deduction, narration

The 'speaker-orientation' system has already been discussed (2.3.2); it can be treated as an evidential system. The 'event verification' system involves speaker and addressee (hearer), whether the speaker alone or both speaker and addressee saw the event, deduced that it occurred or were told about it. Lowe provides the following glosses:

•	individual, observation:	'I report to you what I saw the actor doing'
	individual, deduction:	'I tell you my deduction of an action that must have occurred because of something I see or saw'
	individual, narration:	'I was told by someone that a certain action occurred'
	collective, observation:	'I report what both I and the addressee saw the actor doing'
	collective, deduction:	'From what the speaker and the addressee saw, they deduce that a certain action must have taken place'
	collective, narration:	'Both speaker and addressee were told that a certain event took place'

His translations of the forms of the verb 'work' are:

> He worked
> He must have worked
> I was told that he worked (past)
> Both you and I saw that he worked
> He worked, as deduced from what we saw
> It was told us that he worked

2.5 **Interrogatives**

In a number of languages the Interrogative fits formally into the modality system. It is worth looking in detail at some that have already been mentioned.

For Menomini (1.1.1) Hockett (1958: 257) places the Interrogative in a five-term system which includes what might be identified as the Declarative and Quotative plus two forms that indicate surprise that the proposition will or will not come true.

In Serrano (2.1.2) the 'dubitative' morpheme is used in questions. With 'Yes–No' questions a rising intonation also occurs (on the verbal complex), but in '*wh-*' questions the dubitative occurs: 'alone marking the construction as a question' (Hill 1967: 20–1), as in:

> naːšt ta-bɨ'   hihi ?   čičinti
> girl   DUB-she+PAST see   QUES boy+ACC
> 'Did the girl see the boy?'

> haiːŋkʷa' ta-bɨ   mi
> to where DUB-he+PAST go
> 'Where did he go?'

The second of these repeats the (only) example of a '*wh-*' question. What is important is that the word translated 'to where' is an indefinite determiner; a translation 'to somewhere' would be more appropriate; it is the dubitative that indicates the question.

There is a somewhat similar situation in Hixkaryana (2.1.2) where there are a number of tense forms which include 'non-past uncertain' (as well as 'non-past certain'). The 'non-past uncertain' form occurs with a variety of modal particles to express 'hearsay', 'deduction', 'uncertainty' and 'positive doubt', but when it occurs alone, the 'non-past uncertain' expresses a question:

> amanheno (a-manho-yano)   (138)
> 2SG-dance-NONPAST UNCERT
> 'Do you dance?'/'Are you going to dance?'

Matthews' (1965: 99–100; see also this volume: 2.3.2, 2.6.1, 2.6.2) analysis of Hidatsa appears *prima facie* to provide a similar picture, in that he includes 'indefinite/question' among his mood morphemes, and remarks 'both indicate that the speaker does not know whether or not the sentence is true. The Indefinite also means that the speaker thinks the listener does not know; whereas the Question indicates that the speaker thinks that the listener does know.' What is interesting here is the suggestion that a question can be treated as a statement by the speaker of his ignorance, with the belief that the hearer has the required information. This would, clearly, explain why interrogatives belong so often to a modal system. Unfortunately, this is not an observation based upon the language, but on the author's own interpretation and rationalization, for there is no actual segmental morpheme of 'question' and so no formal reason for linking it to 'indefinite' or even for including it in the modal system at all (see also 2.7.1).

Even more surprising, perhaps, in Huichol (Mexico – Grimes 1964) there is a specific marker for the 'assertive' mood. Although questions may be indicated by the 'interrogative transformation', there are sentences with no 'mode' (mood) marker, and these are often to be interpreted as questions. What Grimes says (p. 27) is:

> Questions not marked by the interrogative transformation . . . have no special marking that identifies them unambiguously. Any assertion can be agreed with or disagreed with, so that a plain assertion is the semantic equivalent of an English 'Yes or No' question. In a conversational context, however, modeless assertions are most likely to be interpreted as questions.

Examples are:

pée-tⁿa
ass-direction go
'He left'

mázá tikuucúu
deer asleep
'Is the deer asleep?'

It is curious that Grimes should regard the unmarked form as a 'plain assertion', since he has indicated that there is a marker for the 'assertive' mood, and it rather looks as if the unmarked form should be the one to be identified with the Interrogative. The point he should, perhaps, be making is that the mere presentation of a proposition, with no indication of mood, can be agreed with or disagreed with. This would be an argument similar to that proposed for the unmarked declarative (see 1.4.2 and 2.6) – that it is merely presented for acceptance. It may be significant too that the 'assertive' mood marker occurs only in main clauses, just as the unmarked form that is identical with declaratives occurs in such clauses in other languages. It is not, then, impossible to accept that the unmarked form is the Interrogative, at least in the sense that unmarked forms in

Huichol are generally taken as questions, and in the sense that unmarked forms in other languages are usually taken as statements, and so identified as Declarative.

All the languages considered so far are American Indian (though from South and Central America as well as the USA). Quite remote from them geographically and linguistically is Ngiyambaa (1.5.4). Here there are the 'knowledge' clitics 'exclamative' and 'ignorative'. The latter is used together with 'counterfactual' and 'hypothesis' to express 'might have' and 'perhaps' respectively (Donaldson 1980):

minjaŋ-gaː-ma-ndu	dha-yi	(253)
what-IGNOR-CNTRFACT-2NOM eat-PAST		
'You might have eaten I don't know what (but you didn't)'		

guya-gila-gaː-lu	dha-yi	(257)
fish+ABS-HYPOTH-IGNOR-3ABS eat-PAST		
'Perhaps he ate fish'		

However, both can be translated as questions when no other clitic occurs:

minja-waː-ndu	dha-yi	(260, 262)
what+ABS-EXCLAM-2NOM eat-PAST		
'What did you eat?'/'You ate *what*?'		

guya-waː-ndu	dha-yi	(260, 262)
fish+ABS-EXCLAM-2NOM eat-PAST		
'So you ate a fish!'/'What? You ate a fish!'		

minjaŋ-gaː-ndu	dha-yi	(260, 262)
what+ABS-IGNOR-2NOM eat-PAST		
'You ate something, I don't know what'/'I don't know what you ate'		

guya-gaː-ndu	dha-yi	(260, 263)
fish+ABS-IGNOR-2NOM eat-PAST		
'Did you eat a fish?'/'You ate a fish, I don't know'		

What is to be noticed is that the 'exclamative' can be interpreted as a '*wh*-question' when it occurs with the indefinite 'something' ('what') while the 'ignorative' can be identified as a 'Yes–No' question in other cases. Both can also be interpreted in terms of surprise or ignorance (surprise being an expression of the speaker's failure to know about the event – see 3.4.3).

Even in English questions may be used to express doubt, as in:

We're expecting him, but will he come?

There are other more formal reasons for associating questions with doubt. The verb WONDER, for instance, can either suggest question or mere rumination:

He wondered whether I would give him a lift

(But see Bolinger 1978 for the potential distinction of question and rumination marked by *if* and *whether*.)

For English it can be safely argued that the Interrogative is used to express doubt. But in all the other languages that have been considered it may be that doubt (ignorance etc.) is the more basic notion; certainly such terms as 'dubitative', 'ignorative' are used, or we are told the 'speaker does not know'. Similarly, for Luiseño (Uto-Aztecan, California) Akmajian, Steele and Wasow (1979: 3; see also this volume: 1.5.3) gloss one of the modal particles 'question and somewhat weak explanation'. It is this fact, perhaps, that leads Lyons (1977: 748) to say that there is possibly no attested language that has a distinct mood for interrogatives, though he adds that a dubitative mood might be regularly used for 'posing questions as well as expressing doubt or uncertainty'. It is difficult to see how this could be justified. If a morphological category is used for both purposes, there is no obvious reason to argue that it is the Dubitative used for questions rather than the interrogative used for expressing doubt, and there is a danger that Lyons' claim is true only by definition (that a morphological (mood) category must be Dubitative rather than Interrogative). Moreover, if these are definitely not Interrogatives, it follows that many languages have no Interrogative at all. That would be a strange conclusion.

2.6   Declaratives

The status of declarative sentences (first discussed in 1.4.2) and even whether they exist, may differ from one language to another. In particular, languages with evidential systems may differ in this respect from languages with judgment systems.

2.6.1   *Marking*

In many languages the Declarative is unmarked morphologically, while the modal categories are marked by a distinctive set of grammatical forms. Thus in English, modality is marked by a modal verb, while the declarative is unmarked, except for tense and aspect.

In inflected languages there are usually no formally unmarked forms, except possibly the imperatives. There is an indicative as well as a subjunctive (i.e. modal) 'mood' in Latin, plus an optative in Greek:

Latin:	amamus	'we love'	present indicative
	amemus		present subjunctive
Greek:	títheːmi	'I place'	present indicative

tithó:	present subjunctive
tithéie:n	present optative

Both languages also have an imperative mood, which may be assigned a place within the deontic system (see 1.4.3 and 3.3).

Similarly, Ngiyambaa has, within its inflectional system, an imperative, two declarative forms (differentiated in tense: present and past) and two modal paradigms, 'purposive' and 'irrealis' (see 1.5.4).

It is not necessarily the case that if the declarative is marked it will be marked inflectionally. For there are some dialects of English in which positive declarative forms (like negatives) use forms of the verb DO:

They do say	(Standard: They say)
He did go	(Standard: He went)

Even when the declarative appears to be of the same formal status as other moods, there may be grounds for treating it as more basic. In Latin, for example, the indicative has six different tense/aspect paradigms: present, future, imperfect, perfect, future perfect and pluperfect; but the subjunctive has only four, there being no future or future perfect subjunctive. In fact, it will be generally the case (perhaps even by definition) that the declarative is the form that maximally marks all the categories associated with the verb, not only tense, but also, where appropriate, number, gender and person (as concordial features). As such, it is the maximally finite form, non-finite forms such as the infinitive being minimally marked for such categories. (See 4.2.5 for further discussion.)

Moreover, if there is a formally unmarked form in a language, it is almost certain that it will be the Declarative. One possible exception has been noted – Huichol, in which the unmarked form may be taken as the Interrogative (2.5). Of particular relevance here is the comment by Lyons:

> It is an established fact that there are languages in which it is not possible for a speaker to make a simple categorical assertion by uttering a subjectively unmodalized declarative sentence. One such language is Hidatsa, . . . in which statements necessarily include one of a set of five modal particles, the function of which is to express the speaker's attitude or degree of commitment or to give some indication of the evidential basis for the proposition that is being conveyed. (Lyons 1982: 110)

The essential point here is that there is no potential candidate for identification as the declarative, that is both formally and semantically unmarked. It would not be very interesting to say that there is no 'declarative' that is only formally unmarked, for there is no formally unmarked declarative in Latin, and it is not easy without a complex philosophical discussion to establish whether a 'declarative' is semantically unmarked (but see 2.6.4). But the suggestion that every term in the system, including the declarative, is contrastively marked both formally and semantically is much easier to establish.

Unfortunately, although there may be languages of which this is true (see 2.6.3), Hidatsa (see 2.3.2) is not one of them. On closer inspection it does not appear to be true that all sentences in Hidatsa contain a mood morpheme. In a footnote Matthews notes that there are exceptions to this rule. In particular, 'period', which expresses what would seem to correspond to simple declarative sentences in other languages (Lyons' (1982) 'unmodalized statements'), does not appear at all with past tense. Matthews accounts for this by saying, in the theoretical spirit of 1965, that it is 'deleted by a transformational rule'. Declarative sentences in the past then, which are perhaps the most common type of 'unmodalized statements', do not in fact have an actual mood marker after all. (It has already been noted too that 'question' also is not marked by a 'mood morpheme' in the formal system – see 2.5.)

2.6.2 Knowledge and belief

In languages in which the epistemic system is wholly or largely in terms of judgments, it seems plausible that the declarative would be concerned with what the speaker believes or knows. But it seems that a distinction between knowledge and belief is made in some languages and is relevant for the interpretation of others.

Hidatsa (see the previous section) is a good example. 'Period,' which can be identified with Declarative, is defined in terms of the speaker's belief and 'emphatic' in terms of the speaker's knowledge. The 'emphatic' in Hidatsa is not, it seems, very different from 'emphatic' in Imbabura (2.3.2) or 'categorical assertion' in Ngiyambaa (1.5.4). For the latter, Donaldson (1980: 254–5) comments: 'The speaker presents the statement ... as significant for its absolute truth.' What is to be noted here is that there is, in the epistemic modality system of these languages, a term that does not weaken or modify the truth value of the proposition, but instead strongly commits the speaker to it. In these languages 'knowledge' is treated within the system, but as a term distinct from and stronger than that for 'belief', which is the form that may be equated with Declarative.

It is probable that there is, in most languages (except those with wholly evidential systems – see 2.3.1), a declarative that expresses belief, not knowledge. It is relevant that Grice (1975), when he deals with the Cooperative Principle between speaker and hearer, offers, as one of his maxims, the maxim of Quality:

> Quality. Try to make your contribution one that is true.
> (1)   Do not say what you know to be false.
> (2)   Do not say that for which you lack evidence.

These are indications of belief, not knowledge. Hearers do not expect the truth, or what is known to be true, but only what the speaker believes to be true.

2.6.3   *Direct evidence*

In Tuyuca, there is a system of evidentials that includes that of 'visual' evidence (2.3.1). The 'visual' evidential is the preferred evidential and must be used whenever visual evidence is available.

Another of Grice's maxims, the maxim of Quantity, is relevant here. Its first part reads:

> Quantity. (1)   Make your contribution as informative as required for the purpose of the exchange.

Lyons (1977: 595) illustrates this with reference to the modal (judgment) system of English by noting that *It may be raining* will imply that the speaker is unable to make the more informative statement *It is raining*. By a similar argument the use of a non-visual, apparent, secondhand or assumed evidential in Tuyuca would imply that the speaker has no visual evidence for what he is saying.

Other languages have a 'direct evidential' as one of the terms in a modal system. In such cases it is a little more plausible to identify it with the declarative, especially if it is morphologically unmarked, as in Serrano (Hill 1967: 18). Here the direct evidential is used only in the case of reporting firsthand knowledge; the speaker, that is to say, identifies himself as a witness. Hill gives as an example:

> 'iːp bɨ'   wahi' pɨnq
> here he PAST coyote pass
> 'The coyote passed here (I saw him)'

However, although the 'direct' or 'visual' evidential is formally 'unmarked' and is translationally equivalent to the Declarative, it is still evidential, and so not completely identifiable with the Declarative. Visual or direct evidence is as much a type of evidence as any other.

The importance of direct evidence is also shown in the account of Hixkaryana (2.1.2). Derbyshire (1979: 145) says that the distinction between 'hearsay' and 'eyewitness' is crucial and that 'in any connected discourse concerning events that have not been witnessed by the speaker', the 'hearsay' evidential occurs in almost every clause. In Sherpa too, there is a contrast between what Givón (1982: 32–5) calls 'direct' evidence and 'indirect/hearsay' evidence, illustrated by:

> ti laĝa ki-yin-no   (32)
> he work do-AUX-be+DIR
> 'He is working (and I have direct evidence to support this)'

> ti laĝa ki-yin-way
> he work do-AUX-be+IND
> 'He is working (I have indirect/hearsay evidence)'

Givón reports that a Lama narrating the *Life of Buddha* told the bulk of the story in the perfective/past using the 'hearsay/indirect evidence' suffix, and that in the entire narrative only two 'direct evidence' suffixes occurred and that these were both in direct quoted speech. Givón comments that the story 'is undoubtedly considered the "truest" of all stories for a devout Tibetan Buddhist such as the story-teller himself, yet is told in the "hearsay/indirect evidence mode" because it was not witnessed by the speaker'.

The complex system of Nambiquara (2.4) is worth considering again. Here there are two independent parameters:

> event verification: individual, collective
> speaker orientation: observation, deduction, narration

There are six possibilities in all, of which four are dependent on direct observation. For it is not only observation itself but also 'deduction' that requires direct evidence; both also distinguish direct evidence by the speaker and direct evidence shared by speaker and hearer. English, by contrast, ignores the nature of the evidence.

However, it is not necessarily the case that, if a language can formally indicate visual evidence, utterances so marked will have a privileged status. An example of a language where this is not so is Ngiyambaa, where all kinds of sensory evidence are marked by a term in an evidential system that is independent of other modal systems, and where all sensory evidence appears fallible (see 2.3.4).

It is worth commenting that in a European society scientific knowledge is often accorded the highest epistemic status. Even Bloomfield (1933: 139) thought that scientific definitions were linguistically more valid than others. Yet almost all such knowledge is based on the evidence of others, on indirect evidence of a 'hearsay' kind. That does not, however, make it less true for most of us, any more than the *Life of the Buddha* is less true for the devout Lama.

There is a grammatical consequence of direct evidence in Japanese, according to the account of Watanabe (1984), though it is not clear whether the evidential auxiliaries of Japanese have a grammatical status. The transitive construction with NOM (*ga*) and ACC (*o*) is not generally used with expressions to report subjective feelings; instead, the reduced transitive NOM–NOM, which expresses a lower degree of certainty, is required. The internal condition of other people cannot be reported in a simple sentence in the present, though this is possible with the past or if an evidential auxiliary is present:

> *Masao-ga   kaminari-ga   kowai
> Masao-NOM thunder-NOM afraid
> 'Masao is afraid of thunder'

> Masao-ga   kaminari-ga   kowak-at-ta
> Masao-NOM thunder-NOM afraid-be-PAST
> Masao-ga   kaminari-ga   kowai rashii
> Masao-NOM thunder-NOM afraid SEEM
> 'It seems that Masao is afraid of thunder'

> Masao-ga   kaminari-ga   kowai soodesu
> Masao-nom thunder-NOM afraid HEARSAY
> 'They say Masao is afraid of thunder'

However, if the auxiliary for 'direct evidence' is used, the transitive NOM–ACC construction is required:

> Masao-ga kaminari-o   kawa-gat-teiru
> Masao-NOM thunder-ACC fear-DIR-ASP
> 'Masao is showing fear of thunder'

2.6.4 The status of the Declarative

It is now appropriate to return to the issue raised in 1.4.2 concerning the status of the Declarative. It was there suggested that the declarative can be seen as epistemically unmarked, and gives no direct indication of the epistemic status of the proposition. This may seem paradoxical, for it implies that declaratives do not strictly assert anything at all, if by assertion is meant that the speaker thereby signals his maximum commitment to the truth of the proposition. The suggestion is rather that he presents it without actually signalling commitment, though it will generally be assumed that the purpose of the presentation is that he thinks it is relevant and probably true. Why, otherwise, would he, normally at least, say anything at all? This suggestion, though not in any sense provable, accounts for a number of facts about declaratives and their formal markers (all these points were briefly mentioned in 1.4.2).

First, *pace* Lyons' suggestion (1977: 809) that ' there is no epistemically stronger statement than a categorical assertion' and that the 'fact of introducing *must, necessarily, certainly*, etc., into the utterance has the effect of making our commitment to the factuality of the proposition explicitly dependent upon our, perhaps, limited knowledge', it is easy to imagine contexts where such markers strengthen the commitment rather than weaken it after a declarative statement, as in the conversation:

> John is at home
> I don't think so
> Oh yes he certainly is/He must be

Expressions of the speaker's commitment do not necessarily weaken it. The point is that the declarative does not indicate commitment at all, even if generally it is assumed that the speaker is telling the truth as he sees it. The same kind of arguments hold for the Imperative (1.4.3, 3.3.1).

Secondly, as was argued earlier (2.6.2), it is belief rather than knowledge which is usually to be assumed, but some languages have indicators of knowledge and they, surely, indicate something stronger than 'categorical assertion', though it is the marker of belief that should be equated with the declarative.

Thirdly, the form that marks the declarative is used in subordinate clauses where the speaker expressly indicates his non-commitment, even non-belief, and also in real conditionals where he does not necessarily accept the proposition expressed by either clause. This is so in English:

> I don't think that John is coming
> I wonder if John is coming
> If John is here, Mary will come too

Undoubtedly, this fact largely explains why there is often some confusion between propositions and statements: the presentation of a proposition in its baldest form is usually to be regarded as a statement. Thus Rescher (1968: 24) says: 'A proposition is presented by a complete, self-contained statement, which, taken as a whole, will be true or false: *The cat is on the mat*, for example.'

When, then, Lyons (1977: 736) says: 'the illocutionary force of a statement is not exhausted by its propositional content: it must be associated with the illocutionary act of assertion', it is easy to understand the purpose of his argument; but it can be argued that there is a sense in which the propositional content is sufficient – it has only to be presented, and does not need a specific type of illocutionary act, assertion. This depends, of course, on the interpretation of the term 'assertion', but the essential point is that this is the most 'neutral' or 'unmarked' kind of illocutionary act, and the declarative is thus the most neutral or unmarked member of the epistemic system.

The situation is different in languages with evidential systems. Here the term nearest to the declarative may indicate the 'strongest' type of epistemic modality. In Tuyuca, visual observation is the strongest evidence and must be indicated whenever it can be. Although this is the nearest translationally to the declarative, it is preferable not to use the same term, simply to emphasize the different place it has in the epistemic system (though such a principle if followed to extremes would make all typological identification impossible).

2.7 Discourse

In most languages, perhaps all, there are discourse features that show the relationship between one sentence and another. These are particularly obvious and necessary in conversation, where each person's utterances are intended as reactions to, or stimuli for, the utterances of the other. Many of the devices are words such as *well*, *yes*, *then*, *surely*, etc., though intonation also plays a large part.

2.7.1 *Grammatical systems*

In general, there is no precise system for such devices, though in some languages a small set of particles can be identified. One such set is that of German (1.5.3); and an interesting comparison can be drawn between them and English intonation (Schubiger 1965 [1972]). More precisely definable is the set of sentence-final particles in Chinese which are glossed as follows by Li and Thompson (1981: 238ff):

le	currently relevant state	(238)
ne	response to question	
ba	solicit agreement	
ou	friendly warning	
a/ya	reduce forcefulness	
ma	question	

Some examples are:

> yíyàng de le   (264)
> same it LE
> 'It's the same (you're wrong in thinking that what you have is different)'

> tāmen yoǔ sān tiáo niú   ne   (301)
> they exist three CL cattle NE
> '(Listen) they have three cows'

> wǒ hē   bàn bēi   ba   (308)
> I drink half glass BA
> 'I'll drink half a glass, OK?'

> wǒ yào dǎ nǐ   ou
> I will hit you OU
> 'Let me tell you, if you do this, I will hit you'

> nǐ   lái   a/ya   cf.   nǐ   lái   (315)
> You come A/YA   You come
> 'You come here'   'You come here!'

> nǐ   hāo ma   (305)
> you well MA
> 'Are you well? (=How are you?)'

It should not be surprising that the question marker is included in this set. Asking questions is an important part of any conversation. But there are good reasons for treating Interrogation as modal (see 2.5); there are examples of 'question' among the modal markers in Menomini, Serrano, Cashibo and Ngiyambaa (but see below, 2.7.2). A rather similar, but smaller, set of particles, including 'question' (but also 'I am telling you', 'I hope you agree', 'It goes without saying') was noted for Japanese in 1.5.3.

Moreover, the auxiliary verbs of Cashibo (Shell 1975; see this volume: 2.3.3) are, perhaps, to be handled in terms of discourse rather than modality. These are largely formed agglutinatively from five elements, with further elements for number and person. The attested combinations are (3rd person singular):

ka	declarative
kaísa	report in independent clause
isa	report in dependent clause
kara	interrogative
ria	response

riapa response where question implies scepticism
karaisainterrogative report

For example:

Jorgenïn ka	aín lápiz	ćasiaşa	(178)

George DECL+3 his pencil break+PAST+3
'George broke his pencil'

Jorgenïn kaísa	aín lápiz	ćasiaşa	(181)

George REP IND+3 his pencil break+PAST+3
'George broke his pencil, it is said'

aín lápiz isa   ćasiaşa   kišon   ka
his pencil REP DEP+3 break+PAST+3 CLOSE OF QUOTE DECL+3

Jorgenïn ʔï	kaaşa		(182)

George   me SAY+PAST+3
'George told me that he broke his pencil'

Jorge kara kʷan			(192)

George INT+3 go+PRES+INT
'Is George going?'

(aş) ria kʷanín		(192)

(he) RESP+3 go+PRES+3
'Yes, he is going'

(aş) riapa kʷanin		(193)

(he) RESP SCEP+3 go+PRES+3
'Yes, he certainly is going!'

an ka   ñokáaša   ʔï karaisna   kʷan
he DECL+3 ask+PAST+3 me INT REP+3 go+PAST+1/2

kišon	(193)

CLOSE OF QUOTE
'He asked me if I went'

It is clear that Cashibo has a very full discourse system, and, in particular, forms for making statements, asking questions, giving replies and giving emphatic replies (Declaratives, Interrogatives, Responsives and Emphatic Affirmatives).

It has not always been noted that, in an indirect way, English too has a formal indication of discourse features, found in constructions associated with the NICE properties of the English modal verbs. This is an acronym suggested by Huddleston (1976: 333) based upon my previous analysis (Palmer 1974: 15). These features are, with examples:

Negative	I can't go
Inversion	Must I come?
'Code'	He can swim and so can she
Emphatic Affirmation	He *will* be there

Only the auxiliary verbs can be used under the conditions illustrated. If there is no auxiliary verb, one has to be supplied – the 'empty' auxiliary DO, as in:

> He goes
> He doesn't go
> Does he go?
> He goes and so does she
> He *dóes* go

The most important (but not sole) function of inversion is in questions, as the examples show. The most important use of code is in responses:

> Can John come? Yes he can
> Has he come? No he hasn't

In the response, the lexical verb is not repeated, but an auxiliary verb is required and, if none is present, DO must be used.

Two of the most important functions of the auxiliary verbs, then, are to signal questions and responses, the two most basic discourse functions. A third is emphatic affirmation, which is used to reply where there is doubt – exactly like the response to a sceptical question in Cashibo. More basic still is the need to make positive and negative statements (to assert and to deny). Assertion, the indication of positive statements, is unmarked in English, but denial, the indication of negative statements, employs the auxiliary verbs, exactly as the discourse features do. It can be argued that the NICE properties share one characteristic, that they do not add to or alter the propositional content, but basically deny, question, repeat or confirm it (see Palmer 1983a: 207). Not only do they have this in common, but they are also, in this respect, very like modal markers.

2.7.2   *Discourse and modality*

It is not easy to draw a clear distinction semantically between discourse features and modality, For in discourse we often express opinion, draw conclusions, etc.; and no doubt, in 'evidential' language speakers regularly indicate in their conversations and arguments the evidential basis for what they are saying. Not surprisingly then, it is by no means always possible to make a clear distinction between a discourse and a modal feature.

To begin with, what are clearly systems of epistemic modality may contain some terms that belong more to discourse. The interrogative (2.5), for instance, may or may not fall formally within a system of epistemic modality. In a similar way, emphatic affirmation may be treated either as a matter of discourse or as a kind of 'strong' epistemic modality expressing complete confidence in, or knowledge of, what is being said. Perhaps the best example of this is the 'emphatic' of Hidatsa (2.6.2). In Imbabura too (2.3.2) there is a particle glossed 'emphatic firsthand information'. In both cases the overall system appears to be one of modality rather than discourse.

A little more problematic is the system of 'belief' clitics of Ngiyambaa (Donaldson 1980: 252–5); these (listed with examples in 1.5.4) are:

Assertion	'used to draw the addressee's attention to a statement'
Categorical assertion	'the speaker presents the statement ... as significant for its absolute truth'
Counter-assertion	'either contradicts a previous statement or is intended to counter some presupposition the speaker suspects his addressee of entertaining'
Hypothesis	'marks a statement as an unconfirmed hypothesis on the part of the speaker'

All but the last of these contain the word *assertion* in the name.

Formally this 'belief' system is independent of other systems in Ngiyambaa (and there are sentences that are unmarked by any of the Ngiyambaa clitics – i.e. 'simple' declaratives). The 'belief' clitics may combine with other clitics, e.g. 'linguistic evidence' in the 'evidence' system, or 'ignorative' in the 'knowledge' system:

waŋaːy-bagaː-dhan-du   ŋudha-nhi   (277)
NEG-CNTR ASSERT-LING EVID-2 NOM give-PAST
'But rumour has it you *didn't* give (anything)'

minja-ŋalmayŋ-gaː-baɽa   gabadaː   badhiyi (267)
what-quantity+ABS-IGNOR-CATEG ASSERT moon+ABS emerge+PAST
'So many moons came, I don't know how many' (i.e. 'I don't know *how* many months passed')

Obviously 'counter-assertion' is basically a matter of discourse, and there are examples which suggest that this is no less true of 'categorical assertion' and even of 'assertion'. Two of Donaldson's examples of 'categorical assertion' are triggered by what was said before. In one example a place is being discussed and someone intervenes with:

ŋadhi-laː-baṟa-dhu   badhiyi   (255)
there+CIRC-EST-CATEG ASSERT-1NOM come+PAST
(CIRC=CIRCumstantive; EST=ESTablished reference)
'That's exactly where I've (just) come from!'

The second example is translated 'I've seen it already'. The 'assertion' example is a reply to 'How are you going to cook it?':

guṟiː-ga-baːla   (254)
coal-LOC-ASSERT
'On the coals, of course'

On the other hand, the distinction between 'He never walked again' and 'He didn't walk again' is made by 'categorical assertion' and 'assertion', and seems, perhaps, to involve strength of speaker commitment. Moreover, there is one term in the system, 'hypothesis', which seems to be wholly modal and not really a discourse feature at all. Such examples show the close relationship between discourse and modality.

It may even be the case that there are languages in which the declarative too belongs essentially to a discourse system – where formally it is not unmarked and does not belong to either a judgment or an evidential system. This may be the most appropriate interpretation for those dialects of English that use DO even for declaratives (2.6.1), giving a four-term system:

affirmative	They do say
negative	They don't say
interrogative	Do they say?
response	They do

(There would be no need to indicate Emphatic Affirmation as another term in such a dialect: it can be dealt with wholly in terms of stress and intonation, whereas in Standard English its occurrence with DO has to be accounted for independently.)

There are two final points. First, in both Ngiyambaa and Inga the modal particles are attached not to the verb, but to elements with discourse function (see 1.5.3, 1.5.4). They are attached to 'topics' in Ngiyambaa (Donaldson 1980: 237), which are defined as the constituents in initial position, but are salient in the same way as the most stressed constituent of a clause in English. In Inga (Levinsohn 1975: 15) it is the rhematic element (the 'comment') that is marked, as shown by:

nispaca   Santiagoma-mi   rini
After that to Santiago-AFF   I went
'After that I went to *Santiago*'

nispaca   rini-mi   Santiagoma
After that I went-AFF to Santiago
'After that I *went* to Santiago'

Secondly, what seem to be discourse features often relate not to the discourse, but to relevant elements of the extralinguistic situation. This is even true of pronouns. Although many linguists have attempted to account for anaphoric pronouns in terms of formal features of the discourse or even syntax, Lyons (1977: 637, 659–63) argues convincingly that anaphoric use is derived from a more basic deictic use. A number of examples in support of this are to be found in Brown and Yule (1983: 215–22).

It should be no surprise then that in Cashibo (Shell 1975: 195) the 'response' form *ria* may be used as a 'response to a puzzling situation':

upí   ɔkin ka   ʔaia   kišan   rina
good make DECL do+PRES CONT CLOSE OF QUOTE RESP+I
  isa
  see+PAST
'(How strange) I saw him doing it so well'

The use of verbal discourse features in Cashibo, no less than the use of 'anaphoric' pronouns in English, is related not only to the purely linguistic context, but also to the wider non-linguistic context. This observation links discourse even more closely to modality, for speaker attitudes are often related to known facts, derived from both the linguistic and the non-linguistic situation.

2.8   A possible typological system

On the basis of the discussion in this chapter it is, perhaps, possible to suggest an overall system within which to handle epistemic modals. This should take into account:

(i)   The two main modal systems, Evidentials and Judgments, plus the related system of Discourse.
(ii)   The sub-systems of Judgments: Inference and Confidence (2.4.2).
(iii)   The different sub-systems of Evidentials in terms of the treatment of sensation, as illustrated by Tuyuca and Ngiyambaa (2.3.4 and 2.6.3).
(iv)   Possible equivalences in different systems, especially Declarative, but also involving Deductive and Assumptive (2.3.2) and the problem of Interrogative (2.5).
(v)   The notion that some terms are stronger than others (2.2.1, 2.3.1), and that one may be unmarked (2.6.1).

A possible system is shown in Figure 1.

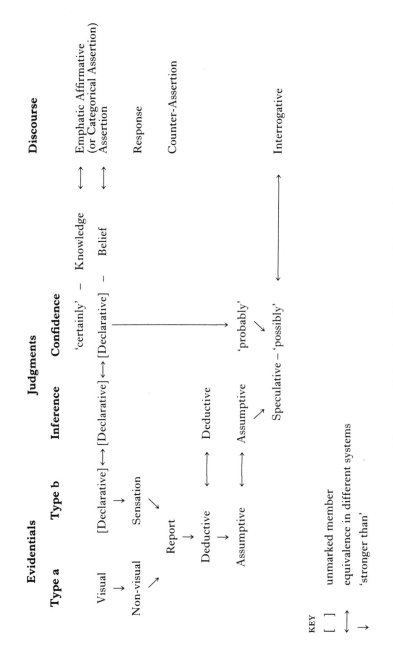

Figure 1. Epistemic modality: a possible typological system

3
Deontic modality

3.1 Definition of the term 'deontic'

'Deontic' is used in a wide sense here to include those types of modality that are characterized by Jespersen (1.2.1) as 'containing an element of will'. It is obvious, however, that the meanings associated with deontic modality are very different from those of epistemic modality. The latter is concerned with belief, knowledge, truth, etc. in relation to proposition, whereas the former is concerned with action, by others and by the speaker himself. It might well be argued that there are two quite distinct categories.

There are two features that they share: subjectivity (see 1.3.2), i.e. the involvement of the speaker, and non-factuality. Yet it must be admitted that the chief reason for treating them as a single category lies in the fact that in English, and many other languages, the same forms (e.g. modal verbs) are used for the expression of both. There are possibly some deeper reasons, which will be discussed in 3.5.

It should not be concluded, however, that the epistemic/deontic system of languages like English is typical of all languages. A very different deontic system is found in Afar (Cushitic, Ethiopia – Bliese 1981: 139–46). Within the same formal system it has not only an 'imperative' but also a 'jussive', a 'subjunctive' and a 'consultative', as exemplified by:

imperative:	ab	'do'
jussive:	nakay	'let me drink'
subjunctive:	rabu	'may I die'
consultative:	a'bo	'shall I do it?'

In English the Imperative does not belong to the same formal system as the modal verbs. The imperative is, however, found in most languages and, undoubtedly, is closely related to, or included within, the deontic system. It is, nevertheless, a problematic category, as has already been shown (1.4.3); further discussion will be needed (3.3).

There is rather less to be said about deontic modality than epistemic modality in a grammatical study. Some types of deontic modality, in the wide sense, are often expressed in lexical verbs, e.g. those of hoping and wishing in English, as in:

> I hope John will come
> I wish John would come

Even where a grammatical form is available, there may be a great deal of variation in meaning expressed by such verbs, e.g. the imperative:

> Come here!
> I beg/urge/entreat/beseech/request/ask you to come here

The most important types of deontic modality in a grammatical study appear to be Directives and Commissives ('where we commit ourselves to do something') which, as Searle (1979: 14) noted, have much in common. (In practice most of the chapter will be concerned with directives, since there is little to say about commissives.) One obvious point is that both are not only subjective, but also performative, they actually initiate action by others or by the speaker. For that reason they will always be related to the future, since only the future can be changed or affected as a result of them being expressed. At the time of speaking a speaker can get others to act or commit himself to action only in the future. In this respect they are clearly different from epistemic modality, where the speaker can commit himself to the truth of propositions in the past, present or future. Of course, deontic modality can be reported in the past, but that is no less true of epistemic modality which is the subject not of this chapter but of Chapter 4.

There are also sections on Volitives and Evaluatives. The status of these is open to some doubt. Volitives (3.4.2) are modal in the sense that they involve non-factuality, and are more like deontic modals in that they are concerned more with possible action than with the truth, etc. of propositions. Evaluatives (3.4.3), however, seem to relate to factual propositions and are possibly not modal at all. However, they are often treated in languages as if they were.

3.2 Directives

Searle (1983: 166) defines directives as 'where we try to get our hearers to do things'. Here again (see 2.2) MUST and MAY are important, and the distinction between them is fairly basic for a typological study. (But if giving permission is included, 'try to get' is rather too strong; it would be better to talk of 'initiating action'.)

3.2.1 MAY *and* MUST

Just as English has a basic system of weak and strong epistemic modality, so it seems also to have a basic system of weak and strong deontic modality (at least of directives), again expressed by MAY and MUST; there are similar verbs in other European languages.

Again the notions of possibility and necessity are involved. MAY, when used for giving permission, may be interpreted as expressing deontic possibility, and MUST, when used for laying an obligation, as expressing deontic necessity. In saying *You may/must come tomorrow*, the speaker imposes the possibility or necessity of coming tomorrow upon his hearer. (In colloquial speech, CAN is more common for permission, but MAY still survives – see Palmer 1979b: 59–60.)

As with epistemic modality, there are relationships between the two in terms of negation. These are clearly and simply expressed for obligation (necessity) where there may be a positive obligation towards a negative course of action or a negative obligation towards a positive course of action. English uses *mustn't* for the first and *needn't* for the second:

> John must come tomorrow
> John mustn't come tomorrow
> John needn't come tomorrow

The second of these expresses 'There is necessity not to come' and the third 'There is no necessity to come'. Yet there is no complete set for MAY. It is possible to deny permission ('It is not possible for . . .') with MAY (or CAN):

> John may/can come tomorrow
> John may not/can't come tomorrow

Yet there is no obvious form of giving permission for negative action ('possible for not . . .'). In appropriate contexts, *may not/can not*, with stress on *not*, is used to give permission not to act:

> You may (can) come or you may (can) *not* come, as you wish

But there is no form that is regularly and unambiguously used for this purpose. The most likely alternative is *needn't*, which is a necessity form and associated with MUST rather than MAY:

> You needn't come tomorrow

This can again be explained in terms of the logical relations between possibility and necessity involving negation – the equivalence of 'not necessary' and 'possible not'. But the situation is the reverse of that found with epistemic modality, where the 'possibility' modals of English were used suppletively for the negatives of the 'necessity' modals (2.2.1). Lyons (1977: 839) comments: 'it is obligation that is distinctively grammaticalized in the structure of English'. But it would be a mistake to emphasize these logical relations too much, for there is a difference between:

> John may/can not come tomorrow
> John mustn't come tomorrow

In purely logical terms, 'not possible' (*may not*) is equivalent to 'necessary not' (*mustn't*), but denying permission is not the same as obliging someone not to act. We only deny permission if we are in a position to grant it, but can lay an obligation not to act when it is not normally up to us to give permission.

In German too there are two verbs DÜRFEN (not MÖGEN as in the epistemic system) and MÜSSEN. MÜSSEN with the negative *nicht* can express either 'no necessity' (*needn't*) or 'necessity not' (*mustn't*):

> Du   musst   das nicht tun
> you (SG) MÜSSEN+2SG+PRES+INDIC that not   do
> 'You needn't/mustn't do this'

DÜRFEN with the negative expresses 'may not' or 'must not' (Hammer 1983: 228). On purely formal grounds this is the negative of the permission modal, i.e. 'may not', but it is often translated by 'mustn't', e.g. (Hammer 1983: 228):

> Aber ich darf   mich nicht loben
> but I   DÜRFEN+1SG+PRES+INDIC me   not   praise
> 'But I mustn't praise myself'

Syntactically *nicht* belongs to the main verb, since it is often, as above, preceded by its object; but in this form of DÜRFEN and in the 'needn't' sense of MÜSSEN, semantically it negates the modal ('no permission'/'no obligation', not 'permission not to'/'obligation not to').

Bouma (1975: 333) notes that in colloquial German, MÜSSEN plus *nicht* is replaced by DÜRFEN in one sense and BRAUCHEN in the other (both with *nicht*). This latter is obviously translatable as 'needn't':

> Ich brauche   nicht hinzugehen
> I   BRAUCHEN+1SG+PRES+INDIC not   to there go
> 'I needn't go there'

If there are only these two negative forms available, there will be no distinction between 'no permission' and 'obligation not to' or 'permission not to' and 'no obligation'. But since DÜRFEN is a permission ('possibility') modal and BRAUCHEN seems to be essentially a form for obligation ('necessity'), it is difficult, if not impossible, to decide whether obligation or permission is basic in German. In Chinese, by contrast, only possibility forms are used for negative deontic, as well as epistemic, modality (6.4).

As with epistemic modality (in English at least), there are no past tense forms for the deontic modals, for obviously one cannot give permission or lay obligation in the past (as opposed to reporting that one did). Although *had to* seems to be suppletive for MUST, it always clearly implies that the speaker is not involved in the laying of obligation, and similarly, although *could* may be used for past permission (but not normally *might*), it, too, suggests that the speaker is not involved. Indeed, the past tense forms are the clearest indications of dynamic, as distinct from deontic, modality (see 3.2.3).

There are non-European languages that have a system of 'strong' and 'weak' deontic modality. Thus in Tamil (Dravidian – Asher 1982: 167–70) the suffixes *-laam* and *-ṇum* are used (as with epistemic modality) for permission and obligation respectively:

> veṇum-ṇṇaakkaa,   naalekki avan peeca-laam
> want-COND   tomorrow he   speak-PERM
> 'If he wants, he can speak tomorrow'
> avan aṇke pooka-ṇum
> he   there go-DEB
> 'He must go there'

3.2.2 Modifications

Just as the epistemic modals can be modified by the use of 'more tentative' forms in English, so the deontic modals appear to have similarly related forms: MUST has *ought to* and *should* (for any difference between these see Coates 1983: 77–83), and MAY has *might* (or CAN, *could*). However, these are not strictly directives at all, although they are clearly attitudinal.

The position is clearest with *ought to* (*should*). There are two points. The first is that these verbs differ from MUST in that the speaker admits the possibility that the event may not take place. This is seen in:

> He *ought to/should* come, but he won't
> *He must come, but he won't

The second of these is most unlikely, if not anomalous; if the speaker thinks that the obligation may not be fulfilled, *ought to/should* would be used. Secondly, *ought to/should* can refer to past events, whereas MUST cannot:

> You ought to/should have come

Must have here could be interpreted only epistemically, never deontically.

The explanation for these two points is that *ought to* and *should* are essentially conditional – referring to what would occur or would have occurred. The conditionality does not refer strictly to the modal, but to the event expressed in the proposition (Palmer 1979b: 102). Thus the following glosses are appropriate:

> You ought to come
> 'You have an obligation to come, and you would come if you fulfilled it'
>
> You ought to have come
> 'You had an obligation to come and you would have come if you had fulfilled it'

The glosses, however, suggest an objective obligation – and this is misleading, for it is the speaker who is, quite subjectively, expressing his attitude towards what 'ought to be' or 'ought to have been'. It is this attitude and the conditionality that explain both why *ought to/should* can be used when the speaker envisages the non-occurrence of the future event, and why there are forms to refer to past events. But it is clear that, in this sense, *ought to/should* is not strictly a directive.

The situation with *might* is less simple. It is often used in questions as a more tentative, more polite, form for asking permission (Palmer 1979b: 68):

> Might I come in at the moment on this, Chairman?

But it is also used to make a quite positive suggestion, as in (Palmer 1979b: 159):

> You might try nagging the Abbey National
> You might have told me

Here again, as with *ought to/should*, there is conditionality, referring to events that would take place or would have taken place under certain conditions. With *ought to/should* the conditions were the carrying out of an obligation; with *might* they seem to be those of behaving in a sensible or proper way. But this is a much stronger notion than mere permission, and it is clear that *might have* does not mean 'You would have acted thus if you had had permission'.

Apparently then, *might* expresses a stronger kind of deontic modality than MAY – a positive suggestion rather than mere permission. *Could* is used in similar circumstances:

> You could try nagging the Abbey National
> You could have told me

This, however, can be accounted for in the dynamic 'ability' sense of CAN – 'You would be able to or would have been able to act' (with an implicit reproach if you did not).

3.2.3 *Subjectivity*

It was suggested earlier that subjectivity might be considered an essential feature of modality (1.3.2) and that epistemic modality, at least, is always subjective. There are problems with this in the analysis of deontic modality, in that some non-epistemic uses of modal elements seem to have no element of subjectivity while others seem to involve varying degrees of involvement of the speaker.

CAN, for instance, is often used to express what seems to be a factual non-modal statement as in:

> John can speak Italian

This involves neither the attitude nor the opinion of the speaker (except that it is true), but simply asserts that John has the ability to speak Italian. But CAN is undoubtedly a modal verb in English, if defined formally.

MUST, rather differently, may be used to indicate the speaker's involvement (if he 'obliges' some one to act, we can assume that he himself wishes the action to be carried out), or it may be used where he is not involved and has no views on the desirability of the action:

> You must come here at once
> You must go now if you wish to catch the bus

It can be argued that there are degrees to which the speaker may be involved. He may be totally involved, he may not be involved at all or he may be involved as a member of the society or body that instigates the action. The same is true of the other modals. With MAY, in particular, the speaker is often clearly totally involved – it is he that normally gives the permission – but equally, he may not be (but see below).

For reasons such as these, I proposed (Palmer 1979b: 36–7) that we should recognize not two, but three, types of modality – epistemic, deontic and dynamic. The third kind is foreshadowed in a footnote in von Wright (1951: 8), where 'dynamic' modality is said to be concerned with 'ability and disposition'. Within dynamic modality, however, I included both 'neutral' or 'circumstantial' modality, as in the MUST examples above, and 'subject-oriented' modality illustrated by CAN or by the 'willingness' use of WILL:

> He'll come, if you ask him

Other scholars have avoided the problem raised by the term 'deontic' by distinguishing not between epistemic and deontic, but between epistemic and 'root' modality. This terminology seems first to have been used by Hofmann (see Hofmann 1976: 85). It has the advantage that it avoids the necessity of distinguishing between 'pure' deontic and dynamic modality, and so avoids the problems of indeterminacy (below). But the term 'root' is a little unfortunate if it is used to include all non-epistemic modality, with the implication that this is more basic. If any kind of modality is basic it is, surely, dynamic modality with its notions of willingness and ability (i.e. subject-oriented modality not neutral dynamic modality), and, of course, WILL still retains its earlier meaning of wishing.

In fact, the subject-oriented use of CAN and WILL raises no problems. They are subject-oriented in that they are concerned with the ability or willingness of the subject, not with the opinion or attitude of the speaker. This type can be omitted from the strict typological classification of modality, although it is of interest that modal verbs have these meanings.

The status of neutral or circumstantial uses of the modals is more problematic, for they are not always clearly distinct from deontic modality, in the strictly subjective sense. There is thus indeterminacy, leaving completely indeterminate the dividing line between what is modal (and subjective) and what is non-modal (and objective, declarative). But, except for CAN and WILL, the 'root' modals are perhaps never wholly objective. This is shown in two observations.

First, a contrast can be drawn between MUST and HAVE TO and between MAY and CAN in terms of speaker involvement, as in:

> He must come tomorrow
> He has to come tomorrow
>
> You may smoke in here
> You can smoke in here

The most natural distinguishing feature is that with HAVE TO and CAN the speaker is disassociating himself from the obligation or permission, and, by implication therefore, associating himself with it in using MUST and MAY.

Secondly, MUST has no past tense form and equally neither does 'permission' MAY (*might* is not used in that sense, to refer to past time). Past obligation can only be expressed by *had to* and past permission by a lexical item:

> He had to come yesterday   (*musted)
> He was allowed to come yesterday   (*might)

In contrast, subject-oriented CAN has a regularly used past tense form *could* as in:

> When he was younger, he could speak Italian

(There are some limitations on *could*, and *would* (='was willing') is also possible with similar limitations – see Palmer 1977: 163–5.)

The absence of past tense, past time, forms of MUST and 'permission' MAY is easily explained. If the speaker actually lays an obligation or gives permission by his utterance, he cannot do so with reference to actions in the past. In a similar way there are no past tense forms of the epistemic modals to express a past time belief, though it is possible to express a (present) belief about past events – see 2.2.1.

There are no similar restrictions on the closely related modal verbs of German (and other languages). Thus German can say (Hammer 1983: 224):

> Ich musste   fleissig arbeiten
> I   müssen+3SG+PAST+INDIC hard   work
> 'I had to work hard'

However, this merely shows that the German verb is semantically, as well as formally (see 1.5.1), less modal than its English counterpart. In the past tense it cannot be a directive but makes a statement about past necessity, while English can use only *had to* – and it is this, above all, that clearly distinguishes MUST and HAVE TO in English, a distinction that German does not make.

For reasons such as these the term 'root' modality is inappropriate and will not be used.

3.2.4 Other systems

There are few languages that have deontic systems quite independent of other modal systems. A partial system is found in Kobon (New Guinea – Davies 1981: 23–4). There are four 'moods' (an unmarked 'indicative', an 'imperative', a 'prescriptive' and a 'counterfactual'), all fully inflected for person and number (singular, dual and plural). Examples of the 'imperative' and 'prescriptive' are:

kale mab ud   ar-laŋ
3PL tree take go-3PL+IMP
'Go and take the wood'

yad gai   han-nam
1SG where sleep-1SG+PRESC
'Where am I to sleep?'

But although these two moods are clearly deontic, the counterfactual, of course, is not.

There are languages that have forms corresponding to 'must' and 'may', but these are not often to be found within a single grammatical system, still less within a clearly deontic system. In Ngiyambaa, for instance (Donaldson 1980: 162), 'must' is indicated by the 'purposive' inflection of the verb, which occurs in the same inflectional system as the tenses (see 1.4.1):

ŋadhu bawuŋ-ga   yuwa-giri
I+NOM middle-LOC lie-PURP
'I must lie in the middle'

Similarly, in Yidiny (N. Queensland, Australia – Dixon 1977: 207, 344) the 'purposive' occurs in a system of tense/mood:

ḏilŋgu mayi   wayu   wunaː-na banaː
down vegetable+ABS long-time he-PURP   water+LOC
'This vegetable food must lie in the water for a long time'

There are similar forms in other Australian languages (see Hale 1976: 81–4). A further example is from Mangarayi, cited by Merlan (1982: 182), who refers to the relevant affix as 'desiderative':

na-mawuɲ-gu   a   nur-miʔmi-wu
PURP-vegetable-food IRR 2 DUAL-search-DESID
'You must look around for vegetables'

The purposive inflection of Dyirbal, however, has a wider 'implicative' use (Dixon 1972: 67–9; see also this volume: 5.2.4):

balan ḏugumbil   baŋgul yaṛaŋgu   balgali
CL   woman+NOM CL   man+ERG   hit+PURP
(CL=CLassifier)
'Something happened to enable or force the man to hit the woman'

An example of 'may', expressed by a 'permissive', is found in Tübatulabal (Uto-Aztecan – Steele 1975: 207, quoting Voegelin):

> hatda:w-aha-bi
> cross-PERM-SM
> (SM=subject marker)
> 'You may cross it'

But the 'permissive' is also used for epistemic modality and wishes (see 3.5), and there is no evidence of a directive system.

This may be more similar to the mood of familiar languages. Latin, for instance, used the subjunctive for *should*:

> Sed maneam etiam, opinor (Pl. *Trin.* 1136)
> but remain+1SG+PRES+SUBJ still I think
> 'But I should still remain, I think'

It also can indicate 'should have' to refer to past events by the imperfect subjunctive:

> At tu dictis, Albane, maneres (Virg. *Aen.* 8. 643)
> but thou to words Alban remain+3SG+IMPERF+SUBJ
> 'But thou, Alban, shouldst have kept thy word'

In Homeric Greek the optative is available to express the 'suggestion' meaning of *might* (above):

> taút' eípois Akhilé:i (Hom. *Il.* 11. 791)
> these say+SG+AOR+OPT to Achilles
> 'You might tell Achilles this'

But these languages have no deontic system. The subjunctive and optative have a wide variety of functions.

3.2.5 *Deontic requests*

A speaker can not only express his own attitudes or deontic modality; he can also ask the addressee about his – whether he considers an action deontically permissible or necessary:

> May I come in?
> Must I go now?

However the use of the interrogative form with the possibility modal *may* does not usually ask for information, but is a request for permission. *May I come in?* is not to be paraphrased by 'Is it the case that I have permission to come in?', but by 'I ask you to give me permission to come in'. By contrast, the use of *must* is essentially a request for information alone. *Must I go now?*

would never be a request for the hearer to place an obligation upon the speaker.

English also uses SHALL in the interrogative. This is different again, for although it is formally the interrogative of a commissive (where we commit ourselves to do something), it neither asks for information nor requests a commitment from the hearer: *Shall I come in?* would not mean either 'Is it the case that I promise to come in?' or 'Do you promise that I shall come in?'

Similarly, Latin and Greek may use the subjunctive:

> Mirer ...,   si vana, patres conscripti, vestra
> wonder+1SG+PRES+SUBJ if vain, fathers conscript your
>   auctoritas ad plebem ... est?   (Liv.3.21)
>   authority to people   is
> 'Am I to marvel, conscript fathers, if your authority towards the people
> is ineffectual?'

> óːmoi egó páːi boː?   páːi
> oh   I   where go+1SG+AOR+SUBJ where
> stóː?   páːi   kélsoː?   (Eur. *Hec.* 1056)
> stand+1SG+AOR+SUBJ where put into harbour+1SG+AOR+SUBJ
> 'Ah me! Where shall I go? Where stand? Where find haven?'

Latin can mark tense here too, while Greek can use the optative for a weaker form:

> Haec cum viderem,   quid agerem,
> these when see+1SG+IMPERF+SUBJ what do+1SG+IMPERF+SUBJ
>   iudices?   (Cic. *Sest.* 19)
>   jurymen
> 'When I saw this, what was I to do, gentlemen of the jury?'

> Teán, Zéu, dúnasin tís ... katáskhoi?   (Soph. *Ant.* 604)
> Thy   Zeus power   who   restrain+3SG+AOR+OPT
> 'Thy power, Zeus, who might restrain?'

Fula, too, uses its subjunctive, with the appropriate particle (Arnott 1970: 299):

> mi-nasta   na   (301)
> come in+1SG+SUBJ NA
> 'May I come in?'

Kobon's 'prescriptive' form has already been noted. This too can be used in questions to express 'Am I to ...' (3.2.4).

Afar (Bliese 1981: 139ff) has a distinct form for what is termed the 'consultative' (the usual traditional term is 'deliberative' – see Moore 1934: 99):

> Aboô   'Shall I do it?'

3.3 Imperatives

3.3.1 *The status of the Imperative*

It was argued in 1.4.3 that the Imperative is best seen as the unmarked member of the deontic system, or rather of the Directive sub-system, just as the Declarative is the unmarked member of the epistemic system (1.4.2, 2.6.4). The basic arguments, which need not be repeated in detail, were that the imperative is often a simple form (e.g. the bare root in Latin for the singular at least), and that the imperative is not necessarily stronger than the modal form MUST, or even MAY. It is merely presented as a deontic 'proposition', and the hearer is left to judge the force of his obligation to act from the circumstances. It would be taken as an order in:

> Stand at ease!   (in the army)
> Take down this poem   (teacher to class)
> Sit at the table   (parent to child)

But it is merely an expression of permission in *Come in*, where the use of either MUST or MAY would be inappropriate. It is clear, then, that the imperative is neither 'stronger' nor 'weaker', neither more nor less polite than MUST.

There are two respects in which the argument differs from that concerning the Declarative. The imperative is not generally used in subordinate clauses at all, and there can be no argument therefore (similar to that used for the declarative in 2.6.4) that it can be used when the speaker also indicates that he does not expect action. We may contrast:

> I don't think John is here
> *I didn't order come

However, this is explainable in terms of the characteristics of reported speech – and in any case is not wholly true of all languages (see 3.3.3 for further discussion).

Secondly, unlike the declarative, the imperative is not marked for most of the other categories associated with the verb, especially for tense and person. The reason for absence of tense is obvious – the fact that the required action is always in the future. The situation with person (and gender as well) is more complex and is discussed in the next section.

3.3.2 *The Imperative and person*

In general, it is assumed that the Imperative will have only 2nd person forms, referring to the hearer. It is easy enough to see why, if the speaker merely presents (to the hearer) a proposition for action. Lyons (1977: 747) argues that imperatives can only be, strictly, 2nd person, and never 3rd person. Nevertheless, there are forms in Greek and Latin that are 3rd person and different morphologically from the subjunctives, and are generally referred to as '3rd person imperatives'. Thus there is in Greek:

> all' ei dokéi,   pléoːmen,   hormásthoː
> but if it seems sail+1PL+PRES+SUBJ set forth+3SG+PRES+IMP
> táchus   (Soph. *Phil.* 526)
> swift
> 'If thou wilt, let us sail and let him set forth with speed'

Here 'let us sail' is indicated by the subjunctive, but 'let him set forth' by the imperative (there is no 1st person imperative form). Similarly in Latin:

> Naviget!   Haec summa est, hic nostri nuntius
> sail+3SG+PRES+SUBJ this   point   is   this of us message
> esto   (Virg. *Aen.* 4 237)
> be+3SG+PRES+IMP
> 'Let him sail! This is the point, let this be our message'

Here both the subjunctive (*naviget*) and the imperative (*esto*) are used; but the subjunctive might be better translated as 'he should sail'.

The status of 3rd person imperatives may be doubtful in Latin, but there is certainly no 1st person imperative. The example discussed in 3.2.4 uses the subjunctive:

> Sed maneam   etiam, opinor   (Pl. *Trin.* 1136)
> but remain+1SG+PRES+SUBJ still   I think
> 'But I should still remain, I think'

There are, however, plenty of languages that have specific 1st and 3rd person forms for exhortation. English, as some translations have already shown, uses *let*, with the shortened form *let's* for 1st person plural. Similarly, Afar (Cushitic, Ethiopia) has the ending *-ay*, which exactly parallels this, as the glosses show (Bliese 1981: 139ff):

> kur-t-ay   'let her divide'
> nak-(ø-)ay   'let me drink'

Similarly, with the appropriate particle, Fula (Arnott 1970: 299ff) uses the subjunctive:

haa njah-en   'Let's go!'

A question to be asked, however, is whether there are languages with complete imperative paradigms, showing all the person, number and gender markers found with other paradigms in the language. One such, possibly, is Maasai (Paranilotic, E. Africa). Tucker and Mpaayei (1955: 63–4) offer the following paradigm of the verb *any* 'sing', which appears to include imperatives:

mataranya	'so that I sing'
taranya	'so that you sing'/'Sing!'
metaranya	'so that he sings'
matarany	'so that we sing'
entarany	'so that you sing'/'Sing!'
metaranya	'so that they sing'

Although the 2nd person forms differ morphologically from the rest in not having an initial *m-*, they do not differ syntactically, for all of these forms can be used in subordinate clauses, e.g. for purpose:

einyo *matodol*
'He stood up so that we could see him'
ebuakita *entoniŋ*
'He is shouting so that you (pl.) may hear him'

It may well be that the same point is true for Kobon (see 3.2.4) and also for Turkish (Lewis 1967: 13–14, 264–6), though clearly there is a problem in attempting to distinguish between imperatives and 'must'-type directives. One might argue that these languages have complete directive paradigms but no imperatives.

In other languages there is a clear morphological distinction between the 'true' 2nd person imperative and a different complete paradigm (with 2nd person forms), but no syntactic contrast between them. Thus Amharic (Semitic, Ethiopia – Cohen 1936: 179–81) has 2nd person imperative forms, which like those of Arabic are inflected only for gender and number:

naggərə	'he said'
nəgər	'Say!' (2msg.)
nəgari	'Say!' (2fsg.)
nəgəru	'Say!' (2pl.)

In addition, it has a complete 'jussive' paradigm which has person prefixes, as does the so-called 'imperfect'. This is used for wishes and greetings:

əgz^yer yaṭnah
God   give strength+1SG+JUSS
'May God give you strength'

badəhna yəsanbətu
well   spend week+3PL+JUSS
'Have a good week!'

An important point, however, is that the 2nd person forms of the 'jussive' are used only when negated and then as negative commands (i.e. the negative of the Imperative).

Cohen, therefore, treats the 'imperative' and 'jussive' as a single mood, the forms being in complementary distribution; moreover, neither of them occurs in subordinate clauses, the 'imperfect' being the form used in such constructions (but see 4.3.1 for one exception). The 'jussive', however, can be used in deliberative questions, whereas this is not possible for the 'imperative':

mən ləwsad
what take+1SG+JUSS
'What shall I take?'

The essential question is whether all or any of these 1st and 3rd person forms are 'true' imperatives. If the Imperative is defined as presenting a proposition for action by the hearer, then clearly it can only be 2nd person. But could it not be presented for action by someone else, even though it is the hearer who is addressed? There is no very definite answer to this. It may be best to restrict the term 'Imperative' to 2nd person forms and to use 'Jussive' for the others.

It is worth adding that, although with the 1st person there may be 'jussive' forms (or 'deliberative' forms using the subjunctive as in Latin), yet speakers can also address themselves, treating themselves as hearers, so to speak:

Keep calm!   (=I must keep calm)

But this raises no real issue – the speaker is both speaker and hearer and the 2nd person form is appropriate.

3.3.3 *Other grammatical restrictions*

There are other features of the imperative related to tense, negation and subordination.

Generally, imperatives have no past tense forms. This is also true of MAY

Deontic modality

and MUST in English. The reason is that directives in general can only refer to the future (3.1); we cannot say:

> *Come yesterday
> *You must come yesterday
> *You may (might) come yesterday

(There are no similar restrictions on the closely related modal verbs of German and some other languages, but see 3.2.3.) Yet the modals can occur in past tense forms in reported speech, while the imperative cannot:

> You may come
> He said I might come
> You must come
> He said I must come
> Come!
> *He said I come

There is, however, in Syrian Arabic (Cowell 1964: 36) a construction that looks extremely like a past tense imperative – the use of the perfect form of KĀN 'be' with the imperative, but with the meaning 'should have':

> kənt   kōl   lamma kənt   fəl-bēt!
> You were eat+IMP when   you were in-the-house
> 'You should have eaten when you were at home'

The way in which imperatives are negated in a number of rather different languages is interesting. Latin generally uses the subjunctive, or rarely, the imperative, with the particle *ne*, which is the negative form used instead of *non* with types of deontic modality:

> Ne sis   patruus mihi   (Hor. *Ser.* 2.3.88)
> not be+2SG+PRES+SUBJ uncle   to me
> 'Don't come the uncle with me'

> Abi,   ne iura   sati'
> go away+2SG+PRES+IMP not swear+2SG+PRES+IMP enough
>   credo   (Pl. *Pers.* 490)
>   I believe
> 'Go on, don't swear; I believe you'

Greek uses either the present imperative or the aorist subjunctive, and in both cases the negative form *mé:* instead of *ou(k)* (see 1.5.3) (just as Latin uses *ne* instead of *non*):

> mé: lue   mé: luseis
> not free+2SG+PRES+IMP   *or*   not free+2SG+AOR+SUBJ
> 'Don't free'

The subjunctive is also used for negative mands in a quite different language, Syrian Arabic (Cowell 1964: 345):

rūḥ	'go!'
la trūḥ	'don't go!'

(The imperative is a bare stem, though it can also indicate gender and number, but the subjunctive has the 2nd person prefix, *t-*.)

Slightly differently, the jussive of Amharic (Cohen 1936: 179), which is also used for wishes, deliberation, etc., has 2nd person forms that are used only with negation, and Amharic does not normally negate the imperative forms (see 3.3.2).

The explanation for this is, presumably, that denial of permission is equivalent to giving instructions not to act, since 'Not-possible' is equivalent to 'Necessary-not' in a logical system (see Palmer 1979b: 75–6). Arguments of this kind have already been presented for both epistemic and deontic MAY and MUST (2.2.1, 3.2.1). The imperative thus expresses 'necessity', but the negated subjunctive, jussive, etc., 'no possibility'.

As mentioned in 3.3.1, the imperative does not occur in English (and most languages) in a subordinate clause, though a deontic modal is possible:

*I tell you that come tomorrow
I tell you that you must come tomorrow

However, it is possible for the imperative to occur, if it is presented as direct, not indirect (reported) speech:

My advice is – come tomorrow

This is possible in other languages, e.g. Syrian Arabic (Cowell 1964: 361):

bənṣaḥak   ᵊnsāha
I advise you forget it
'I advise you to forget it' ('I advise you "Forget it!" ')

The alternative here would be to use a conjunction and the subjunctive (4.2.4). However, the imperative is actually required in Maasai (Tucker and Mpaayei 1955: 96–8) when the main verb is imperative (see 4.3.1).

There is one attested use of a subordinate imperative in Greek:

all' óisth   hó   dráːson   (Ar. *Av.* 54)
but you know what do+2SG+AOR+IMP
'Do-you know what?'/'Do you know what you must do?'

This is unusual, and may, perhaps, be largely explained in terms of taking 'you-know-what' as a nominal object of 'do'.

However, since the form that marks the declarative is often used in subordinate clauses, and this fact actually points to its unmarked status, it might be expected that the imperative would be similarly used for similar reasons. But there is a difference. Reported speech requires deictic shift (see 4.6), so that a 2nd person form is often replaced by a 3rd person form, e.g. in Latin:

> Veni!
> come+2SG+PRES+IMP
> 'Come!'

> Imperat ut veniat
> he orders that come+3SG+PRES+SUBJ
> 'He orders him to come'

If the imperative in practice, or by definition, has no forms other than 2nd person, there is often no form available for subordinate usage.

3.3.4 *Non-finite forms*

Although the traditional definition of non-finite forms is that they are not marked for person, a more satisfactory and general definition is that they do not occur as the verbs of main clauses (see 4.5.1). Yet many languages use what are considered to be non-finites in the giving of prohibitions. Thus in English and Italian smoking is forbidden by:

> No smoking
> Non fumare

English uses the participle, Italian the infinitive, and there are plenty of examples from other languages, e.g. Russian:

> Ne razgovárivat'
> 'No talking!'

This is hardly surprising if the account of the imperative is correct. The infinitive simply indicates what is the forbidden action and does not even give an indication of the person being addressed, since the prohibition is general.

The positive form is also found, but usually for generalized instructions or merely advice or permission, as in:

> Smoking
> Circolare (Italian)
> 'Pass along please'

In Russian, however, it is also used to give a peremptory command:

> Molchat'
> 'Be silent!'

3.4   **Other modalities**

There are three other possible types of modality that are expressed formally in some languages; these are here called 'Commissive', 'Volitive', and 'Evaluative', terms adopted in the discussion of Searle and Rescher (1.2.2, 1.2.3).

Commissives are defined by Searle (1983: 166) as 'where we commit ourselves to doing things'; volitives and evaluatives both seem to fall within his 'expressives' 'where we express our feelings and attitudes'. This includes both the 'boulomaic' and the 'evaluative' modalities of Rescher (1968: 24–6), and would include the feelings and attitudes of fear, hope, wishes, regret, etc. Obviously these are not strictly deontic – it could be argued that 'deontic' should be restricted to directives. Yet they are equally not epistemic, since they do not express the degree of the speaker's commitment to what he is saying, and the term 'deontic' will be used, for convenience, to include them.

A distinction can be made, however, between attitudes towards known facts and attitudes towards those that are not known to be true. The first type, towards factual propositions, seems seldom to be grammaticalized (in main clauses) in languages, though there are a few possible examples, and it would seem reasonable to use Rescher's term 'evaluative' for these (see 3.4.3). (If so, REGRET is evaluative, not 'boulomaic' as Rescher suggests.)

3.4.1   *Commissives*

These are defined by Searle (1983: 166) as 'where we commit ourselves to do things', i.e. promises and threats (and the only difference between these seems to be in what the hearer wants). These are rarely expressed by a specific grammatical form, though English SHALL with 2nd and 3rd person forms is clearly of this type:

> You shall go to the circus
> John shall have the book tomorrow

Here the speaker commits himself to ensuring that the event takes place: he promises to arrange that the person addressed will go to the circus and that John will receive the book.

SHALL is also used together with WILL, in some dialects of English at least, for future time reference, but in this use SHALL occurs only with 1st person subjects. SHALL used with 2nd or 3rd person subjects specifically signals a commissive. The situation is complicated, however, by the fact that future time markers in general, including English WILL and the inflected futures of such languages as French, may be interpreted as promises, but this is best seen as a derived or indirect meaning (6.2.3).

It should also be noted that in Ngiyambaa (Donaldson 1980: 161) one of the inflectional modal paradigms, the 'irrealis', is used epistemically for 'might' and 'likely' but deontically for authoritative 'shall':

> waŋaːy-ndu-gal dhagurma-gu yana-y-aga
> NEG-2NOM-PL   cemetery-DAT go-CM-IRR
> 'You shall none of you go to the cemetery'

(Ngiyambaa has a different, but still inflectional, form as its imperative – the 'purposive'.)

3.4.2 *Volitives*

Jespersen (1924: 320–1) distinguishes between 'optative' and 'desiderative' in terms of what is realizable and what is non-realizable (see 1.2.1). His contrasting examples are:

> May he still be alive
> Would he were still alive!

Traditional grammars often make a distinction between wishes for the future and 'impossible wishes' (e.g. Moore 1934: 99). Examples from Greek are:

> óː paí génoio   patrós   eutukhésteros
>   (Soph. *Aj.* 550)
> o child become+2SG+AOR+OPT of father luckier
> 'My child, mayst thou be luckier than thy father'

> ei gár m' hupó géːn ... héːken   (Aesch. *P.V.* 152)
> oh that me below earth   send+3SG+AOR+INDIC
> 'Would he had sent me under the earth'

Neither of these distinctions is satisfactory. There is a much simpler relevant distinction that is a very familiar one – that between wishing and hoping. This is essentially the same as that between 'unreal' and 'real' in conditional sentences (see 5.4.1). With unreal conditionals and wishes the speaker indicates some kind of negative belief – that the event is unlikely or impossible, while with real conditionals and wishes, he leaves the possibility completely open. Moreover, in subordinate clauses the grammatical distinction between hopes and wishes is expressed in the same way as that of real and unreal conditionals – by the use of change of tense. This is clearly illustrated in the following examples, with the lexical items HOPE and WISH (see 4.3.2):

> I hope John (will come/comes) tomorrow
> I wish John would come tomorrow
>
> I hope John is here now
> I wish John were here now
>
> I hope John came yesterday
> I wish John had come yesterday

The distinction is valid whatever the time relation – for future as much as for past and present. Moreover, wishes do not relate only to what is unrealizable, as Jespersen suggests, or to what is 'impossible' or 'counterfactual', since wishes in the future are none of these. But even in the future the 'hope'/'wish', real/unreal, distinction is valid in terms of the speaker's opinion of the possibility of the event (see also 5.4.1).

Wishes, then, can be for the future, the present or the past. Classical Greek uses the optative for the future, the imperfect indicative for the present, and the aorist for the past. All are introduced by *ei gár* (and it is no coincidence that *ei* is also the conjunction ('if') of conditionals):

> ei gár genoíme:n téknon, antí soú nekrós
> (Eur. *Hipp.* 1410)
> oh that become+1SG+AOR+OPT son, instead of thou corpse
> 'O that I might be a corpse, my child, instead of you!'
>
> ei gár tosaúte:n dúnamin eíkhon (Eur. *Alc.* 1072)
> oh that such strength have+1SG+IMPERF+INDIC
> 'Had I such strength'
>
> ei gár m' hupó gé:n ... hé:ken (Aesch. *P.V.* 152)
> oh that me below earth send+3SG+AOR+INDIC
> 'Would he had sent me under the earth'

Latin uses present, imperfect and pluperfect subjunctive respectively (often with *utinam*):

> Atque utinam ipse Varro incumbat in causam
> (Cic. *Att.* 3. 15)
> but that self Varro apply self+3SG+PRES+SUBJ in cause
> 'But if only Varro would apply himself to the cause'

Modo valeres! (Cic. *Att.* 11. 23)
only   be well+2SG+IMPERF+SUBJ
'If only you were well'

Utinam ne ... tetigissent   litora   puppes
(Catull. 64. 171)
that   not   touch+3PL+PLUP+SUBJ shores ships
'Would that the ships had not touched the shore'

In English both hopes and wishes are usually expressed by lexical verbs *I hope* ..., *I wish* ... (4.3.2), though forms such as those given by Jespersen are found in literary texts. These are, in fact, examples of a hope and a wish for the present, with *may* for a hope and *would* for a wish, but the distinction is possible for all time relations:

> May he come tomorrow!
> Would that he came tomorrow!
>
> May he be here now!
> Would (that) he were here now!
>
> (?) May he have come yesterday!
> Would that he had come yesterday!

The Latin and Greek examples were all of wishes; hopes can be expressed, at least for the future, by the same moods (subjunctive and optative respectively, without the particles). An example for Greek is given above:

ό: paí   génoio   patrós   eutukhésteros
(Soph. *Aj.* 550)
o child become+2SG+AOR+OPT of father luckier
'My child, mayst thou be luckier than thy father'

Quite different languages have grammatical forms for expressing volition, at least with reference to the future. Thus for Fula, Arnott (1970: 299) offers:

njuutaa   balde
be long+2SG+SUBJ in days
'May you live long!'

Particles are used for the same purpose in Serrano (Hill 1967: 88), and in Huichol together with a 'desiderative' suffix (Grimes 1964: 60–1; see also 1.6.4).

Under Volitives should be included expressions of fear (which is listed by Rescher under 'boulomaic'). But fear is essentially the counterpart of hope (not of wish), always towards what is real or possible. Greek may express fear for future events by using the subjunctive with the negative *mé:* (essentially the 'modal' negative – see 1.5.3):

> mé: ... soús diaphtheíre:i   gámous   (Eur. *Alc.* 316)
> not   your destroy+3SG+PRES+SUBJ marriage
> 'I'm afraid she may ruin your marriage'

But these Greek expressions of fear usually have the very weak meaning of (English) 'I'm afraid' or even of 'perhaps':

> mé: ti   kakón rékso:si   (Hom. *Od.* 16. 381)
> not some ill   do+3PL+AOR+SUBJ
> 'Perhaps they may do some mischief'

There is in Greek, moreover, a distinction between fear and negative wish (which requires the optative, but the negative *mé:* still):

> egó thrasús ... oút'   eimí,   méːte
> I   bold   neither be+1SG+PRES+INDIC nor
> genoíme:n   (Dem. 8.68)
> become+1SG+AOR+OPT
> 'I am not, nor may I be, foolhardy'

3.4.3 *Evaluatives*

If Evaluatives are defined as attitudes towards known facts, they are not strictly modal at all. But they must be briefly considered, because they are sometimes included within, or as semantically closely related to, modal systems.

Two of the particles of Hixkaryana that have already been discussed are of this nature (Derbyshire 1979: 144, see also this volume: 2.1.2):

> nomokyaha hampɨnɨ
> 'He's coming – be warned!'

> nomokyatxow hampe
> 'They are coming! I don't believe it!'

Derbyshire glosses these as 'certainty' 'prediction' or 'warning', and 'positive doubt' 'scepticism', respectively. These suggest that they may express the degree of speaker commitment to the truth, but the translations suggest rather that they express the speaker's attitude towards what he already accepts as true.

Another example which has been discussed already (1.1.1) is in Menomini (Hockett 1958: 237–8):

pi·w	he comes, is coming, came
pi·wen	he is said to be coming, it is said that he came
pi·ʔ	is he coming, did he come?
piasah	so he *is* coming after all! (despite our expectations to the contrary!)
piapah	but he was going to come! (and now it turns out that he is not!)

The last two of these express failure of expectation, surprise or disappoint-
ment at the fact of his coming or not coming. But they are within a system
that includes interrogative and quotative.

For Ngiyambaa, Donaldson (1980 – see 1.5.4) mentions the particles for
'good job' and 'bad job':

> mandaŋgul-dhi:-ndu waŋa:y ŋiyiyi (242)
> GOOD JOB-1OBL-2NOM NEG say+PAST
> 'Good job you didn't tell me!'

> ga:mbada yana-nhi
> BAD JOB go-PAST
> 'Bad job (she) came!'

These express approval and disapproval of certain observed facts.
However, the particles that indicate them are not clitics attached to topics
as are the other relevant particles of Ngiyambaa, and the category is thus
very marginally grammatical. Indeed there are closed systems of evaluative
adverbs in many languages that are not to be discussed here.

There is one use of a modal verb in English that may prove more
important than might seem at first. It is the use of *should* in the
exclamatory:

> That he should do such a thing!

This is evaluative, in that it expresses surprise; but it is not an isolated
grammatical idiom, for it is found also in complement clauses (see 4.3.3):

> I regret that he should do such a thing

Moreover, Spanish uses the subjunctive, not the indicative, in similar
sentences (Klein 1975: 355):

> Lamento que aprenda
> I regret that learn+3SG+PRES+SUBJ
> 'I regret that he should learn'

What appears to be involved is that although these are factual ('factive') they are not 'assertive' (see 1.3.3, 4.2.3, 4.2.4). The speaker or subject does not present the facts, he merely evaluates them. This then supports the idea that evaluatives are modal, and since they are concerned with attitudes rather than commitments to truth they belong with (widely defined) deontic modality (but see 4.3.3 for an extended discussion).

3.5   Epistemic and deontic modality

Semantically, epistemic and deontic modality might seem to have little in common. One is concerned with language as information, with the expression of the degree or nature of the speaker's commitment to the truth of what he says. The other is concerned with language as action, mostly with the expression by the speaker of his attitude towards possible actions by himself and others. Indeed, all that they seem to share is the involvement of the speaker. Yet in English and many other languages the same forms are used for both types. The following (see 1.3.4) can all be interpreted either epistemically or deontically:

> He may come tomorrow
> The book should be on the shelf
> He must be in his office

Similar examples can be found for French, German and other European languages (see 1.5.1, 2.2.1, 3.2.1).

This is not a purely European phenomenon. The same point is true of the Dravidian language Tamil (Asher 1982: 171), where the same two suffixes are used for both epistemic and deontic modality (see 2.2.1, 3.2.1):

> Kantacaami   vantaalum   vara-laam
> Kandaswami come+CONCESS come-PERM
> 'Kandaswami may perhaps come'
>
> veeṇum-ṇṇaakkaa naaḷekki avan peeca-laam
> want-COND   tomorrow he   speak-PERM
> 'If he wants, he can speak tomorrow'
>
> Gaṇeecan ippa Mannaarkuṭiyile irukka-ṇum
> Ganesan now Mannargudi+LOC be-DEB
> 'Ganesan must be in Mannargudi now'
>
> avan aŋke pooka-ṇum
> he   there go-DEB
> 'He must go there'

Deontic modality

There is, it will be noted, a distinction with the 'may' examples in terms of a 'concessive' and a 'conditional' marker on the verb, but the modal form itself is the same.

There are other non-Indo-European languages in which a single form may be used either deontically or epistemically, as has already been noted for Ngiyambaa (1.5.4; Donaldson 1980: 160–2):

Purposive:

ŋadhu bawuŋ-ga yuwa-giri   (162)
I+NOM middle-LOC lie-PURP
'I must lie in the middle'

yuruŋ-gu ŋidja-l-i   (162)
rain-ERG rain-CM-PURP
'It is bound to rain'

Irrealis:

waŋaːy-ndu-gal dhagurma-gu yana-y-aga   (161)
NEG-2NOM-PL   cemetery-DAT go-CM-IRR
'You shall none of you go to the cemetery'

yuruŋ-gu ŋidja-l-aga   (160)
rain-ERG rain-CM-IRR
'It might/will rain'

Similarly, in Tütatulabal (Steele 1975: 207, quoting Voegelin; see also this volume: 3.2.4) the 'permissive' suffix is used in a variety of senses, e.g.:

hatdaːw *aha* bi
'You may cross it'

wiː-*aha*-dza
'It might run'

tan-*ahaː*-giluts-tiːtɨk
'Would we were eating'

However, it has already been seen that the forms used for epistemic and deontic modality are not, in fact, identical even in English (1.3.4). There are, in particular, differences with negation (see 2.2.1, 2.3.1). Languages vary according to the degree to which they use the same forms for both kinds of modality. In one form of Chinese (see 6.3 for details) there are different forms for epistemic and deontic necessity, but partially the same forms for the two kinds of possibility:

kŏe lén	'may'	epistemic
kŏe ï	'may'	deontic

In literary Arabic (Zayed 1984: 92–141; see also this volume: 2.2.1) the forms are:

Epistemic:	'may'	rubbama
	'must'	labudda
Deontic:	'may'	yumkin
	'must'	yagib

In contrast with this, however, in colloquial Cairene Arabic (Gary and Gamal-Eldin 1982: 98–9) the same form is used for both kinds of necessity, but there are different forms of possibility:

laazim tiX̱allas   bukra
must you+SG-finish tomorrow
'You must finish tomorrow'

laazim jikuun hinaak
must he be there
'He must be there'

ti?dari   tifuuti   min hina
you+SG can/may you+SG pass from here
'You can/may pass through here'

jimkin   jikuun hinaak
probable/possible he be there
'He may be there'

A language may have deontic, but no epistemic, forms. Thus for Kobon Davies (1981: 23–4; see also this volume: 3.2.4) notes a paradigm that contains an 'imperative' and a 'prescriptive', but he explicitly states that 'there is no morphologically distinct category with which the speaker can indicate his authority for making an assertion'. Conversely, it seems likely that the forms of an evidential system are not used deontically. In Tuyuca (2.1.2) the 'apparent' evidential can be translated as 'must', but not, presumably, in its deontic sense.

The close relationship between them has, of course, been noted before. Joos (1964: 195) comments 'within the modal system English does not distinguish between duty and logic'. But it has seldom been noted that there is no immediately obvious reason why the same forms should be used for expressing the speaker's degree of commitment to truth and for getting other people to do things. It is by no means obvious that permission is a 'related notion' to possibility, or requirement to certainty, as Steele *et al.* (1981: 21) comment without justification or explanation.

The most detailed and plausible explanation is found in Sweetser (1982), who argues (p. 492) that the 'epistemic world is understood in terms of the sociophysical world', an idea that is virtually identical with that of locative case theory (Anderson 1971). Sweetser suggests that while MAY is 'an absent potential barrier in the sociophysical world', epistemic MAY is the 'parallel case in the world of reasoning' and that its meaning would be that 'there is no barrier to the speaker's process of reasoning from the available premises to the conclusion expressed'. Both are covered by Ehrman's (1966) *nihil obstat*. Similar arguments hold for MUST.

This would be no more than plausible speculation if it were not the case that Sweetser adduces evidence from other forms in English. She finds a similar ambiguity in verbs such as INSIST, SUGGEST, EXPECT:

> I insist that you go to London
> I insist that you did go to London

> I suggest that you leave the room now
> I suggest that you left the room to avoid being seen

The following sentence is ambiguous between the two senses:

> I expect him to be there

She notes a similar ambiguity in causal conjunction:

> He came because he heard me screaming
> He heard me screaming, so he came
> (You say he's deaf, but –) He came, so he heard me screaming
> (You say he's deaf, but –) He heard me screaming, because he came

Similar arguments can be found for *therefore, since, although, despite* and *anyway*, though with all of these Sweetser sees a further distinction, not present with the modals, relating them to the reasoning for the speech act itself.

To these observations can be added the fact that verbs such as *ask*, *promise* and *swear* can be used epistemically or deontically:

> I asked if he had come
> I asked him to come

> I promise you he's here
> I promise you he'll come

> I swear he's here
> I swear I'll give it to you

Similar points can be made about other language: for example, INSISTER in Spanish is used in both senses, though with the indicative indicating the epistemic and the subjunctive the deontic, sense (Klein 1975: 356, who does not specifically note the epistemic/deontic distinction):

> Insisto que *aprende*
> I insist that learn+3SG+PRES+INDIC
> 'I insist that he's learning'

> Insisto que *aprenda*
> I insist that learn+3SG+PRES+SUBJ
> 'I insist that he learn'

But there is, as might be expected, some idiosyncrasy or idiomaticity, as shown by the different sense of SENTIR 'to feel':

> Siento que aprende
> I feel that learn+3SG+PRES+INDIC
> 'I feel he's learning'

> Siento que aprenda
> I feel that learn+3SG+PRES+SUBJ
> 'I regret that he's learning'

Sweetser's arguments are convincing and have been partly followed in this book, but she goes much too far in suggesting that an advantage of the approach is to allow us to give a single semantic analysis to the modal verbs. For not only is this not fully convincing intuitively – it also fails to explain why, even in English, there is such variation in the syntactically related or similar forms. Why are the negatives so different? Why is CAN so easily substitutable for MAY only when deontic? What her arguments should be allowed to show is that it is quite 'reasonable' that languages use the same or similar forms for deontic and epistemic modality – that we should not be surprised if they do. But observations about what is 'reasonable' in languages are not reducible to rigorous formal statements about their semantics (or their syntax). Indeed, if Sweetser were to attempt to proceed to a semantic analysis of modality on the basis of her 'single semantic analysis', she would soon find quite insuperable difficulties. (See Palmer 1983a, for discussion of the notion of what is 'reasonable' in languages.)

4
Complement clauses

The previous chapters have discussed how what, loosely, may be called 'the opinions and attitudes' of speakers may be expressed by modal forms in main clauses. But modal forms also occur in subordinate clauses, where they do not usually (but see below) indicate the attitudes and opinions of the actual speakers. They are, however, of relevance for several reasons.

First, modal forms certainly occur in subordinate clauses, and it is therefore necessary to give an account of them. The subjunctive in many European languages is of particular interest (4.2.4, 4.3). Secondly, many subordinate clauses, especially object complements (see 4.1.1), report the attitudes and opinions of the subjects of the main clauses, who are presented as the original speakers who expressed, or may be thought to have expressed, some kind of modality. This is clearly illustrated by comparing the two (epistemic and deontic) uses of MUST with verbs with object complements:

> You must be there
> He concluded that she was there
> He urged her to be there

Thirdly, 'modal' lexical items with complement clauses, mostly verbs with a 1st person subject (where the speaker and subject are identical) can be used performatively to indicate (not report) the opinions and attitudes of the speaker, as in:

> I think he's there
> I urge you to come

Indeed, because the number of lexical verbs in a language is likely to be far greater than the number of distinct modal grammatical forms, this device permits a much greater range of modal expressions by the speaker (see 4.1.2, 4.7).

4.1   Classification

4.1.1   *Types of clause*

There are basically three types of subordinate clause. The first type – the complement clauses of this chapter – are introduced by a lexical subordinator, or 'predicator', most importantly a verb which can be interpreted as reporting something that was said or might have been said by the subject of the main clause, who is thus portrayed as having expressed some kind of opinion or attitude, as in:

> He requested that they should arrive early
> Mary asked John to do it
> I thought that it was a good idea

In such examples it is natural to see the subordinate clause as the object of the main clause, and traditionally they are noun clauses, though this has not been universally accepted (see Rosenbaum (1967), who distinguishes between 'noun phrase complementation' and 'verb phrase complementation').

There are, however, some clauses that typically, but not exclusively, occur with adjectives and where the sentence is usually introduced by *it*, as in:

> It is essential that they should come
> It is likely that they will come

These seem again to be modal, in that they express deontic and epistemic modality (respectively). But they differ from the other type in that there is no animate subject of the main clause to indicate whose opinion or attitude is being reported. They can then be interpreted either as reporting the attitudes or opinion of the actual speaker, or as being objective.

There are semantic and syntactic arguments for suggesting that a complement clause of this kind is not the object, but the subject of the main clause. Semantically, what, in our examples, is 'essential' is 'that they should come', what is 'likely' is 'that they will come'. Syntactically, *it* often functions as a dummy subject, which is used solely to ensure that there is a grammatical subject (which is an absolute requirement in English), the 'real', 'original' or 'deep' subject having been moved to a later position in the sentence. This was the solution of the Standard Theory of Transformational-Generative Grammar (see Rosenbaum 1967: 77ff, 102ff). Yet in most respects these 'subject' complements are very similar to the 'object' complements. They appear in the same position in the sentence and have, in general, the same markers of subordination. They cannot, then, be treated as unrelated, but a detailed discussion of them is left until the end of this chapter (4.7).

The second type of subordinate clause, the oblique clauses of Chapter 5, are not dependent upon a lexical item, either verb or adjective, and have an adverbial or oblique, rather than nominal, status in relation to the syntax of the main clause. The most typical, and perhaps the only genuinely modal, type is the clause of purpose illustrated by:

> I did it so that they should come

However, there is a problem concerned with clauses of result, and something can be said about other types of oblique clauses, especially temporal and causal clauses.

A third type of subordinate clause is the relative clause, which is essentially adjectival in character. There will be no separate discussion of relative clauses, since there appears to be nothing relevant that can be said except in conjunction with one or other of the other types. Thus 'relative purpose' (5.2.3) is closely related to purpose, and the distinctive use of the subjunctive in relative clauses in indirect speech is obviously a matter within the discussion of complement clauses.

4.1.2 *Lexical classes*

One way of approaching the analysis of complement clauses would be through a detailed classification of the lexical items. Indeed, it could even be argued that such a classification is basic to the whole analysis of modality, and that, therefore, this chapter should have preceded, and have been the basis for, the analysis in the preceding chapters. This view is implicit in the remarks of Rescher (1968; see also this volume: 1.2.3):

> A proposition is presented by a complete, self-contained statement, which, taken as a whole, will be true or false: *the cat is on the mat*, for example. When such a proposition is itself made subject to some further qualification of such a kind that the entire resulting complex is itself once again a proposition, then this qualification is said to represent a modality to which the original proposition is subjected.
>
> (1968:24)

All the types of modality suggested by Rescher are expressed as complex sentences in subordinate position (1.2.3). The same idea is found in the theory of abstract performatives (see 4.7).

Not all subordinate clauses introduced by lexical items are concerned with modality. It is for this reason that the notion of reporting of attitudes and opinions is important (see also 4.1.4), and may perhaps be why Rescher spoke of 'proposition' (though this term may be too wide and too vague). A very common type of subordinate clause, that is not of interest here, is concerned with aspect, or involves verbs such as BEGIN, KEEP ON, STOP, etc. Some languages have a wider range of such verbs than English, for example Maasai (Tucker and Mpaayei 1955: 96ff), where they are glossed 'do first', 'do in future', 'do soon', 'do afterwards', 'do early', 'do again', 'succeed', 'know how to', 'finish'; or Tzotzil (Mexico – Cowan and Merrifield 1968: 294 fn. 9) where they are glossed 'come', 'go', 'go and return', 'arrive home', 'arrive away from home', 'begin', 'finish'. Other verbs are almost 'adverbial' in meaning, expressing how or why the event took place, e.g. English HAPPEN, CONDESCEND. Others that are more similar to the modal verbs and may even overlap semantically or formally with them are those of causes (GET, HAVE, ALLOW, etc.) and perception (SEE, WATCH, HEAR, etc.); the former are partially related to deontic modality, the latter to epistemic, and very often have the same syntactic constructions.

The most obvious way of classifying these might seem to be in terms of their semantics, but it is also possible to deal with them in terms of their syntax alone, with no reference to modality, aspect, etc. One such study is that of Rosenbaum (1967).

Even if the investigation is restricted to modal types, it will be found that there are far more lexical items than the types of modality indicated by the grammar, and that there is no one-to-one correspondence between the verbs and the types of modality already established. In the case of directives, alongside the imperative and MUST there are many verbs (INSTRUCT, ORDER, COMMAND, REQUIRE, TELL, EXHORT, URGE, ASK, BEG, TELL, etc.) and, except perhaps for ORDER and COMMAND, all could be used as counterparts of either the imperative or MUST. By contrast, English appears to have no verb that relates directly to deontic MAY. LET, PERMIT and ALLOW all indicate permission, but not necessarily by the use of language (though PERMIT suggests linguistic permission more than the other two), as seen in:

> He allowed/let the bird fly away
> (?) He permitted the bird to fly away

Similarly, there is no lexical item that corresponds exactly to epistemic MAY in English; THINK expresses far more confidence than MAY. (But CONCLUDE is much more closely related to MUST.)

Complement clauses

For reasons of this kind the complement clauses should be seen as reports of attitudes and opinions which the original speaker may be thought to have expressed, or might have expressed, rather than accurate reports of what he actually said, as can be seen (see 4.1.4, 4.2.1) by contrasting:

> John says 'It may rain'
> John thinks it will rain
>
> John said 'You must come'
> John urged her to come

There are many verbs that express some degree of modality in that they suggest 'opinions or attitudes', but which carry other meanings as well. Thus DECIDE is in part commissive in that the (original) speaker clearly indicates what he will do, but it also indicates some deliberation. Similarly, PERSUADE is directive but also indicates that the required action will take place (unlike URGE which is 'purely' directive). WAIT often has a sense of purpose but also indicates temporal inaction. There are many other such verbs, e.g. CHALLENGE, CONSTRUE, FANCY, MAKE, NAP, PLEDGE, PRESUPPOSE, REVEAL, SPUR, SUSPECT, VOTE, VOUCH (see Van Ek 1966). All of these carry some of the meanings of modality and all function grammatically like some of the modal predicators. They should, therefore, be considered at least for exemplification of the modal types and their related constructions.

One important corollary of the fact that there are so many lexical items that can express modality is that since the modality is so clearly expressed in the lexical item it may not also be expressed in the subordinate clause. An example of this is the common use of infinitives and other nominal forms, which mark few or none of the categories that are usually associated with the verb, including modality (see 4.5). Thus in English the infinitive may be used with CONSIDER, which has epistemic qualities, and ORDER, which is clearly deontic:

> He considers him to be a fool
> He ordered him to come

Moreover, the declarative is often used in subordinate clauses with verbs that express epistemic modality, although clearly this does not indicate that the speaker presents the proposition in the subordinate clause as factual. This has already been discussed (1.4.2, 2.6) and will be briefly discussed again (in section 4.2.5).

4.1.3 Markers of subordination

Traditionally, when two clauses are combined to form a single sentence they are joined either by coordination or subordination. Informally the distinction is a simple one: with coordination there are two independent sentences simply linked together, while with subordination one of the clauses forms an essential part of the structure of the other. There is some difficulty, however, in deciding whether in given cases there is coordination or subordination, or even whether the two clauses form one sentence rather than two. There are, however, at least four types of criteria for subordinate clauses.

First, they are, by definition, a part of the syntactic structure of the main clause. In most causes the verb of the main clause can be seen as a transitive verb and the complement clause as its (obligatory) object, as in:

> John wanted me to come
> (cf.*John wanted)

(In some cases it may be that the clauses are the subjects rather than the objects of the main verb – see 4.4.)

This simple fact, however, does not distinguish indirect speech, which is of interest here, from direct speech, which is not. This is discussed in sections 4.1.4 and 4.6.

Secondly, there are conjunctions, but there is very little to be said about them, for although individual languages may have specific conjunctions to indicate subordination, e.g. *that* in English, they are language-specific and have no typologically shared characteristics that would indicate subordination in different and unrelated languages. It is not even necessary for a conjunction to be present:

> John said he was coming

The absence of the conjunction seldom raises problems because there are usually markers. Nor should it be surprising if some languages regularly use no conjunction for indirect speech.

Thirdly, mood is of relevance in inflected languages. It was noted earlier (1.3.6) that the term 'subjunctive' has the etymological meaning 'subordinate' (Greek *hypotaktikē*), and that subordination is among the subcategories tentatively suggested in Jespersen (1.2.1). Indeed, it appears that the function of the subjunctive in a subordinate clause is often to do no more than indicate the subordination, or rather to indicate that it is one particular type of subordinate clause. Thus, in Latin an indirect (reported) question requires the subjunctive:

Quid agis? → Rogo quid agas
What do+2SG+PRES+INDIC → I ask what do+2SG+PRES+SUBJ
'What are you doing?' 'I ask what you are doing'

Rogavi pervenisset-ne Agrigentum
(Cic. *Verr.* 2.4.12.27)
I asked arrived+3SG+PLUP+SUBJ-INT Agrigentum
'I asked if he had arrived at Agrigentum'

In contrast, a direct question in Latin uses the indicative, unless it is of a particular type that requires the subjunctive, e.g. a deontic request (3.2.5). There are other uses of the subjunctive related to reported speech that are discussed later (4.2.4).

Mood is, however, far from being a reliable indication of subordination, for it often merely reflects the mood of an independent clause. Thus both volitives (wishes) and reported volitives are marked by the subjunctive in Latin (3.4.2, 4.3.2). It is this fact that has led to some misleading statements concerning parataxis (for which see 5.5.1). Moreover, one important type of subordinate clause, that of reported speech, is not generally marked by mood in most Classical and modern European languages, or, at least, the subjunctive is used there for specific purposes, e.g. 'non-assertion' in Spanish (see below 4.2.4).

There are other languages in which there is a particular verbal paradigm or set of verbal paradigms that are regularly used, following fairly strict rules, in subordinate clauses of various types; these may appropriately be called 'subjunctive'. Thus for Syrian Arabic, Cowell (1964: 345ff) has a long list of predicators used with the subjunctive: 'overt expressions of exhortation, suggestion, wish, fear, intention, etc.'. In addition, it is found with 'must', 'may' 'be able', 'know how to', 'forget to' and many others, not all of them describable as modal (but the subjunctive is not used for reported statements or questions – see 4.3.2). Examples are:

ʔana bəddi ʔəržaɛ ɛal-bēt
I I want+INDIC I go+SUBJ to the-house
'I want to go home'

lāzəm ʔūfi bwaɛdi
must I keep+SUBJ to promise my
'I must keep my promise'

Similarly for Fula, Arnott (1970: 305–6) indicates that the 'subjunctive' is used with verbs of (i) enjoining, (ii) wishing, (iii) fearing, taking care, (iv) requesting, (v) permitting or agreeing, (vi) causing or arranging, as well as in other types of clause.

132

In a very different language, Mangarayi (Merlan 1982: 178, 184), there is an 'irrealis' prefix that is used for epistemic possibility, but which is also often the only marker of subordination:

> a-ɲani-yug
> IRR-talk-AUX
> 'He might talk'

> gawa-j   muyg jaŋʔ   ya-ma-ɲ
> bury-PAST PUNC dog   die   IRR-AUX-PAST PUNC
>
> 'He buried the dog $\left.{\text{when it died}\atop\text{that died}}\right\}$'

Some languages have more than one mood that is particularly associated with subordinate clauses. Greek has both subjunctive and optative, but the choice between them is determined not by the type of subordinate clause but by sequence of tenses rules relating to the tense of the main verb. By contrast, Maasai (Tucker and Mpaayei 1955: 61ff, 96ff) has no fewer than five different paradigms that are used with different sets of lexical subordinators. These Tucker and Mpaayei call 'subjunctive (a)', 'subjunctive (b)', 'infinitive (a)', 'infinitive (b)' and the 'N-tense'. The infinitives lack some of the person markers, while the 'N-tense' is the one also used for serial coordination (see 5.5.2). The subjunctives are mostly used in purpose clauses or in main clauses as exhortations and wishes. For subordinate clauses there are (at least) five classes of predicator:

(i)   'Let' takes either of the two subjunctives.
(ii) Verbs of wanting, liking, disliking, etc. (including 'ought') take the 'N-tense'.
(iii) 'Infinitive (a)' is used mostly after verbs of motion, but also after verbs of liking, 'help', 'do again', 'do in the near future', 'start', 'repeat', 'do early in the morning'.
(iv) 'Infinitive (b)' is used with 'get to do', 'know how to', 'finish', 'be able to', 'dare'.
(v)   Either 'infinitive (b)' or the 'present' tense is used after 'refuse', 'be afraid', 'forget', 'lack'.

Fourthly, and related to the third point, non-finite forms are also typically and critically markers of subordinate clauses. This may seem not to have a great deal to do with modality, but non-finite forms are, like modal markers, indications of non-factuality. However, the issue of non-finite clauses and their relation to finite clauses is a fairly complex one and is left until section 4.5.

4.1.4 *Complements as reports*

Complement clauses of the type considered here can be seen as reporting attitudes or opinions; in the case of object complements these are attitudes or opinions of the subject of the main clause of the sentence – the original, as opposed to the actual, speaker.

It is generally accepted that there are two ways of reporting what has been said: direct and indirect (or reported) speech. In direct speech the actual words of the original speaker are simply repeated, whereas in indirect speech this is not so, for example:

> John said 'I'm coming tomorrow'
> John said that he was coming the next day

These do not differ, however, in terms of the relation to the rest of the sentence of the clause that indicates the words spoken (see 4.1.3). In terms of the structure of the whole sentence both types involve complement clauses, for both *I'm coming tomorrow* and *that he was coming the next day* are the object complements of *said*, SAY being a transitive verb that requires an object. Because of this, there are examples where it would not be possible to distinguish direct and indirect speech, as in:

> I say 'I am coming'
> I say I am coming

Here the conventions of writing, the punctuation, make the distinction, but in the spoken language there would be no such features. In most cases, however, the distinction is made by the choice of deictic markers of person, place and time. Indeed it is this that must be considered the essential criterion. The situation is, however, complex and a detailed discussion is left until section 4.6.

Although an essential characteristic of the complement clauses being considered here is that they can be seen as reports, the most accurate reports (those of direct speech) are, paradoxically, of little interest, for since they merely repeat precisely what was originally said they have no further characteristics of their own, but express modality in exactly the same way as it is expressed in main clauses. It is only when changes are made to the original utterance in the report that there is indirect speech, and essentially, therefore, it is these changes that are the topic of this chapter.

Traditionally there are three basic types of indirect speech, indirect statements, indirect questions and indirect commands, reflecting the three sentence types discussed in 1.4.1:

I'm coming
John said he was coming

Are you coming?
John asked if he was coming

Come!
John told him to come

Yet clearly there can also be indirect wishes and evaluatives. The three-term distinction has some usefulness and plausibility, but is not basic to the discussion.

In theory, a language can use direct speech for all its complement types, leaving nothing more to be said. In practice, it is not certain whether this is wholly true of any language. Amharic (Semitic, Ethiopia – Cohen 1936: 363) illustrates the extent to which this is possible. With many complementizers of all types a direct question is used, with the participial form (the so-called 'gerund') of the verb 'to say' occurring at the end of the quotation, as in:

> mængædum aagaññaum   bəyye   əfarallaüh
> the road   he will not find it I saying I fear
> 'I am afraid he won't find the road'

It is even possible to express refusal with the verb 'to say' with inanimate subjects:

> səga albasləmm   ala
> meat I will not cook   said
> 'The meat refused to cook'

There are languages in which direct speech is the norm for reporting statements, question and commands. Two which are geographically and linguistically far apart are Kobon (New Guinea – Davies 1981) and Hixkaryana (Brazil – Derbyshire 1979). Similarly, the languages of Australia described by Dixon (1972, 1977) and Donaldson (1980), Dyirbal, Yidiny and Ngiyambaa, make extensive use of direct speech (this is not actually stated but is clearly shown in the textual material). However, Amharic also has indirect speech forms; there is some evidence of indirect speech in Ngiyambaa (indirect commands – see 4.3.1); and Derbyshire's positive assertion that there is no indirect speech in Hixkaryana can be accepted only with reservations (see below 4.6.1).

More importantly, the indirect speech forms are very commonly used in a whole variety of languages for what are not strictly reports of anything said. In particular, in most of the languages with which we are familiar they are used for all kinds of epistemic judgments. The construction used with verbs of saying is also used with verbs of thinking, knowing, guessing, concluding, etc.:

> John said/thought/knew/guessed/concluded that Mary would come

Traditionally, such sentences are simply treated as examples of indirect or reported speech, though the term 'reported' is misleading, since there is no implication that any words are actually spoken. This is clear enough from:

> My dog knew that there was someone there

Yet the traditional treatment is easily justified:

(i) There is usually very little formal difference between constructions with epistemic verbs and those with verbs of saying.

(ii) Although no words may have been uttered, the speaker can 'put into words' what might have been said.

(iii) Even with verbs of saying, it does not follow that the indirect speech is a faithful representation of the words that were uttered. The second sentence below is not a false report of the first:

> 'I'll be there'
> John said he was coming

By contrast, it would be untrue to say in a direct report of the first sentence:

> John said 'I'm coming'

4.2 Epistemic modality

4.2.1 *Judgments and reports*

As suggested in 4.1.3, the complement clauses discussed in this book are by definition those that, in some sense, report attitudes or opinions. Object complement clauses report the attitudes or opinions, of the subjects of the main clauses.

Reports of opinions, of epistemic judgments, are treated in many languages exactly like reports of actual speech; traditionally all are subsumed under 'indirect speech'. Thus in English, both THINK and SAY are followed by *that* or no conjunction and a declarative form of the verb:

> He said/thought (that) John was coming

There is a similar construction in Syrian Arabic, with the verb in the indicative (Cowell 1964: 347):

bəṭẓənn ənno byaṛref   l-ᵊḥkāye
you think that   he knows+INDIC the-story
'Do you suppose he knows the story?'

Other languages use different constructions, but still do not differentiate grammatically between reports of speech and of epistemic judgments.

The nature of the judgment is expressed lexically in the verb, and there is often no grammatical indication of modality within the subordinate clause. Indeed, it can be suggested that such grammatical marking would be semantically redundant. Thus in both English and Arabic the declarative (indicative) is used (but see 4.2.5). Yet the lexical judgment verbs are far from being identical with any of the markers of epistemic modality in main clauses. In particular, there is no verb that comes near in meaning to epistemic MAY; THINK is by no means equivalent to it, and may occur either with no modal verb in the subordinate clause, or with any of the modal verbs:

> He thinks John comes
> He thinks John may come
> He thinks John must come

In some languages there are fairly firm rules or tendencies relating to the use of mood in such subordinate clauses. This may directly depend upon the type of judgment (especially the degree of certainty) indicated in the verb, or there may be a choice of mood to indicate the subject's degree of commitment. For a more detailed discussion see sections 4.2.3, 4.2.4, 4.2.5.

It is possible to make a judgment about a deontic attitude, too:

> He thinks John ought to come

Indeed, if the speaker expresses his own judgment about such an attitude he cannot do so by using a modal form, but must employ a verb of judgment in a performative structure (see 4.7):

> *John may ought to come
> I think John ought to come

For a language that uses mood to express deontic modality, but a non-finite clause to indicate indirect speech, it is usually necessary to use some other device for indicating the deontic modality in such cases. However, Latin can (rarely) use the subjunctive instead of the accusative and infinitive for this purpose, as in (see also 5.5.1):

Censeo ad nos Luceriam venias (Cic. *Att.* 8.11A)
I think to us Luceria come+2SG+PRES+SUBJ
'I think you should come to us at Luceria'

Languages that do not have indirect speech forms or which use direct speech very commonly, not unexpectedly use direct speech with judgment verbs, as, indeed, even English can. Thus in Amharic and Kobon (Cohen 1936: 363; Davies 1981: 3):

aldənəm massalaw
I shall not recover it seemed to him
'He thought he would not recover'

yad gasi nöŋ-bin möŋ al-aŋ a gasi nöŋ-bin
I think-PERF+1SG rain shoot-IMPERF+3SG QUOTE think-perf+1sg
'I think it is going to rain'

(The deictic markers show that the Amharic example is one of direct speech, while Kobon has no indirect speech with finite verb forms.) It appears, too, that in Yidiny (Australia – Dixon 1977: 529) thoughts are indicated as talking to oneself:

waɲɖa yiŋu wuɽuː
where+LOC this+ABS river+ABS
'Where is the big river?' [Damari said to himself]

4.2.2 Mood and indirect speech

The subjunctive is directly associated with indirect speech in some languages. In German, for instance, it may be used in indirect statements (Hammer 1983: 267–8):

Ich glaubte er wäre krank (267)
I thought he be+3SG+IMPERF+SUBJ ill
'I thought he was ill'

Er sagte er wäre krank (268)
he said he be+3SG+IMPERF+SUBJ ill
'He said he was ill'

This depends, however, not on any degree of commitment, but on the tense of the main verb, the past tense normally requiring the subjunctive (but see also 4.2.5).

Latin does not use the subjunctive for reported statements, but it uses the subjunctive in various other ways relating to indirect speech (some of which have already been noted). First, it uses the subjunctive for indirect questions (see 4.1.3). By contrast, Syrian Arabic (Cowell 1964: 569), although it has a subjunctive mood, uses the indicative:

> taʕal,   nəsʔalo   šū   šār   maʕo
> come on, let's ask him what happened INDIC with him
> bət-talavəzyōn
> on the television
> 'Come on, let's ask him what happened to him on the television'

Secondly, a subordinate clause within a subordinate clause of reported speech in Latin is also placed in the subjunctive:

> Dicit   se   de   Gallis ... postulare   triumphum quos
> he says self from Gauls   to demand triumph   whom
> acie   vicerit   (Liv. 36.40.3)
> by battle defeat+3SG+PERF+SUBJ
> 'He says he claims a triumph from the Gauls, whom he has defeated in battle'

More strictly (and significantly), this is so only if the subordinate clause is part of what is reported. If it is part of the information being provided by the speaker (not the subject, but the original speaker) the indicative is used:

> Diogenes ... dicere solebat Harpalum, qui temporibus illis
> Diogenes   to say used   Harpalus who in times   those
> praedo felix   habebatur,   contra deos
> brigand happy be held+3SG+IMPERF+INDIC against gods
> testimonium dicere   (Cic. D.N. 3.34)
> witness   to speak
> 'Diogenes used to say that Harpalus (who at that time was generally thought to be a fortunate brigand) was a witness against the gods'

There is an exactly parallel situation in German (Hammer 1983: 268):

> Er sagte, er werde   das Buch kaufen da sein
> he said   he be+3SG+IMPERF+SUBJ the book to buy as his
> Onkel ... es ihm   empfohlen   hätte
> Uncle   it to him recommended have+3SG+IMPERF+SUBJ
> 'He said he would buy a book as his uncle ... had recommended'

> Er sagte, er bewerbe   sich um diese Stelle,
> he said   he apply+3SG+PRES+SUBJ self to this job
> für die   er gar   nicht geeignet ist
> for which he at all not   suited be+3SG+PRES+INDIC
> 'He said he was applying for this job, for which he is not at all suitable'

Thirdly, Latin uses the subjunctive in certain types of oblique clause to indicate that the propositions they contain were maintained by someone other than the speaker (see 5.3.1).

There is not much material available for the situation in languages with quite different, for example evidential, epistemic systems. In general, it seems that where a language has an epistemic 'hearsay' marker, this is used in reported speech after a verb of report. However, in Cashibo (Peru – Shell 1975) report in a main clause requires both the declarative and the report marker, but in a subordinate clause only the report marker:

Jorgenïn kaísa   aín lápiz ćasiaşa   (181)
George   REP IND+3 his pencil break+PAST+3
'George broke his pencil, it is said'

aín lápiz isa   ćasiaşa   kišon   ka
his pencil REP DEP+3 break+PAST+3 CLOSE OF QUOTE DECL+3
Jorgenïn ʔï kaaşa   (182)
George   me say+PAST+3
'George told me that he broke his pencil'

The subordinate form is not subjunctive in the sense in which the term has been used, but it is clearly marked as non-declarative.

4.2.3   Factivity and assertion

Lyons' (1977: 794) suggestion that factivity is a possible criterion for modality was briefly discussed in 1.3.3 with the comment that 'factuality' is a more appropriate term. The issue to be discussed here, however, is not factuality (or 'factivity') in general, but what have been called 'factive complements'. Paradoxically, it appears that in several languages (e.g. Spanish) the subjunctive is associated with factive complements and the indicative with non-factive ones – precisely the opposite of what might be expected.

Before discussing the Spanish examples, it would be wise to look at the original use of the term 'factive' within linguistics. A shortened and simplified account of the proposals of Kiparsky and Kiparsky (1971) is as follows:

(1)   Only factive predicates can have as their objects the noun *fact* with a gerund or *that* clause:
      I want to make clear the fact that I don't intend to participate
      *I assert the fact that I don't intend to participate
(2)   Gerunds can be the objects of factive predicates, but not freely of non-factive predicates:
      I regret having agreed to your proposal
      *I believe having agreed to your proposal

(3) Only non-factive predicates allow the accusative plus infinitive construction:

> I believe Mary to be the one who did it
> *I resent Mary to be the one who did it

According to this analysis, BELIEVE is a non-factive predicator and RESENT a factive one, yet in Spanish non-factive appears to be associated with the indicative and factive with the subjunctive (see 4.2.4 and 4.3.3):

> Creo   que vendrá
> I believe that come+3SG+FUT+INDIC
> 'I believe that he will come'

> Siento que ud lo haya   perdido
> I feel that you it have+3SG+PRES+SUBJ lost
> 'I regret that you have lost it'

There are problems in English, too, when semantic and formal criteria are compared. By the formal criteria, KNOW is a non-factive predicator:

> *I know the fact that John is here/John's being here
> I know John to be here

Yet KNOW is, rather obviously, semantically factive, for what is known must be true. Indeed, Coates (1983: 235), while quoting Kiparsky and Kiparsky, says 'KNOW is the classic example of a factive predicator'! There are problems too with WANT TO MAKE CLEAR and ASSERT (examples under (1), above), one being factive and the other non-factive. None of this should be surprising, however, for the Kiparskys are essentially concerned not with 'statements of fact', but with presupposition, with what is presupposed by speakers (which can be contrasted with what is asserted – see Strawson 1964). Moreover, most of their factive predicators turn out to be evaluatives, while the non-factives are epistemic in the wide sense that includes reporting statements of fact.

4.2.4 Mood and assertion

A rather different approach to the concept of statements of fact and modality is provided by Hooper (1975), with her distinction between 'assertive' and 'non-assertive', which is used by Klein (1975) to account for alternations between indicative and subjunctive in Spanish. Hooper's assertive predicators are precisely those that can be seen as predicators for indirect speech: THINK, BELIEVE, ASSERT, SAY, etc.

The chief formal test of these assertive predicators is that they can be postposed, as in:

He thinks John is coming
John is coming, he thinks
He says John is coming
John is coming, he says

She distinguishes, however, between 'weak' assertives such as THINK and BELIEVE and 'strong' assertives such as ASSERT and SAY. This is clearly a distinction between reports of modal judgments and reports of actual utterances, with the subject of the main verbs shown as fully committed to the truth of the proposition only with the latter (and with a much closer relationship between the words of the subordinate clause and words actually spoken).

Hooper accepts the Kiparskys' factive/non-factive distinction. These verbs are, then, assertive but non-factive. She suggests that there are non-assertive, non-factive predicators too, e.g. BE LIKELY, BE POSSIBLE, plus the negatives of weak assertives. It follows that verbs such as REGRET will be non-assertive, but factive, and the problem with KNOW is solved by saying that it is assertive but 'semi-factive'. The assertive/non-assertive distinction thus cuts across the factivity distinction, providing the four main possibilities shown in table 2.

Table 2. *Assertion and factivity*

NON-FACTIVE		
assertive		non-assertive
weak assertive	strong assertive	
think	assert	be likely
believe	claim	be possible
suppose	report	be unlikely
seem	say	doubt
etc.	etc.	neg+strong assertive
FACTIVE		
assertive (semi-factive)		non-assertive (true factive)
find out		regret
know		resent
learn		forget
remember		be odd
etc.		etc.

There is, unfortunately, a considerable amount of confusion and implausibility here about the use of the term 'assertive'. In what sense does THINK assert, while the negative of SAY does not? Both express some kind of opinion about a proposition, but neither asserts that it is true. The confusion is shown, too, when Hooper sees a problem in her conclusion that semi-factives appear both to assert and to presuppose, since it is generally assumed that assertion and presupposition are mutually exclusive. (It will be noted that factive and semi-factive are equated with presuppositional.) The problem arises from the failure to see that 'assertion' in the sense in which it is used here is quite independent of presupposition. 'Assertion' refers to assertion by the subject of the main verb, but presupposition to what is presupposed by the actual speaker. There is no conflict: what the subject may have asserted may or may not be believed to be true by the speaker.

The difficulties become even more apparent when the situation in Spanish is considered. Following Hooper's distinction, Klein (1975) claims that it is assertive/non-assertive that determines the use of indicative/ subjunctive in subordinate clauses in Spanish. She notes the contrast:

Insisto que aprende
I insist that learn+3SG+PRES+INDIC
'I insist that he's learning'

Insisto que aprenda
I insist that learn+3SG+PRES+SUBJ
'I insist that he learn'

Siento que aprende
I feel that learn+3SG+PRES+INDIC
'I feel that he's learning'

Siento que aprenda
I feel that learn+3SG+PRES+SUBJ
'I regret that he should learn'

These particular examples raise no problem concerning 'assertive'. The first pair illustrate the distinction between the epistemic and deontic uses of 'insist' (see 3.5), and it is often the case that deontic complements are marked with the subjunctive. The second pair indicate a difference between indirect speech that is assertive but non-factive, and an Evaluative (see 4.3.3) which is non-assertive, but factive.

However, although these examples show the indicative being used with assertive predicates, it is clear that the issue is not one of factivity, as might have been thought from the arguments in 4.2.3. Indeed, evaluatives, though clearly factive, are here marked by the subjunctive.

There is still a problem with the precise definition of 'assertive'. It cannot be equated with reported speech because the negatives of weak assertive verbs are, according to Hooper, non-assertive in Spanish, and for that reason may occur with the subjunctive. But Hooper (1975: 359 fn. 21) actually defines 'weak' non-assertive in terms of taking the subjunctive when negated – which is circular.

Klein notes that the verbs considered earlier may occur with either the indicative or the subjunctive when the assertive is negated (though the negation of the non-assertive is still marked by the subjunctive):

> no insisto que aprende
> not I insist that learn+3SG+PRES+INDIC
> 'I don't insist that he's learning'

> no insisto que aprenda
> not I insist that learn+3SG+PRES+SUBJ
> 'I don't insist that he's learning'
> 'I don't insist that he learn'

> No siento que aprende
> not I feel that learn+3SG+PRES+INDIC
> 'I don't feel that he's learning'

> No siento que aprenda
> not I feel that learn+3SG+PRES+SUBJ
> 'I don't feel that he's learning'
> 'I don't regret that he should learn'

Klein had noted (1975: 353) that 'doubt' is similarly followed by the subjunctive:

> Dudo   que aprenda
> I doubt that learn+3SG+PRES+SUBJ
> 'I doubt that he's learning'

This is very like the negative of a weak assertive such as 'believe' or 'think', which function similarly:

> No creo   que aprenda
> not I think that learn+3SG+PRES+SUBJ
> 'I don't think he's learning'

She could also have noted that 'be possible', 'be probable', etc. (and their negatives) are followed by the subjunctive:

> Es posible que aprenda/aprende
> is possible that learn+3SG+PRES+SUBJ/INDIC
> 'It is possible that he is learning'

All of these are non-assertive for Hooper and it seems that doubt or disbelief is what is at issue. Klein notes, however, that 'admit' may also be used with the subjunctive, to indicate 'grudging admittance':

> Admito que aprenda/aprende
> I admit that learn+3SG+PRES+SUBJ/INDIC
> 'I admit that he's learning'

This is not a matter of non-commitment, but rather unwilling commitment, to the proposition, and is possibly to be treated as an evaluative.

The conditions under which the subjunctive is, or may be, used are thus very varied (doubt, disbelief, 'weak' commitment, unwilling commitment, possibility, etc.). The claim that these mood distinctions can be accounted for in terms of assertion and non-assertion is not very meaningful, and may even be circular, unless an independent definition of 'assertion' is given.

In fairly general terms, it is fairly obvious what the situation is. The indicative is used where the subject shows some positive degree of commitment to the proposition, either total as with ASSERT, or partial as with THINK. Where there is no degree of positive commitment but either non-commitment as with BE POSSIBLE, or negative commitment as with DOUBT (partial negative commitment) or *don't think* (total negative commitment), the subjunctive is used. But 'assertion' and 'non-assertion' are no more than rather convenient labels for this, and do not in themselves explain the situation. The issue of 'grudging admittance' even further weakens any explanatory function of the terms, but it can be seen in terms of the subject not having a positive degree of commitment, though not to the truth of the proposition – rather in his attitude towards it.

These uses of the subjunctive in Spanish are not, of course, confined to that language. Generally, in the Romance languages negation with a verb of thinking seems to require a change of mood; thus Bloomfield (1933: 273) notes for French:

> Je pense qu'il   vient
> I   think that he come+3SG+PRES+INDIC
> 'I think he'll come'

> Je ne pense pas qu'il vienne
> I not think not that he come+3SG+PRES+SUBJ
> 'I don't think he'll come'

Prince (1976: 412) argues that the subjunctive is used only where there is 'negative raising', i.e. where the negative belongs syntactically (according to one school of thought) or semantically to the subordinate clause (see 4.5.4):

        Guy ne croit   pas que Fifi soit   bête
        Guy not believe not that Fifi be+3SG+PRES+SUBJ ugly
        'Guy doesn't think Fifi is ugly' (He thinks she isn't)

        Guy ne croit   pas que Fifi est   bête
        Guy not believe not that Fifi be+3SG+PRES+INDIC ugly
        'Guy doesn't think Fifi is ugly' (He does not hold the opinion that she is)

So also in Italian (see Hall 1964: 222):

        Non credo   che sia   Corelli
        Not I think that be+3SG+PRES+SUBJ Corelli
        'I don't think it's Corelli'

But this is, perhaps, not a matter of 'negative raising' at all, but of the use of the subjunctive where the epistemic modality reported is that of doubt – at the 'lower' end of the modality scale.

Italian, like Spanish, uses the subjunctive widely, including after *è probabile*, *può essere*, *è bello che*, *stupirsi* ('it is probable', 'it may be', 'it is nice', 'to be surprised'), all of which parallel Spanish uses; but the choice is often merely stylistic (Lepschy and Lepschy 1977: 224ff.).

A detailed study of the subjunctive in all such languages would be interesting and would undoubtedly show considerable parallelism of use, all related to lesser degrees of subject commitment. But an explanation in terms of 'assertion' would require a very flexible definition of that term.

Finally, it is worth noting that there are some similar features in a very different language. For although Hixkaryana (Derbyshire 1979) has no indirect speech form proper, some modal particles require the non-past 'uncertain' form of the verb (2.1.2). These are the particles of 'hearsay', 'deduction', 'uncertainty', 'positive doubt or scepticism'. In contrast, the particles for 'certainty, prediction or warning' and 'opinion, recollection or counter-affirmation' do not take the 'non-past uncertain' form. Again the epistemic modalities seem to fall into 'weaker' and 'stronger' types, and it would not be implausible to see the modal particles as in a sense superordinate to the lexical verb. In that case, the 'non-past uncertain' form of the verb would be very like the subjunctive in some complement clauses, especially those of the Romance languages.

4.2.5 *Speaker's commitment*

The discussion so far has concentrated on the commitment of the subject, the original speaker. But languages have devices for indicating the commitment of the actual speaker to the proposition expressed in the subordinate clause.

It was noted in 4.2.2 that German uses the subjunctive, with past tense main verbs, in indirect speech. The indicative, however, can be used to indicate confidence by the speaker:

$$
\begin{array}{l}
\text{Ich glaubte dass} \\
\text{I \quad thought \ that}
\end{array}
\left\{
\begin{array}{ll}
\text{er \ krank \ war} & \\
\text{he ill \quad be+3SG+IMPERF+INDIC} & \\
\text{er \ wäre} & \text{krank} \\
\text{he be+3SG+IMPERF+SUBJ ill} &
\end{array}
\right\}
$$

'I thought he was ill'

But the choice of mood depends also on stylistic and sociolinguistic factors (see Hammer 1983: 265–8). English, by contrast, may change the tense of the subordinate verb:

He said he is coming
He said he was coming

The former indicates that the speaker believes the reported statement; but there is no complete parallelism, for with verbs expressing knowledge, certainty, etc., German uses the indicative not the subjunctive, though, like English, it still uses the past tense (Hammer 1983: 267):

Ich wusste, dass er krank war
I knew that he ill be+3SG+IMPERF+INDIC
'I knew that he was (*is) ill'

The use of tense in English, however, is related to a wider issue – that of deixis in the subordinate clause – and this is discussed in detail in section 4.6.

Classical Greek similarly uses the optative mood with past tense verbs of reporting, but may also use the indicative, with the original (direct speech) tense:

eːngélthe   autóːi hóti Mégara aphésteːke   (Thuc. 1.114)
it was reported to him that Megara revolt+3SG+PLUP+INDIC
'News came to him that Megara had revolted' (*not* 'has revolted')

eːpeíleːs'   hóti ... badioímeːn   (Ar. *Pl.* 88)
I threatened that   go+1SG+FUT+OPT
'I threatened that I would go'

There are some examples with both in the same sentence, with presumably some indication of speaker commitment, as in:

élegon   hóti Kúːros mén   téthneːke,
they said that Cyrus on the one hand die+3SG+PLUP+INDIC

Ariaíos dé   pepheugó:s ... eíe: (Xen. *An.* 2.1.3)
Ariaeus on the other having fled   be+3SG+PRES+OPT
'They said that Cyrus had died, but that Ariaeus had fled'

Other languages employ different conjunctions to express similar contrasts of commitment by the speaker. Japanese does not switch tenses in indirect speech (see 4.6.2), but has three different conjunctions, *no*, *koto* and *to* (Kuno 1973: 213–22). These are, in part, determined by the main clause lexical verb:

Watakusi wa John ga Mary o butu *no* o mita   (214)
I   John   Mary   hits that saw
'I saw John hitting Mary'

Watakusi wa nihongo muzukasii *koto* o mananda   (214)
I   Japanese difficult   that   learnt
'I learned that Japanese is difficult'

John wa nigongo ga muzukasii *to*   itta   (214)
John   Japanese   difficult   that said
'John said that Japanese was difficult'

The particles *no*, *koto* and *to* are not interchangeable here, but elsewhere there is a choice, with *to* always indicating that the speaker does not presuppose the truth of the proposition:

John wa Mary ga sinda *to*   sinzinakatta   (216)
John   Mary   died that not-believed
'John did not believe that Mary was dead' (She might or might not have been)

John wa Mary ga sinda *koto* o   sinzinakatta   (216)
John   Mary   dead that   not-believed
'John did not believe that Mary was dead' (She was)

For this reason 'forget' cannot occur with *to*, but only with *koto* (or *no*):

John wa Mary ga tunbo de aru *koto/no* (**to*) o *wasurete-ita* *(217)*
John   Mary   deaf   is   that   had-forgotten
John had forgotten that Mary was deaf'

Similarly, in Kinya Rwanda (Bantu, Rwanda – Givón 1982: 26–32, quoting Givón and Kimenyi 1974) there are three conjunctions *ko*, *ngo* and *kongo*, each expressing different kinds of commitment by the (actual) speaker:

ya-vuze   *ko* a-zaa-za
he+PAST-say that he-FUT-come
'He said that he'd come' (and I have no comment)

ya-vuze   *ngo* a-zaa-za
he+PAST-say that he-FUT-come
'He said that he'd come' (but I have direct evidence which makes me
doubt it)

ya-vuze   *kongo* a-zaa-za
he+PAST-say that   he-FUT-come
'He said that he'd come' (but I have indirect/hearsay evidence which
makes me doubt it)

Factive, non-assertive, complementizers such as 'regret', 'forget' require
ko, the marker of the strongest degree of commitment.

Kinya Rwanda has no verb that corresponds to 'know' and presupposes
the truth of the proposition. The nearest, 'be sure', can take either *ko* or
ngo:

ya-r-a-zi *ko/ngo* amazi yari mare-mare
'He was sure that the water was deep' (and it was/but it wasn't)

Yet another language to make a similar distinction is the Jacaltengo
dialect of Jacaltec (Mayan, Guatemala – Craig 1977: 268). There is a
contrast between *chubil* ('corresponds to a factive "that" ') and *tato*
('introduces an expected, supposed or believed fact'). Both can be used
with a verb of saying to indicate the reliability or unreliability of what is
said:

xal naj *tato* chuluj   naj presidente
said he that will come the president
'He said that the president is going to come'

xal naj alcal   *chubil* chuluj   naj presidente
said the alcalde that   will come the president
'The alcalde said that the president is going to come'

The first indicates an unreliable source of information, the second a reliable
source.

There is one final comment. If the subjunctive often shows that the
speaker is not committed to the truth of the subordinate proposition, it is
not the case, conversely, that the indicative (or any other indication of a
declarative) shows that he is. As argued earlier (1.4.2, 2.6), declaratives in
subordinate clauses do no more than present the proposition, but are
unmarked in terms of modality. In this respect they say no more about the
speaker's commitment than non-finite forms. All indications of modality
are in the lexical main clause verb.

4.3 Deontic modality

There is not much to be said about deontic modality; this is very largely expressed by the lexical items, with an undifferentiated modal marker in the subordinate clause.

4.3.1 *Directives*

The most clearly establishable class is that of Directives – verbs that indicate 'getting other people' to do things.

As with the epistemic verbs it is possible for directive verbs to be used with direct speech – simply indicating the words that were actually spoken. Thus in Kobon (Davies 1981: 2), Yidiny (Dixon 1977: 524) and Syrian Arabic (Cowell 1964: 450):

nipe ip   hag-öp   ne ñel   ud-ag-ø   a
3SG 1SG say-PERF+3SG 2SG 2SG firewood take-NEG-2SG QUOTE
g-öp
do-PERF+3SG
'He said to me "Do not take the firewood" '

damariŋgu buḍiːɲ banaː   budi   ḍiga
Damari+ERG tell+PAST water+LOC put+IMP pour water on+IMP
mamba
sour+ABS
'Damari told him "Put it in the water, pour water on it, it's bitter" '

marra w-marrtēn ʔəlt-əllo   lā   təl̥ab   bəṭ-ṭarīʔ
time and-time I told-to him not play+IMP in the-street
'Time and time I've told him "Don't play in the street" '

Although, however, this appears to be the only way of reporting directives in Yidiny, Ngiyambaa, which is another Australian language and may have no forms for indirect statements (see 4.1.4), has indirect command forms using the purposive suffix (Donaldson 1980: 280):

ŋadhu-na   ŋiyiyi   girma-li   ŋinuː
1+NOM-3ABS say+PAST wake-PURP you+OBL
'I told her to wake you'

The form for 'you' is deictically appropriate to the actual speaker, not the original speaker – the original words were 'Wake him/her' (see 4.4.3). (In fact the original speaker and actual speaker are the same person, but talking to different people, involving different deictics for the addressee – hence 'her'/'you'.)

Syrian Arabic (Cowell 1964: 346), too, has indirect forms with the subjunctive:

l-malek ʔamar ᵊṣ-ṣayyād   ʔənno yžəblo
the-king ordered the-fisherman   that he bring him+SUBJ
ʔarbᶓ samakāt
four fishes
'The king ordered the fisherman to bring him four fish'

Latin uses the subjunctive with or (rarely) without the conjunction *ut*, or for a few verbs (notably IUBEO 'I order') the accusative and infinitive:

Oppidanos hortatur, moenia defendant   (Sall. *J.* 56)
townsmen he urges walls defend+3PL+PRES+SUBJ
'He urges the townsmen to defend the walls'

Rogat et orat   Dolabellam ut de sua provincia
he asks and he begs Dolabella that from his province
decedat   (Cic. *Verr.* 1.29.7)
withdraw+3SG+PRES+SUBJ
'He asks and implores Dolabella to leave his province'

... cum ... eos ... suum adventum expectare
  since   them his arrival   wait for+PRES+INF
iussisset   (Caes. *B.G.* 1.27)
he had ordered
'... since he had ordered them to wait for his arrival'

Amharic also uses the form normally used in subordination, which Cohen (1936: 304) called the 'imperfect':

ənd-imaṭu   azzaza
that-they come+IMPERF he ordered
'He ordered them to come'

However, if the superordinate verb is in the imperative the jussive may be used:

yəzazwaccaw yəmṭu   (357)
order them they come+JUSS
'Order them to come'

This is certainly not direct speech, which would require the imperative 'Come'; it could be interpreted as parataxis (5.5.1), 'Order them – let them come', but the use of the jussive is a regular rule of syntax in Amharic. The interesting point is that the imperfect corresponds to the subjunctive in subordinate clauses in other languages, and the jussive has many of its functions in main clauses, yet with an imperative main verb it is the jussive, not the imperfect, that is used.

In Maasai (Tucker and Mpaayei 1955: 96, 98) the imperative is actually required after verbs such as 'begin', which normally requires one of Maasai's two infinitives, if the main verb is itself imperative. This seems to be a significant grammatical restriction, but formally it is not possible to disprove parataxis again.

4.3.2 *Volitives*

There is very little to be said about other modalities except Volitives, and in particular, wishes.

English normally uses the verb WISH performatively to express wishes rather than the now obsolete *May . . .*, *Would . . . .* But the construction required in the subordinate clause is one that involves the unreal forms, which are essentially the past forms of the verb and exactly the same as those used with unreal conditions (see 3.4.2 and 5.4):

> I wish John would come
> I wish John came every day
> I wish John had come yesterday

These may be compared with the forms used to express the real, expected, event:

> John will come
> John comes every day
> John came yesterday

In each case there is a change to a past tense, *would* for *will*, *came* for *comes* and *had come* for *came*. This use of unreal forms is not restricted to English. Unreal forms are used for wishes in independent sentences in Greek and Latin (see 3.4.2).

The verb WISH, however, is often used almost equivalently with WANT to express intention or a directive (with the infinitive):

> I wish/want to come
> I wish/want you to come

The same is true of the corresponding Greek and Latin verbs, e.g. Latin (subjunctive with, or commonly without, *ut*):

> Ut   mihi   aedis   aliquas conducat   volo (Pl. *Merc.* 560)
> that to me house   some   buy+3SG+PRES+SUBJ I wish
> 'I want him to rent a house for me'

Nolo   me in tempore hoc videat   senex
                                          (Ter. *And.* 819)
I don't wish me in time   this see+3SG+PRES+SUBJ old man
'I don't want the old man to see me now'

As was suggested in 3.4.2, fear is the counterpart of hope and in Modern English FEAR like HOPE simply functions as a verb of reporting with *that* and the deictically appropriate forms (see 4.6), except that both may occur with the infinitive to express the speaker's intention or reluctance:

I hope/fear to do that

In Greek and Latin, however, while the verbs of hope function as verbs of reporting, the verbs of fear require a different construction. The construction used in Greek is identical with that used for fearing in independent clauses, the negative 'modal' particle *mé:* with the subjunctive:

Dédoika gár mé: oud' hósion é:i ...   apagoreúein
                                          (Plat. *Rep.* 368B)
I fear   for MÉ: not righteous   be+3SG+PRES+SUBJ to refuse
'For I am afraid it will not be righteous to refuse'

But as in independent clauses the sense of 'fear' is often little more than that expressed by 'perhaps', as in the example above.

4.3.3   *Evaluatives*

Many of the factive predicators discussed in 4.3.3 are Evaluatives. As non-assertives, it was argued by Klein (1975: 355, 360), they are found with the subjunctive in Spanish, as in:

Lamento que aprenda
I regret   that learn+3SG+PRES+SUBJ
Siento que aprenda
I feel   that learn+3SG+PRES+SUBJ
'I regret that he should learn'

Siento que aprendiera
I feel   that learn+3SG+IMPERF+SUBJ
'I regret that he learnt'

Similarly, Italian has the subjunctive in (Lepschy and Lepschy 1977: 227):

Mi stupisce   che non sia   fatto vivo
Me it surprises that not be+3SG+PRES+SUBJ done alive
'I'm surprised that he did not get in touch'

But the notions of assertive and non-assertive are far from clear (see 4.2.4), and it could well be argued that the subjunctive is used in these examples because evaluatives are essentially modal. There is further evidence for this from the fact that in English the form *should* is commonly used in such evaluative, but factive, complements as one translation above illustrates, or in:

> It is odd that she should have gone

Should is not obligatory here, however, though it is very common. Yet *should* does not follow the non-assertive patterns of Spanish; it is only used with BELIEVE, BE POSSIBLE, etc. with the added sense of obligation:

> I believe that he should act like that   (='ought to')
> It is possible that she should have gone   (='ought to')

This seems a fairly clear example of the use of a modal form as an evaluative. There is a similar, but perhaps rarer, use of *should* in main clauses (3.4.3).

Searle (1979: 15), too, notes that what he calls the 'paradigm expressive verbs' (which are THANK, CONGRATULATE, APOLOGIZE, CONDOLE, DEPLORE and WELCOME) will not take a *that* clause in their performative occurrence, but need a gerundive nominal:

> I apologize for stepping on your toe
> *I apologize that I stepped on your toe

> I congratulate you on winning the race
> *I congratulate you that you won the race

He argues that with 'expressives' the speaker does not try to 'get the world to match the words' (as with his assertives) 'nor the words to match the world' (as with directives and commissives), but that the truth of the expressed proposition is presupposed. This does not, however, really explain why a *that* clause is not used, nor why other languages use the subjunctive, but at least it shows the idiosyncratic syntax of these verbs.

4.4 Subject complementation

There was mention in 4.1.1 of the possibility of distinguishing between subject and object complements, as illustrated respectively by:

> It is likely that they will come
> I think that they will come

In the first it can be argued, *they will come* is the subject (the deep subject) of the main clause, the surface subject position being held by the dummy *it*. There are fairly plausible arguments in favour of this analysis, but it does not greatly affect issues of modality. Semantically, there is, in both types of complement, an epistemic judgment on the proposition, while syntactically the surface structures are more suitable for comparison than the deep structures since they present the same type of subordinate construction after the subordinators. The same remarks hold also for deontic modality (with minor differences), as in:

> I ordered them to come/that they should come
> It is necessary for them to come/that they should come

One important difference, however, is that with subject complements the modality is not ascribed to anyone but is presented as objective, though usually with the implication that the speaker accepts the judgment.

There is a possible syntactic–semantic issue where there is what has been called 'subject-raising', as in:

> John is likely to be here
> John seems to be here

For here, although *John* appears as the main clause subject, an analysis in terms of deep structure would suggest that *John* is the subject of a subordinate clause *John to be here*, and that this whole clause is itself the subject of the main clause, raising being a syntactic device for placing animates (mostly) in initial or subject position. It could be argued (and, indeed, has been argued) that even with main clause modality and modal verbs there is subject-raising, so that in *John may come*, *John* is the deep structure subject of *John to come*, which in turn is the subject of MAY. The interpretation would be:

> John seems to be here
> [John to be here] seems

> John may come
> [John come] may

But this analysis is unnecessary and implausible; *may* is an auxiliary verb, and *may come* a single verbal unit – 'the verb' of the whole clause.

However, it is worth noting that there are related constructions without subject-raising:

> It seems that John is here
> (John seems to be here)

The same is true of the passive of SAY:

> It is said that John is here
> (John is said to be here)

The subject-raising constructions are more like constructions with modal verbs, and can, perhaps, be seen as showing a greater degree of grammaticalization of the modality. The list of predicators that permit subject-raising is interesting: SEEM, APPEAR, BE LIKELY, BE CERTAIN, BE SAID, BE REPORTED, BE ALLEGED (but not BE POSSIBLE, BE PROBABLE, BE HOPED), i.e. those verbs that indicate appearance, reasonable certainty and report.

4.5 Non-finite clauses

It was suggested in 4.1.3 that the presence of non-finite forms is an indication of subordination. Clauses containing such forms are referred to here as non-finite clauses.

4.5.1 *Definition of the term 'non-finite'*

The traditional definition of 'non-finite' is in terms of a form unmarked for person (see 3.3.4), but the term is usefully extended to refer to forms that are unmarked for aspect, tense, mood, as well as the concordial features of number, gender and person (at least some of these features).

Non-finite clauses are almost entirely restricted to subordinate clauses (but see 3.3.4) and, indeed, it seems highly unlikely that there are any languages in which subordinate clauses are finite and main clauses non-finite. It would be very strange if this were so, since the absence of the grammatical marking in non-finite clauses is possible with little loss of relevant information, because the relevant information is mostly indicated in the main clause. For example, in *I want to go* the fact that it is 'I' who will go and that the going is in the future is deducible from the main clause. The use of non-finite clauses as markers of subordination is, then, a typologically relevant fact.

The most common names for the non-finite forms used in complements are 'gerund' and 'infinitive', these being distinct in many languages; but such terms (and certainly the distinction between them) can have no universal definition. Thus in English either the infinitive or the 'gerund' (the *-ing* form) may be used in:

> John intends to arrive tomorrow
> John intends arriving tomorrow

In strictly formal (morphological) terms, these non-finite forms are marked for aspect (progressive and perfect), but not tense:

> John intends
> $\begin{cases} \text{to work} \\ \text{to be working} \\ \text{to have worked} \\ \text{to have been working} \end{cases}$

However, the forms with *have* have all the functions (semantic and syntactic) associated with the past tense as well as the perfect, as shown by:

> John worked yesterday
> John has worked for the last three hours
> I believe John to have worked $\begin{cases} \text{yesterday} \\ \text{for the last three hours} \end{cases}$
> (or more naturally, perhaps, John is believed . . .)

Latin and Greek similarly have a number of infinitive forms of the verb, but these are more matters of aspect than tense. Greek, for instance, has a present, a future, an aorist and a perfect infinitive, but present covers both present and imperfect tense and perfect both perfect and pluperfect (but the system is complex and not wholly 'logical').

Generally, the distinctions made within the system of non-finite forms are those that relate semantically to the verb – tense, aspect, etc. – not the concordial features that relate to other nouns within the clause. Yet in Maasai (Tucker and Mpaayei 1955: 54) the two 'infinitives' are marked for number, though not for person:

> a-rany a-ta-rany   to sing (sg.)
> aa-rany aa-ta-rany   to sing (pl.)

Another clear indication of a non-finite clause, but not directly of a non-finite form of the verb, is the absence of a subject where the 'understood' subject is identical with the subject of the main clause or its object with directive verbs, as in:

> John wants to come
> I told John to come

There are, however, languages for which the notions of subject and object are not strictly appropriate. With these there may be a similar, but not identical, situation. In Tagalog, for instance (Philippines – Schachter 1976), it is 'agents', not 'topics', that are omitted in subordinate clauses, although it is the 'topics' that are usually equivalent to subjects.

In a number of European languages a common construction is the 'accusative plus infinitive', the subject of the subordinate clause being in the accusative case, the normal mark of an object, and the verb in the infinitive. This effectively marks the whole clause as the object of the main verb. Not all languages, of course, have case systems to make this possible.

English marks case only in its pronouns, but still has an accusative and infinitive construction:

> I intend them to come tomorrow

There is, however, a parallel construction with a conjunction and a finite verb:

> I intend that they should arrive tomorrow

There is, then, a choice between two constructions, one with a non-finite clause, the other with a finite one. With other verbs, e.g. HOPE, the infinitive can be used only when the subjects of the two clauses are identical (and the subject of the subordinate clause is omitted):

> I hope to come
> I hope that I shall come
> *I hope them to come
> I hope that they will come

There is, naturally, variation across languages. Thus English and French may be contrasted:

> John wants to come
> Jean veut venir
>
> John wants you to come
> Jean veut que vous veniez
> (*Jean veut vous venir)

Some languages make little or no use of non-finite clauses (see 4.5.2).

The accusative plus infinitive construction is the normal one for reported speech in Latin, and it is used in Greek together with a construction with a conjunction and a finite verb (for the mood and tense see 4.2.5):

> oíesthe   Khalkidéas   tézn Héllada sózsein   (Dem. 9.74)
> you know Chalcideans+ACC the Greece save+FUT+INF
> 'You know that the Chalcidians will save Greece'
>
> ezngélthez   autózi hóti Mégara aphésterke   (Thuc. 1.114)
> it was reported to him that Megara revolt+3SG+PLUP+INDIC
> 'News came to him that Megara had revolted'

There are, however, other possibilities, In Greek and in Latin verse the nominative is used if the subject of the indirect speech is also the subject of the verb reporting. Thus the first quotation above continues:

```
... huméis d'   apodrásesthai    ta   prágmata
you+NOM  but escape+FUT+INF  the  troubles
```
'... and you (nom.) will escape the troubles'

Also in Greek, verbs of perception often take accusative and participle (not infinitive):

```
puthómenoi ... Artaksérkse:n ... neo:stí tethne:kóta  (Thuc. 4.50)
hearing          Artaxerxes+ACC  newly  die+PERF PART+ACC
```
'hearing that Artaxerxes had just died'

Often the verbal form, especially when it occurs alone, is nominalized, i.e. it contains formal markers associated with the noun. Thus in Hixka-ryana derived nominals are the 'dominant form of subordination' (Derbyshire 1979: 23), and with intransitive verbs the subject is marked as a possessive in a noun phrase, as in:

```
koseryehyaha ryehurkanɨr hona                    (24)
I am afraid   my falling   to
```
'I am afraid of falling'

```
tɨtonɨrɨ       yokarymano                        (22)
his own going  he told it
```
'He said that he was going'

The mark of nominalization here is the possessive *-r(ɨ)*. Some languages use such nominalization even more widely for subordinate clauses. Turkish, for example, forms relative clauses in this way (see Comrie 1981: 135):

```
Hasan-ın Sinan-a ver-diğ-i        patates-i  yedim
Hasan-of Sinan-to give-NOMIN-his  potato-ACC I ate
(NOMIN=NOMINalizer)
```
'I ate the potato that Hasan gave to Sinan'

Welsh, too, has nominalized forms for a whole variety of subordinate clauses – see 5.1.1.

It is, however, misleading simply to label the non-finite form as a 'verbal noun', even though it is often the only word in the subordinate clause. To do so may lead to some problems with the so-called 'gerund' of English, the *-ing* form. The case for treating it as a noun seems plausible enough in:

I don't like swimming

But there is no way of explaining the use of a noun in:

I don't like John swimming

For this reason it is sometimes pedantically argued that the correct form is:

I don't like John's swimming

This, however, has a different sense. The problem has been discussed by many grammarians, e.g. Sweet (1903: 121) and Jespersen (1909–49: IV, 44); but there is no real problem, any more than there is with *I don't like John to swim*. In both cases it is the whole clause that is nominal with the non-finite forms *swimming* and *to swim* as the verbal elements; within the clause they do not function as nouns at all.

4.5.2 *Finite and non-finite*

As was briefly noted in the last section, there is considerable alternation and variation in languages between clauses with infinitives and clauses with a conjunction and finite verbs. There are several factors affecting the choice.

In some cases the choice is determined by the choice of lexical verb. Thus Latin has two verbs of ordering, IUBEO and IMPERO; the first requires the accusative and infinitive, the second the dative and a clause with *ut* and the subjunctive:

Eum venire iubet
Him come+PRES+INF he orders

Ei ut veniat imperat
To him that come+3SG+PRES+SUBJ he orders
'He orders him to come'

There is a very similar situation in a quite different language, Jacaltec (Craig 1977), where the alternative constructions are uninflected verbs plus 'irrealis' suffix and omitted subject or finite verbs (unmarked for aspect with ergative subjects). Verbs of movement and desire take the first, 'know how' the second, while 'order' takes either:

xc-ach to sajch-oj (310)
you go play-IRR
'You want to play'

choche naj cañal-oj (311)
likes he dance-IRR
'He likes to dance'

w-wohtaj hin-chemli (312)
I-know I (ERG)-weave
'I know how to weave'

choñ schej ya' wajoj   (317)
us   order he sleep-IRR

choñ schej ya' cu-wayi
us   order he we (ERG)-sleep
'He orders us to sleep'

Often a deciding factor, apart from the type of predicator, is whether the subject of the complement clause is the same as that of the main clause or not. There is a greater likelihood of the infinitive if the subjects are the same (but are omitted or 'deleted') in the subordinate clause. Thus in French and German:

Jean   veut venir
Johann will kommen
John wishes come+INF

'John wants to come'

Je veux que vous veniez
I wish   that you   come+2PL+PRES+SUBJ

Ich will dass du   kommst
I wish   that you come+2SG+PRES+INDIC

'I want you to come'

Although English uses the infinitive as the translational equivalent of these verbs, it uses both constructions with HOPE, depending on the identity or non-identity of the subjects:

I hope to come
I hope (that) you will come

English makes considerable use of the infinitive construction, yet Spanish can use the infinitive where English would not:

Dudo   tener   tiempo
I doubt to have time
'I doubt if I have time'

The situation varies from language to language and affords interesting contrasts between languages (for English/German, for instance, see Bynon 1983). It has also been noted that there is sometimes a switch, historically, from one construction to the other. Latin has more infinitive uses than modern Romance languages, but more striking is the disappearance of the infinitive in most of the Balkan languages – the subject of an entire book

Complement clauses

(Joseph 1983). This affects even Modern Greek, as can be seen by comparing Classical and Modern Greek:

> . . . sungnóːmeːn heoːutóːi keleúoːn ékhein   autón
>   (Hdt. 1.116)
> pity   to him   ordering have+PRES+INF him
> '. . . telling him to have pity on him'

Modern:
> léɣontas na   ton   lipiθí
>   that him pity+3SG+PRES+PERFECTIVE

> léksai théloː soi . . . há   bóulomai   (Eur. *Alc.* 281)
> to tell I want to you what want+1SG+PRES+INDIC
> 'I want to tell you what I want'

Modern:
> θélo   na   su   po   ti   θélo
> I want that to you tell+2SG+PRES+PERFECTIVE what I want

Where Classical Greek has the infinitive, Modern Greek has the conjunction *na* plus a finite verb.

It could be argued that there is no clear distinction between finite and non-finite forms, rather a gradation of finiteness. If the declarative form is considered to be the maximally finite form (see 2.6.1), other forms can be considered to be less finite in relation to the degree to which they do not mark the other categories (tense, aspect, number, gender, person) that may be marked on declarative forms. The infinitive may well be maximally non-finite (unless it marks tense), but the subjunctive, if it does not have full tense marking (see 2.6.1), is less finite than the declarative. Givón (1980) talks of verbs being reduced (i.e. in 'finiteness'), and argues that the degree of reduction is related to the degree to which the event described in the subordinate clause is 'bound' to the agent or experiencer in terms of his influence over it. Thus in English MAKE and HAVE are at the 'top' of the binding scale and take the highly non-verbal ('non-finite') bare infinitives; slightly lower, ORDER takes the *to*-infinitive, INSIST takes *that* with a 'subjunctive' and THINK a fully finite verb, e.g.:

> I made him go
> I ordered him to go
> I insist that he go
> I think that he goes

This analysis, however, does not take into consideration the status of the subjunctive in relation to subordinate clauses. Although it may be 'partially non-finite' in Latin, say, in that it does not make all the tense distinctions, it

162

is nevertheless clearly marked for the relevant category of mood, in contrast with the other non-finite forms whose characteristic is absence of marking. Non-finiteness and mood are thus very different indicators of subordination, and are not to be handled in a single parameter.

4.6 Deixis and indirect speech

Although there has been some discussion of direct and indirect speech, there has been no attempt to provide a definition for the distinction. In this section it will be argued that the formal definition must be in terms of deixis (4.6.1). However, deixis is also related to the issue of speaker's commitment, as discussed in 4.2.5, and this too must be reconsidered.

4.6.1 *Deixis as a criterion*

The most regular, and most important marker of an indirect speech clause is found in the deictic markers it contains. In general there is a switch from the deictics used by the original speaker to those appropriate to the actual speaker, now reporting what was or might have been said.

The pronouns are the most consistently used markers of indirect speech. The languages that have a pronoun system that identifies speaker, hearer and 'third' persons, simply use the pronouns appropriate to the actual speaker in reported speech. Thus we may compare:

> John said 'I saw you'
> John said that he saw me

The persons referred to by John as *I* and *you* are, for the speaker, *he* and *me*. But pronoun systems are not always of this familiar type. In Hopi (Uto-Aztecan, USA) for instance, a distinction is made between 'proximate' and 'obviate' person markers (Voegelin and Voegelin 1975: 385). One function of this distinction is its use in reported speech in a way similar to that of person in languages such as English. There is a contrast between:

> im pɨt yɨkɨqa-y-ʔɨm   'aw paŋqawni
> you it -make-PROX-you to him will tell
> 'You should tell him you made it'

> im pɨt yɨkɨqa-t-ʔɨm   'aw paŋqawni
> you it make-OBV-you to him will tell
> 'You should tell him he made it'
> 'You should tell him "You made it"'

Here in both cases the subject of the subordinate clause is indicated as 'you the hearer', but in the first sentence the proximate marker shows that it is the person addressed by the actual speaker, while in the second the obviate marker shows that it is not. In the English translation either 3rd person 'he' must be used or 'you' with direct speech. But to argue that the occurrence of 'you' illustrates direct speech in both cases in Hopi would be to judge in terms of the English system. What is relevant is that where the original speaker would have used the proximate marker, the actual speaker reports it with the obviate marker. This deictic change is a clear indication of indirect speech.

These examples from Hopi illustrate a point made earlier, that only some of the deictic markers are changed in indirect speech. There is a change from proximate to obviate to accommodate the speaker's deictic reference, but no change in the expression of 2nd person 'you'. Indirect speech lies half way, in this respect, between direct speech, which ignores the actual speaker's deictic system, and main clauses (including coordinated clauses) which wholly use the system of the speaker. In a curious and paradoxical sense, indirect speech seems to show fewer indications of subordination than direct speech.

There is a rather different situation in Navaho (Athabaskan, USA – Akmajian and Anderson 1970) which uses 'fourth' person pronouns to indicate persons mentioned but different from those already referred to by 3rd person pronouns, or to 'someone'. Both uses of 4th person pronouns are illustrated in:

> Jáan be'esdzáa 'ayóí yó'ni, n̄t'éé' Bill hatsi'   'ayói 'ajo'ní
> John wife   loves   but Bill his+4 daughter loves
>   halní
>   told+4
> 'John loves his wife, but Bill told someone he (John) loves his daughter'

Here the first 4th person marker is used to refer to John, because Bill is the 'third person' in the second half of the sentence, while the second 4th person marker refers to 'someone'. But the original speaker (Bill), the subject of the verb of saying would have used a 3rd, not a 4th, person pronoun in the direct speech form.

Several scholars have claimed that the languages they are describing have no indirect speech, yet, on close inspection it can be argued that there is deictic switch and, therefore, indirect speech. Thus for Hixkaryana Derbyshire (1979: 4) says 'Indirect speech does not occur in the language except in a weak restricted form.' The exception relates to the use of the quotative form (see 2.3.3). However, Hixkaryana also uses non-finite 'derived nominals' for reported speech (4.5.1), and these are no stranger than the accusatives and infinitives of Latin and other languages. Derbyshire's statement, then, means no more than that indirect speech using finite clauses does not occur, i.e. that indirect speech is not expressed as it is in English. Even this seems doubtful, for he cites (1979: 22):

> henta ya na　　 ïten ha mutuhwano
> where to UNCERT I-go INT you+IMM PAST+know
> (IMM PAST=IMMediate PAST)
> 'Where am I going? You already know' (='You already know where I am going'?)

As the translation suggests, Derbyshire treats this as a rhetorical question followed by an answer, but a perfectly reasonable alternative solution is that this is indirect speech with the translation 'You already know where I am going'. (Moreover, the use of the 'uncertain' marker may be significant here, as an indication of the modality.) At the very least, this is a transitional or marginal form (see 5.5.1 on parataxis), and whether it should be treated as an indirect speech construction would depend on whether it is regularly used, and, in particular, whether it is used to report actual utterances.

Similarly for Kobon, Davies (1981: 1) says 'Indirect speech does not occur', and this seems to be true of the reporting of all actual utterances. However, he offers:

> nöŋ-a　　　　　　 nömam　 le　 wañib　 rauł
> perceive-3+REM PAST his brother bone string bag inside
> laŋ　 mïd-ei-a
> above be-DUR-3+REM PAST
> (REM PAST=REMote PAST)
> 'He saw that his brother's bones were inside a string bag'

Here the choice of the 3rd person pronoun ('his') marks this as indirect speech. Unfortunately, the superordinate verb is a verb of perception, and it is not clear whether this is an illustration of reported speech. As with Hixkaryana, it would be helpful to have more examples.

4.6.2 Tense and speaker involvement

Until now the discussion has concerned the use of pronouns, but there are other deictic indicators in language, e.g. the forms used to indicate space and time relations, which often directly relate to the speaker's own spatial and temporal location. Time and space reference may then also be adjusted, as in:

> Bill said 'She *will* see them *here tomorrow*'
> Bill said that she *would* see them *there the next day*

The switch in the adverbial forms *here* to *there*, *tomorrow* to *the next day* requires no further comment. But the switch in the tense of the verb form, *will* to *would* requires some discussion.

The change in the tense of verb forms is usually handled in terms of a grammatical 'sequence of tenses' rule, which requires that a verb in the present is changed into a verb in the past, when the verb of reporting is in the past. Yet this is essentially the same type of feature as the change of pronouns and of the place and time references. Consider:

> Bill said 'I am working'
> Bill said that he was working

At the time Bill spoke he was working in the present; but when this is reported (in indirect speech) the relevant time is past, and a past tense verb form is appropriate.

English even uses a 'past-past' form in the same type of circumstances as in:

> Bill said 'I was working yesterday'
> Bill said he had been working the day before

The forms with *had* indicate in English not only 'past perfect', but equally a 'past of a past', and such a form is appropriate here because the time referred to is previous to the time of Bill's speaking, which itself is previous to the present time in which the speaker is reporting it. To handle this in terms of an automatic 'sequence of tenses' rule is not only to miss the point of deictic switch, but actually fails to account for the fact that this 'automatic' rule does not always apply. To begin with, the sentence above could be reported as:

> Bill said he was working the day before

Here the speaker uses a simple past quite correctly because the events are past for him, but he does not indicate the sequence of two events, that of working and that of saying – a speaker is not obliged to provide all relevant information.

The situation is not quite as simple as this. It is not just that the speaker

indicates the time of the events from his own temporal standpoint. This is
shown very clearly by an example from Jespersen (1909–49: IV, 156):

> The ancients thought that the sun moved round the earth; they did not
> know that it is the earth that moves round the sun

The point here, quite clearly, is that the first proposition, with *moved*, is
not accepted by the speaker, while the second with *moves* is accepted as
true by him. It would be incorrect to say that 'the sun moved round the
earth' was true at the time of the ancients; the use of the past tense does not
show the time at which it was true, but rather the time at which it was held
to be true. It associates the proposition, in time, with the epistemic act of
thinking, whereas the present tense associates it with the present – with the
speaker himself.

The speaker is free to choose, very often, whether he uses the tense form
appropriate to the original speaker or the form appropriate to himself. In
the example above, *moved* could have been used in the second sentence.
Jespersen (1909–49:IV, 152) sees this as due to the speaker's 'mental
inertia', but this misses the point that it is not the time of the event or the
state of affairs that determines the tense, but the speaker's decision to relate
the proposition either to the time of the original utterance or to the
(present) time of his own utterance. Tense is still deictic on this interpretation, but it does not relate to the time of the event or state of affairs, seen
from the speaker's standpoint, rather to the time of the validity or relevance
of the proposition. Not all languages make this deictic shift with tense.
Japanese, for instance (Kuno 1973: 261), does not:

> John wa hon o kaite   iru to   itta
> John   book writing is   that said
> 'John said he was writing a book'

> John wa hon o kaite   ita to   itta
> John   book writing was that said
> 'John said he had been writing a book'

But Japanese has another way of indicating speaker commitment (4.2.5).

4.7 **Performatives**

The usefulness of the notion of speech acts in the treatment of
main clause modality as the expression of speakers' attitudes and opinions
was noted in section 1.2.4. This is closely associated with the notion of
performatives as discussed by Austin (1962). Austin, however, begins his

discussion with what he calls 'explicit performatives', in which the speaker names the speech act, as in:

> I bet you five pounds
> I name this ship 'The Queen Elizabeth'

The first actually makes the bet, the second names the ship; both explicitly state what actions are being performed. The same is true of modal predicators:

> I urge you to come at once
> I think that is a good idea

The first actually urges the hearer to come, while the second is a direct expression of the speaker's epistemic judgment. As speech acts, they differ little from forms with main clause modality expressed by the imperative or a modal verb:

> Come at once!
> That may be a good idea

Most importantly, they are not reports about what the subject is doing, as were most of the examples discussed earlier: they actually express the subject's modal attitude or opinion, with a condition that, as here, the subject is also the speaker.

The performative use of these lexical modal predicators serves two purposes. First, the number of lexical items to report modality is far greater than the number of grammatical devices available (see 4.1.2). Using a verb performatively allows all the variations that are available lexically. Thus it is possible to express all the following directives:

> Come at once
> You must come at once
> I beg you to come at once
> I urge you to come at once
> I order you to come at once
> etc.

In particular, it is possible to be much more precise about the meanings expressed by the imperative (see 3.3.1); it is equally possible to make a variety of epistemic judgments. It may also be the case that a language has no grammatical modal form for a common modal function: thus modern colloquial English has no way of expressing a wish other than by the performative use of the verb WISH:

I wish he would come

Although English uses this performative construction to express a wish, Latin expresses wishes by the particle *utinam* with the subjunctive, and even in literary English a wish may be expressed without a verb of wishing:

> Utinam veniat
> that   come+3SG+PRES+SUBJ
> 'May he come!'

Secondly, much greater differentiation of meaning can be derived from the greater complexity of the syntax if a lexical verb is used. For, although with MAY judgments may be made about present, past or future events, they cannot be made about propositions that express necessity or possibility in either an epistemic or deontic sense – because the modals do not occur. This is, however, made possible by the use of a lexical verb:

> He may be there now
> He may come tomorrow
> He may have come yesterday
> *He may may come tomorrow
> *He may must come tomorrow
> I think he may come tomorrow
> I think he must come tomorrow

It might be expected that languages have formal devices to distinguish these performative uses from purely descriptive uses (to report the modality); but there is very little evidence, if any, of this. There is, however, one point to notice: Lyons (1977: 775–6) suggests that *I don't think he'll do it* is not to be treated as descriptive if *don't* is unstressed. It does not report my belief or disbelief, but expresses it. This negative usage has been analysed in terms of 'negative raising' (but see 4.3.3).

The issue of negative raising is considered for Modern Greek by Veloudis (1982), who argues that only what he calls 'the epistemic modal use' of verbs of thinking permit negative raising. Thus we find the equivalence:

> ðe nomízume pos írθe
> Not I think   that he comes
> =nomízume pos ðen írθe
> I think   that not he comes
> 'I don't think he'll come'
> (='I think he won't come')

Veloudis further notes that this negative raising is not possible with the subjunctive or with the imperative. This is equally true of comparable English forms:

> You shouldn't think he'll come
> Don't think he'll come

These are not equivalent to *You should think he won't come*, *Think that he won't come*. Moreover, it is not the case that negative raising always indicates the performative use. This is shown by:

> I didn't think he would come
> John doesn't think he will come

Both the past tense and the 3rd person subject rule out a performative interpretation, but there is still negative raising. Negative raising, then, does not always imply performative use, but the converse is true. With a negative verb the performative use can always be interpreted in terms of negative raising.

The idea that a sentence with a performative verb could function as one with main clause modality is turned on its head by the theory of 'abstract performatives'. The theory, first suggested by McCawley (1968: 155–61), is developed for Latin by Lakoff (1968) and for Greek by Lightfoot (1975). Where mood is used in the main clause to express one type of modality, Lakoff and McCawley postulate an underlying 'abstract performative' verb. Thus Lakoff postulates the abstract verb [vel] when the subjunctive is used for wishes in Latin, as in:

> Ut   illum di ... perduint   (Pl. *Aul.* 785)
> that him   gods   destroy+3PL+PRES+SUBJ
> 'May the gods destroy him!'

The evidence for this is found in the fact that Latin has the verb of wishing, VOLO, which takes the subjunctive:

> Volo   ut   quod iubeo   facias   (Pl. *Bacch.* 988a)
> I want that what I order do+2SG+PRES+SUBJ
> 'I want you to do what I tell you'

She postulates [poss] in view of:

> Iam apsolutos censeas,   quom incedunt infectores
>   (Pl. *Aul.* 520)
> now paid off   think+2SG+PRES+SUBJ when   come in   dyers
> 'You may think they are already paid off when in come the dyers'

Similarly, she postulates [imper] (IMPERO, 'I order'), [hort] (HORTOR, 'I urge'), [lic] ('though' – LICET 'it is allowed'), [oport] (OPORTET, 'must'). In all cases examples are provided of the use of the subjunctive in a main clause and the allegedly corresponding use of a lexical verb with a subordinate clause.

The syntactic theory on which this was based is no longer fashionable and it need not be taken too seriously. It clearly reverses the traditional idea about parataxis (see 5.5.1). Instead of the subordinate modality clauses being seen as originating from independent main clauses, the main clauses with modality are interpreted as being subordinate to an 'abstract' verb. Moreover, there is no way of controlling the number of verbs required. There would be little point in setting up just one verb for the imperative and one for the subjunctive, and this Lakoff does not do. She suggests two to correspond to the imperative, [imper] and [hort]; but why two only? Why not another for permission, another for requesting, another for begging? If this line of thought is followed, not only will there be an almost unlimited set of abstract verbs, but also it will often be impossible to decide, in a given example, which verb among many is the appropriate one.

However, there are occasions when something similar seems to be needed; there is the idea of verbs being 'understood' in traditional grammar. Consider the Latin example:

> Quid nunc faciundum censes?   Egon
> what now to be done think+2SG+PRES+INDIC I
>   quid censeam?   (Pl. *Most.* 556)
>   what think+1SG+PRES+SUBJ
> 'What do you now think should be done? (You ask) What do I think?'

The use of the subjunctive *censeam* shows that this is not to be taken as a simple question 'What do I think?', but as an indirect question or an 'echo' question, which would be clearly indicated in English in the intonation. It would be very difficult to explain this use of the subjunctive in terms of main clause modality (presumably it would have to be handled within the discourse system – see 2.7). But there is no problem if it is postulated that the verb of asking is 'omitted', 'understood', 'deleted', 'abstract' (the choice of terms depends on the theory adopted). There is then an indirect question following the regular pattern of such questions in Latin (see 4.1.3). However, a whole theory should not be built on a rare example such as this.

5
Oblique clauses

This chapter is concerned with subordinate clauses that do not function as complements, either 'subjects' or 'objects', of the main clause, but have an 'adverbial', 'adjunctive' or oblique status. The most important type is that of purpose, though it will also be necessary to look in a little detail at conditional clauses, whose theoretical status and typological characteristics are very difficult to determine. There are, however, other types of clauses that are formally, at least, treated as modal or partially modal by many languages; these include temporal and locative clauses.

5.1 Markers of subordination

Early in the discussion of complement clauses (4.1.3), it was suggested that a complement clause can, in principle, usually be recognized because it is an essential, often obligatory, element of the main clause. This basic test is not available in the case of oblique clauses because, since they are rather like adverbs or adjuncts, they are often inessential or optional elements of the main clause. It is not always possible, therefore, to distinguish them from quite independent clauses, merely coordinated or paratactic with the other clauses, though there are often language-specific markers.

As with complement clauses, there are basically three types of marker of subordination: conjunctions, mood and non-finite forms.

The conjunctions are again of very little typological significance. There is no general way of deciding whether a particular conjunction is being used for subordination rather than coordination. This is easily illustrated from English, where there is no way of distinguishing the following pairs, though each member is traditionally interpreted in terms of subordination and coordination respectively:

> John came although Mary stayed away
> John came, but Mary stayed away

He ran away because he had been seen
He ran away, for he had been seen

Meaning is of no help here either, since the first two make a very similar kind of contrast, while the second pair both give reasons. It might be argued that a clause with *although* and *because* never stands alone, but that is true only of the written form, which merely reflects the traditional view that these are subordinating conjunctions; the argument is, therefore, circular.

Subordination is also marked by mood, e.g. the subjunctive, which is used in Greek and Latin with purpose clauses. However, even with this it is not always possible to distinguish a subordinate purpose clause from an independent clause where the subjunctive has some other function. The problem is familiar and is what is referred to in traditional grammars as 'parataxis', as in the Greek examples:

> epímeinon, Aré:ia teúkhea dúo: (Hom. *Il.* 6.340)
> Wait   of Ares equipment put on+1SG+PRES+SUBJ
> 'Wait, let me put on my war harness'

> epískheton, mátho:men   (Soph. *Phil.* 539)
> Hush   learn+1PL+AOR+SUBJ
> 'Hush, let us hear'

These seem to have the meanings 'Wait for me to put on my war harness' and 'Hush, so that I may hear.' But the subordinate construction (one of 'purpose') that is implied in those glosses would normally require a conjunction in Greek, and it may be, therefore, that the translations given above, which treat the two parts of the sentences as coordinated or merely sequential, are the more appropriate. There seems to be no way of deciding in principle whether that is the correct grammatical analysis or whether these are examples of subordination without the usual conjunction. There are similar issues in other languages – see 5.5.1.

By contrast, there can be no problem when an oblique subordinate clause is marked by the use of a non-finite clause, since non-finite clauses are, by definition, subordinate clauses, and are a well-established typological category (see 4.1.3, 4.5).

English uses the infinitive to express purpose:

> John did it to please me

Other languages use non-finite forms more extensively, even for non-modal types of clause. The nominalized clauses of Hixkaryana have been noted

(4.5.1). Turkish (Comrie 1981: 135) uses nominalization for relative clauses:

> Hasan-in Sinan-a ver-diğ-i   patates-i   yedim
> Hasan-of Sinan-to give-NOM-his potato-ACC I ate
> 'I ate the potato that Hasan gave to Sinan'

Welsh, too, uses non-finite clauses for temporal and other types of clause:

> Cyn   i   mi fynd, agorais   i'r   ffenestr
> Before to me go,   I-opened I the window
> 'Before I went I opened the window'

> Gwisgais i got   fawr rhag i   mi gael annwyd
> I-wore   I coat big   lest   to me get   cold
> 'I wore an overcoat so that I shouldn't get cold'

5.2 'Implicated' clauses

The term 'implicated' is taken from Dixon (1972: 67) and includes both purpose and result clauses. Both are linked to the main clause in a kind of causal or 'implicational' relationship, and in some languages the two types are not formally distinct.

5.2.1 *Purpose*

Most, possibly all, languages have a means of indicating a subordinate clause of purpose. These are semantically modal in that they express an attitude by the subject of the sentence, explaining what intentions he has in carrying out the action indicated.

There are, naturally, many different ways of indicating such clauses. One is the use of a specific inflection of the verb. This is found in many Australian languages, where the 'purposive', which expresses 'must' in independent clauses, is used (see 3.2.4), e.g. Yidiny (Dixon 1977: 345):

> ŋayu   bilaːɲ   duguːda   wunaː-na
> I+NOM go+PAST house+LOC lie-PURP
> 'I went to the hut to lie down'

In Latin and Greek the subjunctive is used (together with the appropriate conjunction), for 'final' clauses:

> Haec acta res   est, ut   ii   nobiles
> this   done thing is   that those nobles

restituerentur   in civitatem
                                                   (Cic. *Rosc.Am.* 51.149)
be restored+3PL+IMPERF+SUBJ in state
'This was done so that those nobles should be restored to the state'

tón gár kákon aeí   déi   kolázein, hín'
the for bad   always it is necessary to punish in order that
    ameíno:n é:i   (Plat. *Leg.* 944d)
    better   be+3SG+PRES+SUBJ
'For we must punish the bad man that he may be better'

There are similar constructions in Syrian Arabic (Cowell 1964: 353) and
Fula (Arnott 1970: 310):

ʔəža   la-yšuf   ʕēlto
he came that-he see his family
'He came to see his family'

'odon-'aata   ŋgam yimɓe paayana-ɓe
3SG+CONT-cry out   so that men   run to help-3SG+SUBJ
'He was crying out so that men would run to help him'

Non-finite clauses are also fairly widespread. English and Greek (with
verbs of motion) use the infinitive:

toús hippéas   pareíkhonto   Peloponne:síois
the   horsemen they provided to Peloponnesians
    sustrateúein   (Thuc. 1.12)
    join expedition+PRES+INF
'They provided the Peloponnesians with the cavalry to join the
expedition'

The essentially oblique nature of the non-finite clause is often quite
clearly marked. Thus Latin, in addition to the *ut* plus subjunctive
construction, has a construction (using the gerundive), that places the
entire clause in the dative:

Q. Fabius comitia   censoribus
Q. Fabius assembly censor+PL+DAT
    creandis   habuit   (Liv. 24.11)
    create+GERUNDIVE+PL+DAT held
'Q. Fabius held an assembly for the creation of censors'

It is of some incidental relevance that the infinitive in Greek (and Sanskrit)
is a dative in its historical formation (see Moore 1934: 86).
    It is not only in European languages that purpose clauses are marked in
this way. In Ngiyambaa, although the purposive inflection belongs to a

verbal paradigm that includes the tenses (see 3.2.4), when it is used in a purpose clause it is further suffixed with a dative ending (Donaldson 1980: 281):

> ŋadhu   yana-nha guṟuŋa-giri-gu
> I+NOM go-PRES   swim-PURP-DAT
> 'I am going to swim'

The purpose clause construction is, as has been seen (4.3.1), used elsewhere in syntax. It is used in Latin for reported commands, while in Ngiyambaa it occurs not only with reported commands but also with 'know how', 'want' and 'intend' (see 5.2.2).

5.2.2 *Purpose clauses and complements*

Purpose clauses are not always formally distinguishable from complement clauses. There are three points to note. First, there is potential ambiguity (in an old-fashioned, literary form of English) in:

> I asked that they should come

This is most naturally to be interpreted as 'I asked for them to come', but could be interpreted as 'I asked in order that they should come'.

Secondly, and more seriously, there may be indeterminacy rather than ambiguity. For instance, it is difficult to be sure of the correct analysis of:

> 'I waited to see the queen'

This could be interpreted either as 'I waited for something (i.e. to see the queen)' or as 'I waited (stayed a long time) in order to see the queen'. The first interpretation would suggest that the clause is the object (complement) of WAIT, while the second would suggest that it is a purpose clause of an oblique or adverbial type. But there is very little semantic difference between these two interpretations and no obvious way in which they could be disambiguated.

Thirdly, the purpose constructions are often used with complementizers as well as in these oblique clauses. Thus in Latin *ut* with the subjunctive is used both to express 'in order that' and after verbs of ordering, requesting, etc.:

> Caesar singulis   legionibus singulos legatos   et   quaestorem
> Caesar to single to legions single   legates   and quaestor
>   praefecit   ut   eos   testis   quisque suae virtutis
>   put in charge that them witnesses each   of his virtue
>   haberet   (Caes. *B.G.* 1.52)
>   have+3SG+IMPERF+SUBJ

'Caesar put the legates and the quaestor each in charge of a legion so that everyone might have them as witnesses of his valour'

Rogat et orat   Dolabellam ut de   sua provincia
he asks and he begs Dolabella   that from his province
    decedat   (Cic. *Verr.* 1.29.72)
    withdraw+3SG+PRES+SUBJ
'He asks and implores Dolabella to leave his province'

So, too, in Russian the infinitive is used both with 'want' and for purpose when the subject of the two clauses is the same, while *chtóby* ('that' plus particle -*by*) with the past tense is also used for both types when the subjects are different (and the past tense with the particle -*by* is often called 'the subjunctive'):

on khochet plavat'
he wants   swim+INF
'He wants to swim'

my prishli   posetit'   bol'novo
we have come visit+INF patient
'We've come to visit the patient'

ja khochu, chto-by vy bol'she eli
I want   that-BY you more   eat+PAST+MSG
'I want you to eat more'

chto-by nikto   ne znal   ob   etom, nado
that-BY no-one not know+PAST+MSG about this   necessary
    molchát'
    be silent
'So that no-one should know about this, we must be silent'

Similarly in Ngiyambaa (Donaldson 1980: 280–1), purpose clauses are used for purpose and for 'knowing how'/'remembering' and for 'wanting' (with the 'caritative' case marker for the latter):

ŋadhu dhiːrba-nha guruŋa-giri
I+NOM know-PRES   swim-PURP
'I know how to swim'

buraːy   wagayma-giri-ŋinda gaṟa
child+ABS play-PURP-CARIT   be-PRES
'The child wants to play'

This is hardly surprising: purpose clauses express what the subject wants or intends, and they are quite close in meaning to complement clauses with the intention, etc. expressed by lexical items, as in:

He did it hoping/intending that they would come
He did it so that they would come

(See also 4.4.1 and the discussion of 'abstract performatives' in 4.7.)

Even in English '*to*-infinitive' is used for both types, and there are even some dialects that use *for to*, e.g. in the song 'Widdicombe Fair':

I want for to go to Widdicombe Fair

5.2.3 '*Relative purpose*'

It '*Relative purpose*'

It is possible in a number of languages to combine a relative clause and a purpose clause; the precise functions vary, however.

In Latin, where the subject of the final clause is identical with a noun phrase other than the subject of the main clause, it is quite normal to express this by a relative clause with the subjunctive:

Scribebat tamen   orationes, quas alii   dicerent
                              (Cic. *Brut.* 56.206)
he wrote however speeches   which others say+3PL+IMPERF+SUBJ
'However, he wrote speeches for others to give'

Here *quas* has the function of *ut ... eas* 'so that ... them'; idiomatic Latin requires this relative construction.

Related to this, though with some differences, is the use of the subjunctive (as contrasted with the indicative) in sentences in Spanish such as (Hopper and Thompson 1980: 277):

Busco   un empleado que hable   inglés
I look for an employee who speak+3SG+PRES+SUBJ English

Busco   a un empleado que habla   inglés
I look for to an employee who speak+3SG+PRES+INDIC English

'I'm looking for an employee who speaks English'

The first means that I am looking for an employee (any employee) who can speak English; the second means that I am looking for an employee (a particular person) who in fact speaks English. This distinction is sometimes handled in terms of 'specific'/'non-specific'. There are similar constructions in Italian and French (examples from Lepschy and Lepschy 1977: 229; Jespersen 1924: 319):

Cerco   una ragazza che sappia/sa   cinese
I look for a girl   who know+3SG+PRES+SUBJ/INDIC Chinese
'I am looking for a girl who knows Chinese'

Je cherche un homme qui puisse   me le dire
I look for a man who can+3SG+PRES+SUBJ me it to say
'I am looking for a man who can tell me'

The meaning of purpose is clear enough here: the subjunctive shows that what is intended is that the girl shall speak Chinese, that the man shall tell me. By contrast, with the indicative there would be merely a factual statement about the girl or the man in question.

This construction can be closely compared with complement clauses of wanting, which equally would require the subjunctive (see 5.2.2). It can be argued that the subjunctive is determined or governed by the main verb, or to make the point in a better way, it is within the semantic scope of the verb. The indicative, by contrast, shows that the relative clause is not within the scope of the verb. It may be recalled that similarly in Latin relative clauses that are within complement clauses of indirect speech are in the indicative only if they are not part of what was said (see 4.2.2). For a different interpretation of this type of construction, however, see 6.4.

A related, but slightly different, construction found in a number of languages is illustrated in Arabic (Cowell 1964; 356) and Fula (Arnott 1970: 307) by:

Mā ʕandi šī ḍīf ʕala hāda
not with-me something I add to this
'I have nothing to add to that'

mi-walaa ko mi-*nyaama*
I-haven't what I-eat
'I haven't anything to eat'

There is clearly a modal sense of 'wanting' or 'being able to' in the complement clause. The noun itself is necessarily indefinite and negation seems also to be essential in such examples. However, there is no negation in the following Tigrinya example (Palmer 1962: 38), where the construction is *zə* (relative) and the 'imperfective' form of the verb with no auxiliary (which is the normal form for subordination):

qʷäl'a ziḥəqqäf, zisənkäl bəḥuq may
child REL+it be nursed, REL+it be cooked dough, water
 zimə'sa', zəḥəqqʷän ṣäba
 REL+it be drawn REL+it be churned milk

'A child to be nursed, dough to be cooked, water to be drawn, milk to be churned'

5.2.4 *Results*

The construction used in Latin to express results (that of 'consecutive' clauses) is almost identical with that used to express purpose. If the clause is positive, *ut* plus the subjunctive is used in both cases; if it is negative, a purpose clause has *ne* instead of *ut* but a consecutive clause retains *ut* with a following *non*. An example of a positive clause, where the two types are identical, is:

> Sicilia, quam iste per   triennium ita vexavit et   perdidit,
> Sicily which he through three years so ravaged and betrayed
> ut   ea restitui   in antiquum statum nullo modo
> that it be restored to old   state   in no in way
> possit   (Cic. *Verr.* 1.4.12)
> can+3SG+PRES+SUBJ

> 'Sicily, which he has so ravaged and betrayed for three years that it can in no way be restored to its former state'

The use of the subjunctive here has puzzled scholars because results are essentially factual and the indicative might therefore be expected. Thus Moore (1934: 108) says 'The subjunctive implies, not that the result is unreal, but that it is *causally connected* and logically subordinate to the main clause.' Alternatively, it can simply be argued that since the true function of the subjunctive is to mark subordination, it is precisely that that is exemplified here.

Hamp (1982: 118) comments 'The generalization of the subjunctive would be a Latin phenomenon'. This may be strictly correct, but is a little misleading, for the similarity between purpose and result clauses is found elsewhere. Even in English *so that* introduces both types, though the purpose clause may also contain *should*:

> He worked hard so that he became rich
> He worked hard so that he should become rich

The first sentence is ambiguous between the two senses.

Even more striking is the situation in the Australian languages. Thus in Yidiny (Dixon 1977: 345–6), the purposive in a subordinate clause usually indicates purpose:

> ḍaḍa   ḍuḍuːmbu gaṛbagaṛbaɳalŋu ɳuḍu
> child+ABS aunt+ERG hide+PAST   not
> wawaːlna
> see+PURP
> 'Auntie hid the child so that it should not be seen'

But it can also be used to express 'a natural result':

> ŋayu burawuŋal dugaːl ḍinbiḍinbiːlna
> I+SUBJ Burawuŋal+ABS grab+PRES struggle+REDUPL+PURP
> 'I grabbed the water sprite woman and as a result she kicked and struggled'

Dixon points out that the semantic distinction between purpose and result may be neutralized in the negative:

> ŋayu guŋgaguŋgaːɽ galiːna garu ŋaɲaɲ
> I+SUBJ north+REDUPL go+PURP by and by I+OBJ
> ŋamuːray ŋudu ɲumaːlna
> smell+ABS not smell+PURP
> 'I must go by the north so that she will not smell me'

Similarly, for Dyirbal Dixon (1972: 68–9) speaks of 'implicated verb complexes' which are again marked with the purposive inflection and indicate either an intended action or a natural consequence (both in relation to a previous event):

> ŋaḍa ḍiŋgaliɲu biligu
> I+SUBJ run+PRES/PAST climb+PURP
> 'I'm running (to a tree) to climb it'

> bayi yaɽa wayɲiḍin yalu
> CLASS+NOM man+NOM come uphill+PRES/PAST towards here
> baŋgun dunduŋgu manḍali
> CLASS+ERG bird+ERG point out+PURP
> 'The man came uphill towards here, resulting in bird's pointing out his presence'

Moreover, there are examples in which it is not possible to decide whether the purpose or result sense is intended, or whether there is simply indeterminacy between the two possible meanings:

> balan ḍugumbil baŋgul yaɽaŋgu balgan
> CLASS+NOM woman+NOM CLASS+ERG man+ERG hit+PRES/PAST
> baḍigu
> fall+PURP
> 'Man hits woman causing her to fall down'

It is possible to have a purposive inflection in an independent clause to express implication:

> balan ḍugumbil baŋgul yaɽaŋgu balgali
> CLASS+NOM woman+NOM CLASS+ERG man+ERG hit+PURP
> 'Something happened to enable or force the man to hit the woman'

Even in independent clauses, then, there are two possible interpretations for purposive clauses, either the obvious one of 'must' or the expression of a result from the situation. Translation into English by *had to* ('The man had to hit the woman') may retain the ambiguity (or indeterminacy?).

Hamp (1982: 118) says, with reference to the *ut* construction in Latin, 'I would say that earlier it was not subordinate but it was non-symmetrically conjoined.' The notion of non-symmetric conjunction is, presumably, similar to Lakoff's (1971: 127) 'asymmetric *and*' which is 'equivalent to *and then*, in either a temporal or causal sense'. In this sense the second clause can be seen as dependent on the first, but not subordinate to it. But such dependence is not wholly unlike subordination in that the second clause is, in a sense, given 'reduced' status and, with the causal sense at least, it is very close to the notion of result. There is a discussion in a later section of the use of the subjunctive and other markers of subordination where there is a symmetric coordination of a similar kind, and even of dependent sentences being formally given reduced status (5.5.2).

There is, then, no great puzzle in the fact that Latin uses the subjunctive in result clauses. Even if Hamp (1982) is correct in arguing that the *ut* of purpose and the *ut* of result have different historical origins, it must be significant that they have now fallen together (except in the negative). It seems that there is a good case for believing that purpose and result are in a variety of languages closely related, and even indistinguishable, concepts.

5.3 Cause, time, etc.

This section is concerned with some other clauses that are marked in some languages, in some circumstances, as modal. Conditional clauses, however, will be left to a later section (5.4).

5.3.1 *Causal clauses*

Causal clauses, introduced by a specifically causal conjunction in Latin and Greek, are followed by the indicative. But a reported reason is indicated by the subjunctive (or the optative also, in Greek). This clearly relates to the use of the subjunctive within reported speech, as in:

> Aristides ... nonne   ob eam causam expulsus est patria
> Aristides   INTERROG for that cause   expelled is from country
>   quod   praeter modum iustus esset   (Cic. *T.D.* 5.36.105)
>   because beyond mean   just   be+3SG+IMPERF+SUBJ
> 'Was not Aristides exiled because (it was said) he was excessively just?'

oístha   epainésanta autón tón Agamémnona ho:s basileús te
you know praised   he   the Agamemnon   as   king   both
eíe: ágathos, kraterós t'   aikhme:té:s
                                                 (Xen. *Symp.* 4.6)
be+3SG+PRES+OPT good   mighty and warrior
'You know he praised Agamemnon because (he said) he was both a
good king and a powerful warrior'

Where the true cause is given, the indicative is used:

Torquatus ... filium suum quod   is contra imperium in hostem
Torquatus   son   his   because he against rule   in enemy
   pugnaverat,   necari iussit   (Sall. *C.* 52)
   fight+3SG+PLUP+INDIC be killed he ordered
'Torquatus ordered his son to be executed, because he had fought
against the enemy contrary to orders'

ke:deto   gár Danaó:n   hóti rha thné:iskontas
he was anxious for of Greeks because dying
   horá:to   (Hom. *Il.* 1.56)
   see+3SG+AOR+INDIC
'He was anxious for the Danaans because he saw them dying'

Only slightly different is the Spanish example offered by Lavandera (1978:
19):

Mientras que a vos no te   falte   nada,   como
as long as to you not you lack+3SG+PRES+SUBJ nothing as
   vos decis ...
   you say
'As long as you don't need anything as you say ...'

Here the comment *como vos decis* clearly indicates that the reason for
inaction (presumably) was given by the addressee.

More predictably, the subjunctive is similarly used in German, as in
other types of report (2.3.2), e.g. (Hammer 1983: 269):

Papa möchte   auch gern   selbst lenken, Mama will   es
Papa would like too rather self   to drive Mama wishes it
   aber   nicht weil   es die Nerven angreife
   however not, because it the nerves strain+3SG+PRES+SUBJ

'Daddy would like to drive, but Mummy doesn't want him to because,
she says, it is a strain on the nerves'

Latin has another use of the subjunctive with causal clauses that is not so
easily explained – to indicate a negated clause (though the indicative is also
used here):

> Pugiles . . . ingemescunt non quod doleant . . .
> boxers   groan   not because be in pain+3PL+PRES+SUBJ
> sed quia   profundenda voce omne corpus
> but because with bursting voice whole body
> intenditur   (Cic. *T.D.* 2.23.56)
> be stretched+3SG+PRES+INDIC

'Prize-fighters groan not because they are in pain, but because their whole body is made more tense by the burst of sound'

The same kind of feature is found in Spanish (Lavandera 1978: 21):

> Yo no lo digo porque a mi me moleste
> I   not it say because to me me bother+3SG+PRES+SUBJ
> 'I don't say it because it bothers me' (i.e. 'not because . . .')

There is something similar in the more stereotyped expression:

> No es que no me guste
> not is that not me pleases+3SG+PRES+SUBJ
> 'It isn't that I don't like it'

Here a possible cause is being rejected.

In all these cases, the explanation is, presumably, that the possible reason or cause is merely presented for consideration, but not for acceptance, and is then rejected; in such circumstances the subjunctive may seem more appropriate than the indicative. But as has already been noted (4.2.4) and will be discussed again (6.3) negation and the subjunctive are associated in other constructions too.

5.3.2 *Temporal clauses*

The use of mood in temporal clauses, in a number of inflected languages, provides an interesting exemplification of the varying functions of the subjunctive (and indicative) in subordinate clauses.

First, as with 'relative purpose' clauses (5.2.3), the use of the subjunctive in Latin may add the sense of purpose:

> Expecta . . . dum Atticum conveniam   (Cic. *Att.* 7.1.4)
> wait   until Atticus meet+1SG+PRES+SUBJ
> 'Wait until I meet Atticus'

This is contrasted with:

> Dum anima est,   spes esse dicitur
>   (Cic. *Att.* 9.10.3)
> while life   be+3SG+PRES+INDIC hope to be is said
> 'It is said that while there is life there is hope'

Secondly, there is a widespread use of the subjunctive to refer to hypothetical future events, with the indicative used for past events. This is closely related to factivity and non-factivity (but see 6.2.3). Examples are to be found in Classical Greek, Spanish and Syrian Arabic (Cowell 1964: 357–9, 528–9). The first of each pair below has the indicative, the second the subjunctive:

    epeí dé eteleúte:se   Dareíos . . ., Tissaphérne:s
    when but die+3SG+AOR+INDIC Darius   Tissaphernes
        diabállei tón Kúron   (Xen. *An.* 1.1.3)
        slanders the Cyrus
    'When Darius died, Tissaphernes slanders Cyrus'

    epeidán dé diaprákso:mai   há   déomai, hé:kso:
                                                (Xen. *An.* 2.3.29)
    when   but finish+1SG+AOR+SUBJ what I want I will come
    'When I have finished what I want to do, I will come'

    Cuando llegó   en Inglaterra, vinó   a   ver-me
    when   arrive+3SG+PAST+INDIC in England   he came to see-me
    'When he arrived in England, he came to see me'

    Cuando se termine   la guerra, volveré
    when   self finish+3SG+PRES+SUBJ the war   I will return
        a Inglaterra
        to England
    'When the war ends, I will return to England'

    b-ʾmžarrad ma zakar   ʔəsma   ḥəḍrət   (528)
    as soon   as he mentioned+INDIC her name she appeared
    'As soon as he mentioned her name, she appeared'

    baɛd ma xalləṣ   šəgli   bişir   ɛandi waʔt   (358)
    after I finish+SUBJ my work it will be with me time
    'After I finish my work I shall have time'

However, there is some variation with indefinite events in the past. Classical Greek uses the optative (the 'past' equivalent of the subjunctive), but Spanish has the indicative:

    epeidé: dé anoikhetheíe: eise:ímen (Plat. *Phaed.* 59D)
    when   but be opened+3SG+AOR+OPT we went in
    'Whenever it was opened, we would go in'

    Cuandoquiera que encontraba   a un niño pobre,
    whenever   that meet+3SG+IMPERF+INDIC to a child poor
        le   daba   dinero
        to him he gave money
    'Whenever he met a poor child, he gave him money'

Oblique clauses

Although these are indefinite events, they are factive, and Spanish chooses the indicative.

Thirdly, mood is sometimes used in Latin simply to distinguish between different kinds of subordinate clause. The conjunction *cum*, for instance, can be used to mean 'when' or (causal) 'since', as indeed can English *as*:

> As I was going to the shop, I saw John
> As I was going to the shop, I couldn't wait

Latin uses the indicative and subjunctive to distinguish these two senses:

> Quae cum ita sint,   Catilina, perge   quo
> which since thus be+3PL+PRES+SUBJ Catiline proceed whither
>   coepisti   (Cic. *Cat.* 1.5)
>   you began
> 'Since this is so, Catiline, pursue the course you have begun'

> Cum haec leges,   consules habebimus
>   (Cic. *Att.* 5.12.2)
> when these read+2SG+FUT+INDIC consuls we shall have
> 'When you read this, we shall have consuls'

Finally, the subjunctive may be used simply to indicate subordination (see 1.2.1, 1.3.6). This became increasingly true of Latin, as shown by the later Latin example:

> Pugnatum ... incerto   Marte, donec proelium nox
> it was fought with uncertain Mars until battle   night
>   dirimeret   (Tac. *H.* 4.35)
>   break off+3SG+IMPERF+SUBJ
> 'The fight went on indecisively until night broke it off'

But even in earlier Latin, it is not always easy to account for an indicative/subjunctive distinction:

> Ante   quam pro L.Murena dicere instituo,   pro
> before that   for L.Murena speak begin+1SG+PRES+INDIC for
>   me ipso pauca dicam   (Cic. *Mur.* 1)
>   me self few   let me say
> 'Before I begin to speak for L.Murena, let me say a little on my own behalf'

> Ante   quam veniat   in Pontum, litteras ad
> before that   come+3SG+PRES+SUBJ in Pontus letter   to
>   Cn. Pompeium mittet   (Cic. *Agr.* 2.20.53)
>   Cn. Pompeius he will send
> 'Before he arrives in Pontus, he will send a letter to Cn. Pompeius'

There are languages, too, where there is a 'subjunctive' which is used in main clauses for a variety of different functions, yet is also used in all types of subordinate clause. One such is Fula (Arnott 1970: 310–11), where it is required with *haa* 'until', *ɗooke* 'before', etc. (for its use in main clauses see 1.5.2):

> ɓe-ŋgaɗay ka remuki *haa* ɓe-*timmina*
> 'They continue farming until they finish'

> *ɗooko* ɓe-*njottoo*, 'o-'yami gorko 'on . . .
> 'Before they arrived, he asked the man . . .'

5.3.3   *Other types*

There are similar features in other types of clause. Spanish, for instance, contrasts indefinite locative clauses in the same way as it contrasts temporal ones (in relation to past and present):

> Dondequiera que era,   me   escribia
> wherever   that be+3SG+IMPERF+INDIC to me he wrote
> 'Wherever he was, he would write to me'

> Dondequiera que yo esté,   te   escribiré
> wherever   that I   be+1SG+PRES+SUBJ to you I will write
> 'Wherever I am, I will write to you'

The same is true of concessive ('although') clauses:

> Aunque estaba   enfermo, siguió   trabajando
> although be+3SG+IMPERF+INDIC ill   he continued working
> 'Although he was ill, he continued working'

> Aunque sea   difícil, lo haré
> although be+3SG+PRES+SUBJ difficult it I will do
> 'Although it is difficult, I will do it'

In Latin, too, there are similar contrasts:

> Quamquam itinere . . .   et   proelio fessi laeti-que
> although   from journey and battle tired happy-and
>   erant,   tamen . . . procedunt   (Sall. *J.* 53)
>   be+3PL+IMPERF+INDIC yet   they proceed
> 'Although they were tired and happy from the journey and battle, yet they keep going'

187

Quamvis sis   molestus, numquam te esse
although be+2SG+PRES+SUBJ troublesome never you to be
confitebor malum   (Cic. *T.D.* 2.25.61)
I will confess evil
'Although you are troublesome, I will never admit you to be evil'

Prima facie it might appear that there is a related construction with indefinite relative clauses:

El que asasinó   a Smith esta loco
he that kill+3SG+PAST+INDIC to Smith is mad

El que asasinara   a Smith esta loco
he that kill+3SG+PAST+SUBJ to Smith is mad

'The man that/Whoever killed Smith is mad'

The precise interpretation of these and the status of the form *asasinara* is a matter of some debate (see Rivero 1975, 1977; Rojas 1977), but it seems that the first refers to a particular person (not necessarily identified), while the second has a 'whoever' sense that links the killing with the insanity, and could therefore be interpreted in terms of scope, rather like the specific/non-specific examples in 5.2.3 – except that here an epistemic judgment is being made, i.e. 'I conclude that whoever killed Smith is, thereby, shown to be insane' as opposed to 'I conclude that a certain person (the one who killed Smith) is insane'.

5.4 Conditionals

Although conditional sentences are important in all languages, and although their 'logic' has been thoroughly, if inconclusively, investigated by philosophers, our knowledge and understanding of them in the languages of the world is very poor. Even in English there is no totally satisfactory account of the reason for the choice between:

If John comes, I shall leave
If John should come, I shall leave
Should John come, I shall leave
If John came, I should leave
If John were to come, I should leave
Were John to come, I should leave

Traditional studies of Latin and Greek show great variation in usage, not all of it well explained, while for most other languages the only information is usually no more than translations with some brief analysis in traditional terms. Undoubtedly, it is difficult for anyone but a native speaker to understand and explain in full the conditional uses of a language, and since this has not been really well done for English, it is hardly surprising that so little is known about other languages.

5.4.1 *The status of conditionals*
Conditional sentences are unlike all others in that both the subordinate clause (the protasis) and the main clause (the apodosis) are non-factual. Neither indicates that an event has occurred (or is occurring or will occur); the sentence merely indicates the dependence of the truth of one proposition upon the truth of another.

There is one distinction that is undoubtedly important typologically, that between real and unreal conditions, the latter being used to refer to events about which the speaker expresses some kind of negative belief. The contrast is clear enough in English between:

> If John comes, I shall leave
> If John came, I should leave

The first leaves open the possibility of John's coming, the second indicates that the speaker thinks it unlikely that he will come.

Modality seems, then, to be doubly marked in conditionals: not only are they non-factual, but in addition there is the distinction between real and unreal, indicating the speaker's degree of commitment. In theory, then, there are two distinct parameters for the marking of modality.

5.4.2 *Real conditions*
In practice, real conditions are unmarked for modality in many languages, in that both protasis and apodosis are presented in the declarative form, the indicative in languages with morphological mood. This is certainly true of Latin, Greek, German and many other languages, including English:

> si hoc facis,   erras
> if this do+2SG+PRES+INDIC, err+2SG+PRES+INDIC

> ei tóuto poiéis,   hamartáneis
> if this do+2SG+PRES+INDIC, err+2SG+PRES+INDIC

> 'If you do this, you are wrong'

> Wenn ich ihm   heute schreibe,
> if   I   to him today write+1SG+PRES+INDIC,
>   bekommt er   den Brief morgen
>   get+3SG+PRES+INDIC the letter tomorrow
> 'If I write to him today, he'll get the letter tomorrow'

Most real conditions refer to future events, and predict that if one takes place, some other one will follow, often with some kind of causal relationship between the two. This is natural enough, since a judgment about the likelihood of some unknown event in the future depending on some other such event is the most useful function of conditionals.

Yet there is no strict rule that this will be so. Any proposition concerning an event at any time may be conditionally dependent upon any other. Thus there is potentially considerable freedom in the choice of tense in protasis and apodosis:

> If John comes tomorrow, Mary will come
> If John comes tomorrow, Mary came yesterday
> If John came yesterday, Mary will come
> If John came yesterday, Mary came too
> etc.

Some scholars, e.g. Dudman (1983), distinguish between 'hypothetical' and 'conditional' sentences, the former relating events (usually in the future) in terms of cause or consequence, the latter merely linking the truth of one proposition with another. Dudman gives as examples:

> If she returns the tickets tomorrow, they will refund the money
> If Grannie is here, she is invisible

Hypotheticals are non-predictive and can be paraphrased 'If it is true that . . ., it is true that . . .' However, this is no more than the distinction between the more common 'future' type and those that do not exclusively relate to the future. It seems very doubtful whether conditionals referring to the future could ever be 'hypothetical' (and clearly distinct from 'conditionals') or whether those referring to the past could ever be 'conditional'. It is difficult, too, to see how one could decide whether a 'mixed' conditional is either a 'condition' or a 'hypothesis', e.g.:

> If John came yesterday, Mary will leave

Moreover, there is no evidence of any formal distinction between the two types.

The distinction is not, then, a useful one linguistically. In all conditionals, the speaker offers two possible, non-factual propositions and makes one dependent for its truth or factuality upon the other. If truth does not seem to be involved in predictions, it is only because of the problem whether statements about the future can ever be seen as strictly true.

As was noted at the beginning of this section, real conditionals in many languages have a declarative form in both protasis and apodosis. Yet the propositions contained in them are not put forward as matters of fact, but simply as propositions to be entertained and indicated as related in terms of cause, conclusion, consequence. This suggests once again (see 2.6.4) that the declarative is not the strongest indicator of the speaker's commitment to the truth of the proposition, but a modally unmarked form that in itself makes no indication of commitment.

5.4.3 *Unreal conditions*

Although traditional grammars discuss unreal (or 'irrealis') conditions, they often distinguish between 'improbable' conditions in the future and 'impossible' or 'counterfactual' ones in the present or past. But this is, once again, no more than the issue concerning the future and truth. Future conditions cannot, by definition, be counterfactual if it is assumed that the future is unknown and that no statements about it can be true.

There is, however, a further point – that it is misleading to see all past time unreal conditions as counterfactual. Clearly they often are, as in:

> If John had come, Mary would have left

This would normally suggest that John did not come, and that Mary did not leave. But it does not necessarily do so: it could be used where the speaker simply does not know whether John came or not; it need not refer to what is known not to be true, but only to what is indicated as unknown. Both types of unreal condition ('improbable' and 'unknown') indicate a negative attitude to the proposition, but the distinction is (largely) dependent upon the tense.

As was noted, real conditions often merely use the declarative form. Unreal conditions, by contrast, use a variety of devices, some of them in conjunction. These include:

(i) past tense
(ii) subjunctive
(iii) modal verbs
(iv) particles

All four can be illustrated from Latin, Greek and English for present unreal conditions. In the following examples Latin uses past (imperfect) tense and subjunctive, Greek past (imperfect) tense and the particle *án*, English past tense and modal verb:

Si hoc faceres, errares
if this do+2SG+IMPERF+SUBJ err+2SG+IMPERF+SUBJ

ei toúto epoíeis, he:mártanes án
if this do+2SG+IMPERF+INDIC err+2SG+IMPERF+INDIC AN

If you did that, you would be wrong

In all cases the past tense occurs in both protasis and apodosis, for both are equally 'unreal'; but both Greek and English have the second feature only (particle or modal verb) in the apodosis.

German is a little more complex. It has the imperfect subjunctive in the protasis but either the imperfect subjunctive or the 'conditional tense' in the apodosis (Hammer 1983: 253):

Wenn ich ihm heute schriebe,
if I to him today write+1SG+IMPERF+SUBJ

$$\left\{\begin{array}{l}\text{bekäme} \qquad\qquad \text{er den Brief morgen} \\ \text{get+3SG+IMPERF+SUBJ he the letter tomorrow} \\[4pt] \text{würde} \qquad\qquad \text{er den Brief morgen} \qquad \text{bekommen} \\ \text{be+3SG+IMPERF+SUBJ he the letter tomorrow to get}\end{array}\right\}$$

'If I write to him today, he will get the letter tomorrow'

However, the 'conditional tense' is, in fact, formed by the imperfect subjunctive of the modal WERDEN (which often marks the future); it thus combines past with mood and a modal.

Spanish also uses 'conditional tenses' and has either the imperfect subjunctive or the conditional in the protasis but the conditional or the conditional subjunctive in the apodosis:

Si yo tuviese/tuviera bastante dinero,
if I have+1SG+IMPERF+SUBJ/CONDIT enough money,
comprara/compraría otro automóvil
buy+1SG+IMPERF+SUBJ/CONDIT other car
'If I had enough money, I would buy another car'

But the conditional here is analysable as the past tense form of the future, and, as such, is exactly like the German conditional if WERDEN is taken to be the future tense marker. However, Spanish, unlike English and German, does not employ a modal verb, but rather its (semantically very similar) future tense, and combines this with past and subjunctive.

These examples concern only present and future unreality. For past unreal conditions there is little new. The general rule is simply to add a past

tense marker in some way. In English this is achieved by the addition of
HAVE:

> If you had done this you would have been wrong

Now both protasis and apodosis are doubly marked for tense (once for
time, once for unreality) by HAVE and a past tense form (*had* and *would*).
HAVE usually indicates perfect, not past; but it also functions as past where
the morphology does not have distinct markers for past (e.g. with the
infinitive):

> to have come yesterday
> to have come today

Compare:

> I came yesterday
> I have come today
> *I have come yesterday

Latin and Greek simply use a more remote past (pluperfect and aorist
respectively), instead of the imperfect (Latin still with the subjunctive):

> si hoc fecisses,   errasses
> if this do+2SG+PLUP+SUBJ err+2SG+PLUP+SUBJ

> ei tóuto epoíeːsas,   héːmartes   án
> if this do+2SG+AOR+INDIC err+2SG+AOR+INDIC AN

> 'If you had done that you would have been wrong'

German uses its 'have' form (HABEN), like English, to add the 'extra' past
tense (yielding what are, predictably, called the 'pluperfect subjunctive'
and the 'conditional perfect'):

> Wenn ich ihm   heute geschrieben hätte,
> if   I   to him today written   have+1SG+IMPERF+SUBJ

> ⎧ hätte   er den Brief morgen   bekommen   ⎫
> ⎪ have+SG+IMPERF+SUBJ he the letter tomorrow got   ⎪
> ⎨   ⎬
> ⎪ würde   er den Brief morgen   bekommen haben   ⎪
> ⎩ be+SG+IMPERF+SUBJ he the letter tomorrow got   to have ⎭

> 'If I had written to him today, he would have got the letter tomorrow'

In a similar way, past unreal conditionals in Spanish simply involve the
addition of HABER (*hubiese* and *habría*).

Similar examples of uses of these various features for unreality could be quoted for other languages. There has already been some mention of the Russian 'subjunctive' (5.2.1), which is in fact the past tense plus a particle. This is used in unreal conditionals (Semeonoff 1958: 167):

> ja chital   by ves' den', esli by u   menja bylo
> I read+PAST+MSG BY all   day   if   BY with me   be+PAST+MSG
> vremja
> time
> 'I should read all day if I had the time'

This is very like the situation in Greek, except that the particle (*by*) occurs in the protasis as well as the apodosis, and that the 'subjunctive' has other functions, especially in complement clauses (4.5.2), whereas Greek has separate moods. There will be further discussion of conditions and modal verbs (5.4.4) and tense and modality (6.2).

Finally, it must be admitted that there are other unreal forms whose precise status is difficult to establish, e.g. English:

> If John were to come, I should leave

This is, perhaps, slightly more unreal than 'If John came . . .'
Latin and Greek have forms which use mood, but not past tense:

> Si hoc facias,   errebis
> if this   do+2SG+PRES+SUBJ err+2SG+FUT+INDIC

> ei toúto poioíeːs,   hamartánois   án
> if this   do+2SG+PRES+OPT err+2SG+PRES+OPT AN

> 'If you were to do that, you would be wrong'

However, Latin uses the present rather than the imperfect subjunctive, so that formally this seems less unreal. Greek uses the present optative (which is in a sense a past subjunctive), but one cannot judge if that is 'more unreal' than the imperfect indicative.

It must, however, be admitted that the neat patterns presented for Latin and Greek are essentially an idealized grammatical presentation of the facts. In the texts there are many examples of 'mixed' conditionals with variations, especially in terms of tense, in the relation between protasis and apodosis (and see 5.4.4).

There are very complex systems in other languages. The varied possibilities quoted for Amharic by Cohen (1936: 371–85) defy explanation for any non-native scholar.

5.4.4   *Modals and unreal conditions*

It was noted in 5.4.3 that English uses a past tense form of a modal in unreal conditions. If the corresponding real condition has no modal, *would* (formally the past tense form of WILL) is used, as a 'dummy', carrying no further meaning of its own:

> If you say that, you are wrong
> If you said that, you would be wrong

But any modal that has a past tense form can be used:

> If you come, you can stay
> If you came, you could stay
>
> If John comes, he may stay
> If John came, he might stay

Ought to and *should* function, in this respect, as either past or present and may occur with both real and unreal conditionals:

> If John comes, he ought to/should stay
> If John came, he ought to/should stay

Because MUST has no past tense form, it cannot occur in an unreal conditional (except when epistemic – see below):

> If John comes, he must stay
> *If John came, he must stay

But it can be argued that this asterisked non-occurring form is simply not required. We cannot lay unconditional obligations in relation to what might happen; if then an obligation is laid, the event related to it must be real, not unreal.

There is one curious use of *should* in English:

> If John should come, Mary will leave

The form of the apodosis (not *would leave*) shows that this is a real, not an unreal, condition. Why then is *should* used? It seems that the proposition is expressed as unlikely, but in an objective sense, not simply expressing the speaker's doubt, and that this accounts for the use of a real condition ('If, though this is unlikely, John comes . . .'). Possibly the use of *should* here is related to the use of *should* discussed in 4.3.3, relating to factive propositions at which the speaker often expresses surprise, etc. (emotional, perhaps rather than intellectual, disbelief).

5.4.5 *Problematic cases involving modals*

There are some rather complex relationships between modals and unreal conditions.

First, it has been argued that there are differences in the use of *could have* in:

> He could have jumped six feet, if he'd trained hard
> He could have jumped six feet, if he'd wanted to

Austin (1956: 163 [1961: 164]) suggests that *I could have* can be either a 'past indicative' or a 'past conditional' and may be equivalent either to Latin *potui* ('I was in a position to') or *potuissem* ('I should have been in a position to'). The 'indicative' sense applies to the second sentence, the subjunctive sense to the first, since wanting to would not have produced the ability, but training would have. In fact, the same arguments can apply to *could*:

> He could jump six feet, if he trained hard
> He could jump six feet, if he wanted to

The essential point is that in the second of each of these pairs of examples the ability indicated by *could have* and *could* is not conditional. However, the distinction between *potui* and *potuissem* is presented by Handford (1947: 132) in terms of what is 'logically preferable' and the facts of Latin language are not as simple as 'logic' would suggest.

It is certainly the case that there are examples of Latin using the indicative in the apodosis and the subjunctive in the protasis not only with POSSE 'be able', but with other 'modal' expressions such as LICITUM ESSE 'be allowed', OCCASIO ESSE 'be a chance', MALLE 'prefer', DEBERE 'ought' (Handford 1947: 131):

> idque   si nunc memorare   hic velim ...   vere
> and that if now to remember this wish+1SG+PRES+SUBJ truly
>   possum   (Ter. *Hec.* 471)
>   can+1SG+PRES+INDIC
> 'If I now chose to recall this, I could do so with truth'

> licitum-est   si velles   (Pl. *Trin.* 566)
> allowed-be+3SG+PRES+INDIC if wish+2SG+IMPERF+SUBJ
> 'You could if you wished'

> quem si interficere voluisset,   quantae   quotiens
> whom if to kill   wish+3SG+PLUP+SUBJ how many how often
>   occasiones fuerunt   (Cic. *Mil.* 38)
>   occasions be+3PL+PERF+INDIC

'If he had wished to kill him, how many chances, how often, there were!'

si ita   sententia esset . . .   tibi   servire
if thus opinion   be+3SG+IMPERF+SUBJ to you to serve
    malui   (Pl. *Miles* 1356)
    prefer+1SG+PERF+INDIC
'If it were your view, I would have preferred to serve you'

eum contumeliis onerasti   quem patris   loco,   si ulla in te
him with insults you loaded whom of father in place if any in you
    pietas   esset,   colere
    affection be+3SG+IMPERF+SUBJ to honour
    debebas   (Cic. *Phil.* 2.38.99)
    ought+2SG+IMPERF+INDIC

'You loaded with insult the man whom, if you had any affection in you, you ought to have honoured as a father'

It should, however, be noted that the 'ideal' grammatical patterns (see 5.4.2, 5.4.3) would be present indicative (instead of imperfect subjunctive) with imperfect subjunctive, and perfect indicative (instead of pluperfect subjunctive) with pluperfect subjunctive, but that these are exemplified only by the second and third examples.

More importantly, there are examples of the indicative being used when the subjunctive is required, according to Austin and the 'logical' arguments presented by Handford. Indeed Handford (1947: 132) comments that (with POSSE at least) 'a Latin author's choice of mood depended largely on personal taste, the whim of the moment, metre or clausula'. He compares (with the perfect indicative and pluperfect subjunctive respectively):

non potuit . . .   fieri   sapiens, nisi
not can+3SG+PERF+INDIC become wise   unless
    natus esset   (Cic. *Fin.* 2.31.103)
    born be+3SG+IMPERF+SUBJ
'He could not have become wise, if he had never been born'

and:

quod certe   si essem   interfectus, accidere
which certainly if be+1SG+IMPERF+SUBJ killed   to happen
    non potuisset   (Cic. *Sest.* 22.49)
    not can+3SG+PLUP+SUBJ
'Which certainly could not have happened if I had been killed'

197

He even notes that the moods may be combined in the same passage:

in qua   quid facere potuissem,   nisi   tum consul
in which what to do can+1SG+PLUP+SUBJ unless then consul
   fuissem?   consul autem   esse qui
   be+1SG+PLUP+SUBJ consul however to be who
   potui,   nisi   eum vitae cursum
   can+1SG+PERF+INDIC unless that of life course
   tenuissem?   (Cic. *Sest.* 22.49)
   hold+1SG+PLUP+SUBJ

'What could I have done in that (crisis) if I had not then been consul? But how could I have been consul, if I had not held to that manner of life?' \

Clearly all that can be said is that with 'modal' expressions the modality associated with the condition is not always expressed by the use of the subjunctive mood, that being, in a sense, redundant. (For further discussion, see Palmer 1977.)

A second complication is that epistemic MUST appears to be used in unreal conditions (although it was suggested earlier that it is not) as in:

> If he had stayed in the army, he must have become a colonel

To explain this, an account should first be given of a similar sentence containing *might*:

> If he had stayed in the army, he might have become a colonel

This appears to raise no problems, since *might* is past tense for the purpose of unreal conditionals. Yet a moment's thought will show that semantically this is not the unreal 'might have'. The correct paraphrase is the second, not the first, of:

> ... it would have been possible that he became ...
> ... it is possible that he would have become ...

Moreover, the epistemic judgment concerns the whole sentence, protasis as well as apodosis, giving the paraphrase:

> It is possible that if he had stayed in the army, he would have become a colonel

By a similar analysis the appropriate paraphrase of the first sentence is:

> It is necessary (necessarily the case) that if he had stayed in the army, he would have become a colonel

Might, it would appear, is used rather than *may* because of the unreality of the proposition about which the modal judgment is made. MUST, however, has no past tense form, but the form *must* is used because it is used elsewhere when a past tense would normally be required, as in:

> You must go
> He said you must go
> cf. You can go
> He said you could go

Alternatively, it might be argued that *might* is the tentative form of MAY and that that alone accounts for its form ('it is tentatively possible'), not that it reflects the unreality of the whole proposition. For it seems possible that *may* could be used here too, exactly parallelling the use of *must*:

> If he had stayed in the army, he may have become a colonel

For discussion see Huddleston 1977: 43; Palmer 1978.

Finally, it may be asked whether an explanation can be given of the relation between conditionals and modality and, in particular, of the use of past tense to indicate unreality. This is discussed in 6.1.1.

5.5   Coordination and subordination

There are some problems concerning the distinction between coordinate and subordinate clauses.

5.5.1   *Parataxis*

There are examples in 5.1 of Greek sentences with one verb in the subjunctive where it is not wholly clear whether there are two co-ordinate clauses or one clause subordinate to the other:

> epímeinon, Aré:ia teúkhea dúo: (Hom. *Il.* 6.340)
> wait   of Ares equipment put on+1SG+PRES+SUBJ
> 'Wait, let me put on my war harness'
> 'Wait for me to put on my war harness'

> epískheton, mátho:men   (Soph. *Phil.* 539)
> hush   learn+1PL+AOR+SUBJ
> 'Hush, let us hear'/'Hush so that we may hear'

In both cases the interpretation in terms of subordination, with a purpose clause, seems the more plausible, but Greek usually marks such clauses with a conjunction, leaving open the possibility that these are two co-ordinate clauses. Of course, in speech the intonation may well have made the distinction. However, the issue here is not simply one of our not knowing which of the two interpretations is correct. The examples suggest rather that even in principle the distinction may not always be clear.

The term 'parataxis' is used to refer to such sentences as these, parataxis being defined in terms of the juxtaposition of two sentences, though with, potentially, a subordinate relationship between them, and typically lacking a conjunction to mark that coordinate relationship.

The examples so far considered were all oblique clauses, but the term 'parataxis' is also often used to refer to what are clearly subordinate clauses lacking a conjunction, as in English:

> John said he was coming
> John knows I am here

In examples such as these the syntactic status of the second clause is not in doubt: it is clearly the object complement of the main clause which without such a complement would be incomplete. The absence of a conjunction raises no problem: it merely has to be noted that some subordinate clauses are not introduced by conjunctions (see Handford 1947: 24).

Paradoxically if mere juxtaposition with no conjunctions were a matter of parataxis, direct speech would be as paratactic as indirect speech, or even more so:

> John said 'I am coming'

Here the second clause is no less subordinate in terms of its relation with the first, yet there is no conjunction. Moreover, it has not undergone the deictic shifts that relate it directly to the speaker.

There is, then, very little point in talking about parataxis in examples such as these, though that is what Cowell (1964: 449–50) does for Arabic in:

> Ɂāl bəddo   yrūḥ   (449)
> he said he wants +INDIC he goes+SUBJ
> cf. Ɂāl Ɂənno bəddo yrūḥ (Ɂənno='that') (449)
> 'He wants to go'

> w-Ɂamar   ᵊž-zənn yərmūni
> and-he ordered the-Jinn he throw me+SUBJ
> b-nəṣṣ ᵊl-baḥᵊr   (450)
> in-middle-the-sea
> 'And he ordered the Jinn to throw me into the middle of the sea'

In both cases the deictic markers show clearly that this is indirect speech, in contrast with the direct speech in:

> marra w-marrtēn ʔəlt-əllo lā təlₑ̣ab
> time and-time I told-him not you play+SUBJ
> bət ṭariʔ   (450)
> in the-street
> 'Time and time again I told him "Don't play in the street" '

There are, however, some examples of clauses that may be interpreted either as coordinated or as subordinated (complements), as in Latin:

> boves aquam bonam ... bibant   semper
> cattle water good   drink+3PL+PRES+SUBJ always
> curato   (Cato *Ag.* 73)
> take care+3SG+PRES+IMPER
> 'Let the cattle drink good water. Let him always take care'
> 'Let him always take care that the cattle drink good water'

However, even here the subordinate interpretation is the more plausible, and this is even more so with other purported examples of parataxis:

> Di   facerent   sine   patre
> gods make+3PL+IMPERF+SUBJ without father
> forem   (Ov. *Met.* 8.72)
> be+2SG+IMPERF+SUBJ
> 'Oh that the gods had brought it to pass that I were fatherless'

> Date   vulnera lymphis   abluam
>   (Virg. *Aen.* 4.683)
> give+2PL+PRES+IMPER wounds with water wash+1SG+PRES+SUBJ
> 'Grant that I may wash my wounds with water'

These could be interpreted as:

> 'Oh that the gods had brought it about! Oh that I were fatherless!'
> 'Grant! Let me wash my wounds with water!'

However, these interpretations would imply that the main clauses are incomplete, with the consequence that there must be a change in the grammatical structure in the middle of them – what is traditionally known as 'anacolouthon'. That may have been the author's intention, for poetic effect. But there may equally be a simple prosaic explanation – that the conjunction has been omitted because conjunctions were omitted more commonly than is supposed. The deictic markers do not help with the decision between the two interpretations, for, either as a clause of an indirect directive or as a wish or request by the speaker, the same (speaker-appropriate) deictics are required.

A more difficult problem arises in the Latin:

> Censeo ad nos Luceriam venias   (Cic. *Att.* 8.11A)
> I think to us Luceria   come+2SG+PRES+SUBJ

This could be interpreted in three ways:

> I think 'You should come to us at Luceria'.
> I think. You should come to us at Luceria.
> I think you should come to us at Luceria.

This multiple interpretation is possible because (a) person-marking in the subordinate clause is appropriate to both verb-subject and to speaker (since they are both 'I'); (b) the subjunctive is used; and (c) there is no conjunction. The first interpretation, in terms of direct speech, seems unlikely, and it is the second that is usually advocated by grammarians (e.g. Moore 1934: 102), thus exemplifying parataxis (with anacoluthon). But the third interpretation, in terms of simple indirect speech, with no parataxis except in the sense of absence of the conjunction, is possible. The only objection to this is that verbs such as CENSEO are normally followed by the accusative and infinitive construction:

> Censeo te   Luceriam venire
> I think you+SG Luceria   come+PRES+INF
> 'I think you are coming to Luceria'

This does not, however, carry the 'should' sense of the subjunctive *venias*, nor is there any obvious and familiar way in which it could be expressed in Latin. It may well be, therefore, that Latin can use a subjunctive even in indirect speech where no alternative is available, and that this is rare, but not 'irregular'.

Parataxis is often adduced as a diachronic explanation of subordination. The evidence consists of a comparison of subordinate clauses with main clauses with identical or similar forms and functions. Thus in Latin *ne* with the subjunctive is used for negative commands, and also for reported negative commands:

> Ne sis   patruus mihi   (Hor. *Ser.* 2.3.88)
> NE be+2SG+PRES+SUBJ uncle   to me
> 'Don't come the uncle with me'

> Mihi ne abscedam   imperat (Ter. *Eun.* 3.5.31.578)
> me NE go away+1SG+PRES+SUBJ he commands
> 'He tells me not to go away'

Similarly, in Greek a 'deliberative question' is expressed by the subjunctive in both main and subordinate clauses:

óːmoi egóː, páːi bóː?   páːi
alas   I   where go+1SG+AOR+SUBJ where
    stóː?   páːi kélsoː?   (Eur. *Hec.* 1056)
    stand+1SG+AOR+SUBJ where put into harbour+1SG+AOR+SUBJ
'Ah me! Where shall I go? Where stand? Where find haven?'

tá d' ekpóːmeta ... ouk oíd'   ei Chrusántaːi
the but cups   not I know if to Chrysantas
    toutoːií dóː   (Xen. *Cyr.* 8.4.16)
    this   give+1SG+PRES+SUBJ
'I don't know whether I am to give the cups to this Chrysantas'

The argument is extended by Moore (1934: 138) to account for the constructions with verbs of fearing, as derived from main clauses expressing fear or negative wishes (with the negative *méː* and the subjunctive). This is particularly striking when both types are used, as with English *I'm afraid that*, to express not real fear, but unwelcome possibilities:

méː déː néːas héloːsi   (Hom. *Il.* 16.128)
MÉː indeed ships take+3PL+AOR+SUBJ
'They may take the ships' ('I'm afraid they'll take the ships')

allá méː ou tóut' éːi   khalepón ... thánaton
but MÉː not this be+3SG+PRES+SUBJ difficult   death
    ekphugeín   (Plat. *Ap.* 39a)
    to avoid
'I suspect it is not the avoidance of death that is the difficulty'

dédoika gár méː oud' hósion éːi ...   apagoreúein
                                         (Plat. *Rep.* 368b)
I fear for MÉː not be+3SG+PRES+SUBJ to refuse
'For I am afraid it may not be righteous to decline'

Of these three only the last contains a verb of fearing (*dédoika*) and therefore a subordinate clause.

However, where appropriate, the subordinate clauses will have formal markers of subordination. In the following sentence the deictic markers are those appropriate to the speaker, not the subject of the main verb. The verb of the subordinate clause is not in the subjunctive but the optative (which, as here, often functions as the past form of the subjunctive) and the person reference is 'he' not 'I':

hupopteúsas mé: té:n   thugatéra légoi   (Xen. *Cyr.* 5.2.9)
suspecting   MÉ: the   daughter say+3SG+PRES+OPT
'Suspecting he might mean his daughter'

What has been shown is that the subordinate clause uses the same introductory particle and the same mood (except for the optative–subjunctive tense relationship) as a comparable main clause. But markers of subordination are still present, and there is thus no parataxis synchronically.

There are similar examples in other languages. Thus Ngiyambaa has (Donaldson 1980: 280–2):

mayiŋ-gu wi: bangiyi   gu:la-giri-gu
person-ERG fire+NOM burn+PAST get warm-PURP-DAT
'The person has built a fire to get warm'

ŋadhu-na ŋiyiyi   girma-li   ŋinu
I-her   say-PAST wake-PURP you+OBL
'I told her to wake you' ('I told her – must wake you')

ŋadhu   dhi:rba-nha gurunga-giri
I+NOM know-PRES   swim-PURP
'I know how to swim'

In the first of these examples it could indeed be argued that there is mere coordination (parataxis), but in the second the pronoun 'you' shows that it is indirect speech. The third makes little semantic sense unless subordination determines the choice of the purposive ending.

The argument that subordinate clauses can be explained historically as derived from parataxis is far from sound. Although this general claim may be plausible if related to distant origins, it is not plausible if related to recent historical development, for that would imply that subordination is a fairly recent phenomenon, which seems most unlikely in view of its very widespread occurrence even in languages spoken by culturally primitive people. Moreover, the similarities can be explained in terms of parallel development. If the use of a particular construction is fairly recent, as often it must be if closely related languages with different constructions are compared, it is hardly surprising if main and subordinate clauses undergo similar changes and adopt similar forms.

5.5.2   *Coordination with modality*

There are languages in which sentences that clearly appear to be coordinated are marked by modal forms. Thus in Fula the subjunctive (which is used in both independent main clauses and in subordinate clauses

– see 1.5.2, 5.2.3, 5.3.2) is also used in 'serial' clauses (Arnott 1970: 313).
Here the first sentence only is presented in the indicative, all the others
being in the subjunctive (in italics):

> tò weetii, 'Ali yahay ladde, *teena* ledɗe, *rimnda* wamnde muuɗum,
> *warta, soora, sooda* nyaamdu
> 'In the morning Ali would go to bush, collect wood, load his donkey
> come back, sell it, and buy food'

Slightly differently, in Maasai (Tucker and Mpaayei 1955: 61) the form
regularly used for serial coordination is also one of the several moods used
for subordination with certain verbs. This Tucker and Mpaayei rather
misleadingly refer to as the 'N-tense' – see 4.1.3:

> ki-etuo aŋ   ni-k-irrag
> we-came home and-we-slept
> 'We came home and slept'

> E-irrit-a   nkishu n-e-rrip
> He-herded-PAST cattle and-he-guarded
> 'He herded the cattle and guarded them'

However, it could well be argued that in Maasai it is not that coordination is
marked by forms used normally for subordination, but the reverse, that the
forms used to express 'and' are also used for subordination with a limited set
of verbs. Something similar might be said of English:

> Try and come
> Wait and see

Here, however, not only is there a restriction on the verbs (TRY, WAIT) but
also on their grammatical forms, since there is no:

> *He tried and came
> *He waited and saw

Not wholly dissimilar from the Fula and Maasai situation is that of some
West African languages that use a fully inflected form only for the first verb
of a serial construction, with the others unmarked for tense/aspect; an
example is Yoruba (Hopper and Thompson 1984: 735, quoting George
1975):

> Mo Ḿ-mú   ìwé bò
> I PROG-take book come
> 'I brought the book'

The same kind of thing seems to happen, though in reverse, in the 'chaining' constructions of Barai (Papua – Hopper and Thompson 1984: 742, quoting Olson 1982):

> agekasa fu ije abe dabe usiae m-uo-e
> agriculture 3SG 3SG take carry arrive give-PL-PAST
> 'The agricultural officer having taken, carried, arrived he gave it to us'
> (Better translated as: 'The agricultural officer took it, carried it, arrived and gave it to us')

Here it is the last verb only that has marking for number and tense; the translation with English 'having' shows a similar, though much less natural, use of non-inflected forms.

The essential point here is that the absence of marking categories such as number and tense is precisely the defining characteristic of non-finite forms (4.5), and non-finite forms typically occur in subordination constructions. More strikingly, perhaps even somewhat paradoxically, such forms are used with coordination, but not with subordination in some Papuan languages (Hopper and Thompson 1984: 742, quoting Haiman 1980 and personal communication). It is coordinated sentences that are given the 'reduced' status usually given to subordinate clauses.

English also uses *and* with the imperative to express conditions:

> Do that and you'll regret it
> (=If you do that, you'll regret it)

But similar constructions are found in other languages without the coordinator 'and', e.g. in Russian (Semeonoff 1958: 193):

> Rebjonka obuchi,
> child   educate+2SG+PERFECTIVE+IMPER
> dash'   miru   cheloveka
> give+2SG+PERFECTIVE+INDIC to world man
> 'Educate a child, and you will give a man to the world'

However, Russian can also use the (2nd person) imperative to refer to persons other than the hearer, as in:

> predi   on ran'she, on zastal   by menja
> come+2SG+IMPER he earlier   he find+MSG+PAST BY me
> 'If he had come earlier, he would have found me in'

This is no longer a clear example of coordination, but could be analysed wholly in terms of subordination with fairly idiosyncratic markers (or in terms of some kind of parataxis).

There are other examples of what can be seen as two particular kinds of main clause juxtaposed with the effect of subordination. Thus in Jacaltec (Mayan, Guatemala – Craig 1977: 72), the 'exhortative', which always requires the 'irrealis' marker, can have the meaning 'even if':

> chiwa-oj   ab s-c'ul   anma tu'   (72)
> get angry-IRR EXH ERG3-stomach people that
> 'Let them get angry'

> c'ul-uj   ab   chu cu cañalwi matzet x̌jicanloj yiñ   (96)
> well-IRR EXH do   we dance   nothing we get   in it
> 'Even if we dance well we get nothing out of it'

Similarly, in Afar (Cushitic, Ethiopia – Bliese 1981: 139) English *either... or* is translated with the subjunctive of the verb 'become' – 'let it be ... let it be'. English, of course, can use *be ... be ...* in a similar fashion for *whether ... or*:

> Be they rich be they poor ...

If intonation were taken into account it might be possible to see subordination in the English:

> I'm not going out. It's too cold.

If spoken with a single intonation tune, this would be interpreted as 'I'm not going out because it's too cold'. But is this parataxis with no conjunction (but the appropriate intonation)? That is a question that can hardly be given an answer in principle.

6

Modality and other categories

There are several ways in which modality is related to other categories.

First, a single formal system may contain some members that are clearly modal in their meaning but also others that seem to belong to different typological–grammatical categories. This is, of course, in addition to the fact that the two main types of modality, deontic and epistemic, as well as dynamic, may be found within the same system, either as quite distinct members or with no distinction between them.

It was also noted that the discourse system is often mixed with a modal system (2.7). Sometimes the discourse system of a language may be quite distinct, but often discourse features and modals seem to occur in the same system. However, it is difficult to draw a very clear distinction between the two concepts, with the result that the members of such a system cannot readily be identified either as 'discourse' or 'modal'. Moreover, some potential members of a modal system, e.g. Declarative and Interrogative, may appear, in some languages, to belong essentially to the discourse system.

Modality seems sometimes to appear in the same formal system as either tense or aspect. For tense, a good example is the inflectional system of Ngiyambaa (see 1.5.4), whose members are 'imperative', 'present', 'past', 'purposive' and 'irrealis'. There is a slightly different situation in Swahili (Ashton 1947: 330; Welmers 1973: 413) where there is a verbal infix that indicates both tense and aspect, but only the modal features of subordinate clauses:

-Ø-	habitual
-na-	progressive
-li-	past
-ta-	future
-me-	completive
-ka-	'and'
-nga-	concessive

| -japo- | suppositional |
| -nge- | hypothetical |

Secondly, and related to this, is the fact that although two systems may be established they are not wholly independent, in that there are restrictions on one in terms of the other. Thus in Latin the present/future contrast is made in the indicative, but not in the subjunctive (see 2.6.1).

Thirdly, and most importantly, a term may belong to (and function quite normally in) one system, but have clear semantic functions that are related to another. Thus in many languages a past tense form has clear modal functions. This is discussed in detail in 6.1.

Finally, the presence of one category in a main clause may determine the presence of a different category in a subordinate clause. Thus, in some languages, negation in a main clause may require the subjunctive in a subordinate clause (6.2).

Two obvious questions are which are the categories most likely to be interrelated with modality and whether there are principles that explain the interrelationship. It is quite clear that, in fact, the closest and most frequent relationship is with tense, but that less frequently negation and person are involved. It might be thought that there would be a purely formal explanation, i.e. that modality is associated with the categories that are usually marked in the same way, by verbal inflection or auxiliary verbs. But this would not explain why there is less of a relationship with aspect and voice. Nor would it explain why person is involved but not gender or number, when all are essentially features of noun phrases and only marked concordially on the verb. The explanation must be semantic – that tense is, in some respects, modal (see 6.1), while negation relates to degrees of speaker belief and confidence and person is involved in speaker–hearer relations.

6.1 Modality and tense

Lyons (1977) has a whole section entitled 'Tense as a modality' (809–23), where he notes that tense logic is treated by logicians as a branch of modal logic. It is not difficult to see how tense could be separated from the proposition and, in line with Rescher's arguments (1.2.3), treated as a qualification to which an original proposition is subjected, such a qualification being said to represent a modality. This, however, is a philosophical rather than a linguistic point, though there are undoubtedly some close connections between modality and both past and future tense in many languages. The future may be thought to be the most 'modal' (see 6.1.3), yet it is the past tense that is in fact mostly interrelated with modality, and particularly with unreality.

6.1.1 *Unreality and past*

In the previous section there were examples from a number of languages of past tense forms being used to indicate unreal conditions. It is easy enough to find further examples: Steele (1975: 200) mentions Garo (Tibeto-Burman), Chipewyan (N. America, Athabaskan) and old Marathi (India, Indo-Iranian), while James (1982: 376) adds Old Irish to the Western European languages exemplified, and also mentions the Bantu languages Tonga and Haya and further North American languages, Cree (Algonquian) and Nitinaht (Wakashan). Steele also argues, perhaps a little speculatively, that the protolanguage of Uto-Aztecan (N. America) had a morpheme reconstructed as *ta*, which combined the notions irrealis and past; the evidence for this is found in morphemes in languages within the family which can be regarded as reflexes of it. These fall into two sets: one contains 'dubitative', 'if', 'polite request', 'counter-to-fact', all reconstructed as 'irrealis'; the other contains 'recent past', 'punctual', 'present', 'neutral time', 'inceptive', 'past' and 'perfective preterite', all to be reconstructed as 'emphasized past'.

Two further examples may be added, both from Ethiopian languages. In Tigrinya (Semitic, Ethiopia) an unreal condition is marked by what Leslau (1941: 84) calls the 'gerundive', but which now functions as a past tense/past time form, the older past tense now being rarer in isolation in main clauses; this 'gerundive' appears on the main verb in the protasis, but on the verb 'to be' plus the other past tense form in the apodosis (Leslau 1941: 148):

> əntäzə-mäṣi'u,   däs mə-bälä-nni   näbiru
> If-you came+GER joy COND-say PAST-me it was+GER
> 'If you came, it would give me joy'

Rather different in form, but equally relevant, is the situation in Bilin (Cushitic, Ethiopia – Palmer 1957). In this language the verbs have a large number of paradigms (inflected for person, gender and number), but these paradigms can be classed in terms of certain features of vowel quality and vowel harmony and of tonal patterns into two types, A and B. With the verb class illustrated below, the vowel immediately after the stem is open and without high tone in B, but front close and with high tone in A:

> (B) jəbäkʷ   he buys
> (A) jəbíxʷ   he bought

(B)	jəbäx^w	which he buys
(A)	jəbéx^w	which he bought
(B)	jəbät	(says) that he buys
(A)	jəbét	(says) that he bought

As these examples show, many of the paradigms are paired, A referring to past time, B to present time. There are two forms for conditionals (used in both protasis and apodosis). These are quite different in form, but, predictably we might now say, the 'unreal' paradigm is of Type A and the 'real' paradigm of Type B (compare the vowels after the stem and the tones):

(B)	jəbän	if he buys
(A)	jəbínädik	if he bought

There is a detailed discussion of the use of the past tense in unreal conditions in James (1982). (She also discusses the past tense in unfulfilled wishes and concludes that it is less widespread in that use.)

An obvious and important question is why is past tense so widely used to express this type of modality? Why is not the future used instead, since the future often seems to be a kind of modality (Lyons 1977: 816) and might even be said to be non-factive (Coates 1983: 61; see also 6.1.3)?

The relation between past and unreality has often been noted, but the explanations seem to be largely circular. Joos (1964: 121–2), for instance, suggests that the essential common feature is remoteness, in time or reality. Similarly, James (1982: 396) speaks of 'remoteness from reality' and Langacker (1978: 855) uses the label 'distal'. But this may be no more than giving a single label to two quite different meanings, and so be uninformative. Steele (1975: 217), too, argues for the 'semantic primitive of disassociative', past time being disassociated from present time and unreality from reality. However, the problem remains.

Steele's article is useful in providing examples from a number of American Indian languages and also in linking the use of unreal past with other uses of the past. She notes, for instance, that past tense is used in English for polite requests, as in:

> Would you pass the salt?
> cf. Will you pass the salt?

Here the past tense is supposed 'to abstract the speaker from the request'. But why? A possible answer is that the use of the past leaves open the possibility that the willingness does not extend into the present, though it may imply that it does. Thus *I want to speak to you* demands attention, whereas *I wanted to speak to you* indicates only past desire and leaves it open for the hearer to make an excuse such as 'I haven't the time right now.'

Steele also notes Hale's (1969: 22) suggestions that intentions in the past are usually unachieved and that unachieved intentions are 'a specific sort of irrealis'. But it is not clear how any of these remarks explain the use of past for irrealis. At best we can only surmise that there are some uses of past tense that are in a sense modal, unreal or tentative, and explainable as such and that the use of past tense has been generalized to cover similar functions, including that of unreal conditions.

James (1982) widens the issue to discuss the relation of past tense and the 'hypothetical', which includes all that is 'hypothetical or uncertain as opposed to real or factual'. Some further examples will be considered in the next section.

There is a rather more sophisticated argument in Dudman (1983). He suggests (see 5.4.2) that there is a distinction between hypothesis and condition, and that with conditionals we imagine a condition and its consequence. This is his 'fantasy' theory of conditionals. But he argues that with unreal conditions in the future we have to put aside present facts, as in:

> If I won the pools tomorrow I would buy a Stradivarius
> cf. If I win the pools tomorrow I will buy a Stradivarius

The gambler can use the second (real) conditional, but not the inveterate non-gambler, who must set aside the fact that he does not gamble. Because of this, Dudman argues, his fantasy, his imagining of conditions and consequences, cannot begin in the present; instead the speaker achieves his purpose by 'switching to fantasy earlier' – hence the use of past tense forms. But this too is no explanation. It is clear enough that the speaker 'must set aside present facts', but why does he do so by switching his fantasy into the past? He wants to show that he is not concerned with a real present situation, but it is the reality, not the present, that is inappropriate, and there is no plausible reason why he should switch to past. Ultimately Dudman's explanation seems as circular as that of Joos.

Almost certainly, no synchronic explanation can be given for the use of past tense for unreality without being circular, but it may be possible to speculate, very tentatively, along the following lines, why the situation has come about historically.

Modality in conditional clauses tends to be *sui generis* – the use of forms is not directly related to the use of other types of clauses (this seems to be largely true in Indo-European at least). The reason is probably the need to make within this 'modal' category the further distinction of unreal and real. As a result, declarative (indicative) forms are used in real conditions (and are available because the declarative does not commit the speaker to the truth of the proposition – see 2.6.4), leaving subjunctives and other forms for use in unreal conditions. But the assignment of forms is liable to be fairly idiosyncratic.

The future is not used because it already has a modal sense (see below, 6.1.3), and there would be a confusion of several senses if it were used. But the past clearly has non-modal functions and is thus available for a modal function without the same danger of confusion. Since there are not enough modal forms to deal properly with conditionals (and languages show some economy in the number of distinct forms they create and employ), the past tenses are the most obvious forms to use.

6.1.2 *Modality and past*

There are a few languages in which the past tense has a modal function other than that of unreality. Thus in Russian what is often called the subjunctive consists in fact of the particle *-by* plus the past tense. This is used in several constructions where the subjunctive would be used in other languages. It is used, for instance, after the verbs 'desire', 'demand', 'insist', in contrast with the accusative/dative and infinitive construction after 'order', while 'suggest' takes either construction:

> Ja zhelaju/trebuju/nastaivaju chto-by ona ushla
> I desire/demand/insist   that-BY she go+FSG+PAST
> 'I desire/demand/insist that she should go'

> On poprosil evo/prikazal emu   uiti
> he asked   him/ordered to him go+INF
> 'He asked/ordered him to go'

> On predlozhil chto-by my ushli
> he suggested that-BY we go+PL+PAST

> On predlozhil nam uiti
> he suggested to us go+INF
> 'He suggested we should go'

It is also used after the negative verbs of thinking, etc., where a Romance language would use the subjunctive (see 4.2.4 and below, 6.2):

> Ja ne dumaju chto-by on byl   glup
> I not think   that-BY he be+MSG+PAST stupid
> 'I don't think he's stupid'

cf. French:

> Guy ne croit   pas que Fifi soit   bête
> Guy not thinks not that Fifi be+3SG+PRES+SUBJ ugly

(These are, of course, examples of the putative negative raising – see 4.2.4.)

Russian also uses the 'subjunctive' in purpose clauses, another type often associated with the subjunctive proper:

> chtó-by niktó   ne znal   ob   étom, nado
> that+BY no one not know+3MSG+PAST about this   necessary
> molchát'
> be silent
> 'So that no one may know, we must keep silent'

A rather more indirect point is the use of past tense in reported speech to indicate that the speaker does not accept the truth of the proposition. Although this was explained in 4.6 in terms of deictic shift (the use of the tense shows that it was valid relative to the past original speaker, but is no longer valid for the present actual speaker), it is related to modality if, as in so many languages, the Quotative is modal. In Tuyuca (Barnes 1984: 265) past tense is used with the 'visual', 'non-visual' and 'apparent' evidentials to indicate the time when the information was obtained, but the 'secondhand' evidential can be used only with past tense. This type of modality is always past.

In Tolkapaya Yavapai (Yuman, California – Hardy and Gordon 1980) the same marker (infix, *th*, which they label 'modal') has a number of functions, which may, for this discussion, be grouped into three types:

(i) It is used for unreal conditions and (unreal) wishes (DS='different subject', SS='same subject'):

> m-vaa-th-m   ny-'u-h   yi-th-a   (189)
> 1-came-MOD-DS 1/2-see-IRR AUX-MOD-INCR
> 'If you had come I would have seen you'

> ma-ch '-yu-th-k wal '-yii-k   '-yu-m   (192)
> 1-SUBJ 1-be-MOD-SS 1-wish-SS 1-be-INCR
> 'I wish I were you'

(ii) It is used after 'try':

> 'wi   '-yoov-a-k   '-wi-th-k   '-yu-m   (191)
> money 1/3-make-IRR-SS 1-do-MOD-SS 1-be-INCR
> 'I'm trying to make money'

(iii) It is used for 'what used to be (but is no longer)':

> ma-ch   m-se-ch   m-yu-th-k   m-yu-m   (192)
> You-SUBJ 2-fat-SUBJ 2-be-MOD-SS 2-be-INCR
> 'You used to be fat'

'-ima-th-k   '-tlahv-k '-yu-m   (192)
1-dance-MOD-SS 1-tired-SS 1-be-INCR
'I was dancing, but now I'm tired'

Here the significant point, perhaps, is that the form expresses some kind of negative ('what is not so') – unreality, unsuccessful attempts, or what was previously but is no longer. The last use suggests a connection with the past in reported speech – propositions that were valid but no longer are. In this sense, a relation can be seen between non-factual mood and non-factual (in present time) tense.

The past tense is also often used in conjunction with modal forms to express some modified form of modality. Thus in Haya (Bantu – Salone 1979: 75; James 1982: 86) it expresses 'may' with the 'unreal' marker:

Kató y-a-ku-chúmbá   bwaigolo
Kato he-RECENT PAST-UNREAL-cook tonight
'Kato may cook tonight'

In Cree it can express purpose, with the future marker (James 1982: 393):

ašay nkanatake:htay
now I will leave+PAST
'I ought to leave now'

Cree uses the same form after 'It's time' (James 1982: 394):

ašay ispaliw   kičikito:hteyahkopan
now it moves for us to go+FUT+PAST
'It's time for us to go'

James (1982: 386) also suggests the conditional in French which is essentially a past-future and expresses what is reported:

Le roi   serait   à Paris
the King be+3SG+CONDIT at Paris
'The King will be in Paris'

The relevance of this is that the French future often has the 'modal' function of English WILL (2.2.2) and Quotative is one type of epistemic modality (2.3.3).

Obviously, there is some similarity between these uses of past tense and its use for unreality, but they do not help to provide any clear explanation of that use.

6.1.3   *Modality and future*
Lyons (1977) says:

> Futurity is never a purely temporal concept; it necessarily
> includes an element of prediction or some related notion.
>
> (p. 677)

> What is conventionally used as a future tense ... is rarely, if
> ever, used solely for making statements or predictions, or
> posing or asking factual questions, about the future. It is also
> used in a wider or narrower range of non-factive utterances,
> involving supposition, inference, wish, intention and desire.
>
> (p. 816)

Similar points were made by Fries (1927), arguing against the view that
English has a 'future tense', and by Ultan (1972) in a typological study of
future tense.

It is certainly the case that the forms traditionally identified as the
markers of the future tense in English, SHALL and WILL (and especially
WILL, which is widely used where normative grammars recommend
SHALL), seldom refer simply to future time. WILL is used commonly
(Palmer 1979b: 108–17) for:

(i)   *Volition*:
      Well, I'll ring you tonight sometime
(ii) *'Power'*:
      Certain drugs will improve the condition
(iii) *Habit*:
      So one kid will say to another ...
(iv) *In conditions*:
      If John comes, Bill will leave
(v)   *Implicit condition*:
      Your nurseryman will probably spare you a few understocks
(vi) *Planned action (often with the planning verb expressed)*:
      My government will make it their duty to protect the freedom of the
      individual under the law
      Is it ever envisaged that the College will hive itself off from the
      University?
(vii) *Epistemic modality*:
      They'll be on holiday

Only rarely does WILL seem to have simple future time reference, notably
when there is specific calendar time reference or in stylized language such
as that of weather forecasts:

My babe-in-arms will be fifty-nine on my eighty-ninth birthday . . .
Most areas will have rain or thundery showers

In English, BE GOING TO is a better candidate for the marker of 'the future tense', but even this is not simply a marker of the future, but rather indicates a progression from the present to the future (see Palmer 1979b: 120–6).

However, WILL is formally a modal verb in English and it is not difficult to see an explanation in terms of a 'modal future', the future expressed by WILL being indicated as a modal judgment by the speaker, in contrast with that expressed by BE GOING TO, which makes an objective statement about current situations relevant to the future. Even languages that have future tenses that are not formally modal, but belong within the inflectional system, often use these tenses for similar purposes; Lyons (1968: 310) notes the French future and the Russian imperfective future tenses as examples:

Ça sera le facteur
that be+3SG+FUT+INDIC the postman
'That'll be the postman' (epistemic)

Ja ne budu rabotat'
I not be+1SG+FUT work+IMPERFECTIVE+INF
'I won't work' (determination)

Moreover, although English uses SHALL with 2nd and 3rd person forms as a commissive (for promises), WILL can be interpreted in the same way, though not as unambiguously as SHALL can; so too can the French future tense:

You shall have it tomorrow
You'll have it tomorrow
Vous l'aurez demain

Similarly for Abkhaz (Caucasian) Hewitt (1979: 176–7) says that actions which are definitely to occur are expressed by the present tense and that the two tenses traditionally treated as future are used rather for:

(i) 'let us', 'I will', a mild imperative or a conditional future
(ii) 'probably', 'possibly' or impulse ('I think I'll . . .')

The examples so far are mostly for future tense forms that have modal meanings (though there is clearly some doubt about the status of English WILL). But there are also examples of modal elements being used to refer to future time. Thus in Homeric Greek the subjunctive is often used as a future:

> ou gár po: toíous ídon   anéras, oudé
> not for ever such   see+1SG+AOR+INDIC men   nor
> ído:mai   (Hom. *Il.* 1.262)
> see+1SG+AOR+SUBJ
> 'I have never seen such men, nor shall I see'

This is also true of colloquial Modern Turkish, at least of 1st person forms (Lewis 1967: 133):

> yarın geleyim
> 'I'll come tomorrow' ('Let me come tomorrow')

Moreover, as was shown in 5.3.2 and 5.3.3, the subjunctive is used in a number of languages (e.g. Greek, Spanish and Arabic) in temporal and locative clauses referring to the future, although the indicative is used in those that refer to the past.

There are also plenty of examples of future tenses that are historically derived from subjunctives; this is true of some Latin forms (see Handford 1947: 15). Other languages have 'future tenses' that have their origins in a modal-type auxiliary. Thus in Modern Greek *tha* is a reflex of THELO: 'I wish', while the futures of modern Romance languages were derived from the infinitive plus HABEO 'I have'.

Rather different, but still very relevant, is the situation in Serrano (Hill 1967 – see this volume, section 2.1.2) with the particle *ta* which appears to be a general marker of modality and is labelled 'dubitative'. It occurs with other modal particles but may be found alone only with interrogative and future. The status of the interrogative as modal has been discussed in detail (2.5); here there is some evidence of the language assigning modal status to the future.

6.2 Modality and negation

The most striking relation between modality and negation was discussed in 4.2.4 – the use of the subjunctive in Romance languages after verbs of thinking where there is putative 'negative raising'. Examples were:

> French:
> Guy ne croit   pas que Fifi soit   bête
> Guy not thinks not that Fifi be+3SG+PRES+SUBJ ugly
> 'Guy doesn't think Fifi is ugly'

Italian:
Non credo   che sia   Corelli
not I think that be+3SG+PRES+SUBJ Corelli
'I don't think it's Corelli'

Spanish:
No creo   que aprenda
not I think that learn+3SG+PRES+SUBJ
'I don't think he's learning'

It was also noted in 6.1.2 that Russian uses its subjunctive under similar circumstances, but that this is essentially the past tense with particle *-by*. A comparison of this with Romance languages links all three categories: negation, past tense and modality.

The subjunctive is also sometimes used in Latin and Spanish with negated causes (see 5.3.1). In both cases the speaker appears to distance himself from the proposition; the subjunctive indicates that he does not guarantee its truth (though in neither case does he actually state that it is untrue).

Spanish also uses the subjunctive where the antecedent of a relative clause has negative quantifiers (Rivero 1970: 646):

Ningún hombre que se   considere (*considera)   honrado
no   man   that self think+3SG+PRES+SUBJ (*INDIC) honest
lo haría
it would do
'No man who considers himself honest would do it'

This is true even where the quantifier is *pocos* 'few', which is semantically negative (='not many' rather than 'a few'):

Pocos hombres que se   consideren (*consideran)   honrados
few   men   that self think+3PL+PRES+SUBJ (*INDIC) honest
lo harian
it would do
'Few men who consider themselves honest would do it'

With *muchos* 'many', by contrast, either the indicative or the subjunctive may be used:

Muchos hombres que se   consideran/consideren ...
many   men   that self think+3PL+PRES+INDIC/SUBJ

Rivero comments 'the speaker does not commit himself to the existence of the men'. The proposition is presumably thus non-factual, but the issue of existence is the subject of 6.4.

A second important relationship between negation and modality concerns the effect of negation with possibility and necessity, as was illustrated in 2.2.1 and 2.3.1. Perhaps the most noticeable feature of this is that it provides some of the differences in English between epistemic and deontic modality (see 1.3.4).

The main problem of interpreting, in a regular way, negation with modals is that there is often no formal way of indicating whether it is the main verb or the modal that is negated. Thus in English *can't* and *may not*, if used epistemically, negate the modal (no permission), while *mustn't* negates the main verb (obligation not to). In German, similarly, there is 'negative lowering' with modals (Hammer 1983: 228):

> Aber ich darf   mich nicht loben
> but I DÜRFEN+1SG+PRES+INDIC me not praise
> 'But I mustn't praise myself'

> Das musst   du nicht tun
> that MÜSSEN+2SG+PRES+INDIC you not do
> 'You mustn't/needn't do that'

The first does not mean 'I may ... not-praise' but denies the modality, while the second can be taken either as denying or asserting the necessity.

By contrast in (at least) one variety of Chinese (data from Lin Wang, Hefei, Anhui, China) the placement of the negative entirely determines the interpretation. There are, however, no negative 'necessity' forms, only negative 'possibility' forms for both epistemic and deontic modality. Consider for example:

> ta míŋ tjen bì ʃy lé
> he tomorrow must come
> 'He must come tomorrow'

There are four possible candidates for the 'modal' slot here:

xùi	'must'	epistemic
bì ỳ	'must'	deontic
koě lén	'may'	epistemic
koě ĭ	'may'	deontic

But the only negatives (formed with the negative *bú*) are:

koě lén bú	'may not'	epistemic
bu koě lén	'can't'	epistemic
koě i bu	'needn't'	deontic
lén koě ĭ	'mustn't'/'may not'	deontic

It will be apparent that the order of the words indicates 'possible not' and 'not possible' in both epistemic and deontic senses (and also that these are equivalent to 'not necessary' and 'necessary not'). In this form of Chinese, it would seem, possibility rather than necessity is to be taken as primitive in both epistemic and deontic modality (Lyons 1977: 802, quoted in 2.2.1).

6.3 Modality and person

The most striking interrelationship between modality and person is found in Nambiquara (Brazil – Lowe 1972), which is discussed in 2.4; but the position is rather different from that discussed in other sections of this chapter, in that it concerns incompatibilities between mood and person rather than shading between modality and other categories.

It will be recalled that there are two parameters within the modal system in Nambiquara:

> event orientation – observation/deduction/narrative
> speaker verification – individual/collective

'Individual verification' is by the speaker alone, 'collective verification' is by the speaker or addressee. Thus 'individual verification' may be glossed 'I report to you what I saw the actor doing'.

Person also has a rather complex system. In the singular there are the familiar three: 1st person (speaker), 2nd person (addressee) and 3rd person (neither speaker nor addressee). The plural forms are various combinations of these with the further possibility of plurality of addressees or others:

1st person plural exclusive:	speaker plus group he represents, but excluding addressee(s)
1st person plural inclusive:	speaker plus addressee(s)
2nd person plural:	plural addressees
3rd person plural:	plural number neither speakers nor addressees
3rd person plural inclusive:	speaker plus plural number neither speakers nor addressees

It will be noted (i) that there is no combination of 2nd person (addressee) and 3rd person (others); (ii) that there is a distinction between two types of 1st person plus 3rd person, depending on whether the group is one represented by the 1st person or not (though the label '3rd person plural inclusive' for the latter is a very peculiar one).

It is not surprising that there are considerable restrictions on person, notably that:

(i) There are no 2nd person forms, explicitly or implicitly (i.e. in the 1st person plural inclusive), for 'individual observation'. There is no way of expressing 'I report to you what I saw you (or I and you) doing'.

(ii) There are no 1st person forms for 'individual deduction'. There is no way of expressing 'I tell my deduction that I did something', e.g. 'I must have worked'.

(iii) There are no 1st or 3rd person forms for 'individual narration'.

For 'collective verification' (by speaker and addressee) the same restrictions hold for 'deduction' and 'narration' but not for 'observation' (where the only restriction is the general one on 2nd person plus 3rd person). These restrictions are easy enough to explain. It is not normal to tell others what they are doing or to deduce the occurrence of one's own action, while narrative is usually about other people. (It is not, however, obvious why there is not a similar restriction on 'collective observation'. It is apparently possible to say 'Both you and I saw that you worked', but not 'I saw that you worked'.)

The situation in Nambiquara is exceptional in that the role of speaker and addressee is specifically indicated in the modal system. Yet there are some restrictions on person in languages where this is not so. In Tuyuca (Brazil and Colombia – Barnes 1984; see also this volume, section 2.3.1), the 'apparent' evidential, which draws a conclusion from evidence, has no forms that can be used to refer to the speaker ('1st' person). In this language there are three forms for 3rd person, masculine, feminine and plural, but only one 'other' form corresponding to 1st and 2nd forms both singular and plural. The 'apparent' evidential has no 'other' forms and although the 3rd person forms may be used to refer to the hearer ('2nd' person) they may not be so used for the speaker.

There is something similar in English. The verb SHALL always has the meaning of commitment ('I promise/guarantee, etc.') with all persons except 1st, where it may be used (in British English at least) as a simple indication of future:

> I shall be ill tomorrow   (future)
> You shall have it tomorrow (promise)
> He shall go   (guarantee, threat)

Less positively, MAY seldom, if ever, gives permission to the speaker. There would normally be a difference in the interpretation (in terms of epistemic/deontic) for:

> I may come tomorrow
> You may come tomorrow

There is no strict rule here, but the degree of restriction is probably not very different from that in Nambiquara.

6.4 Modality and 'existence'

There has been some discussion of two contexts in which the subjunctive is used, with some effect upon the interpretation of a noun phrase. Both can be illustrated from Spanish.

First there is a distinction between (5.2.3):

Busco   un empleado que hable   inglés
I look for an employee who speak+3SG+PRES+SUBJ English

Busco   a un empleado que habla   inglés
I look for to an employee who speak+3SG+PRES+INDIC English

'I'm looking for an employee who speaks English'

The first example refers to any employee who speaks English, the second to a particular employee who (in fact) speaks English. This can be interpreted in terms of the non-specific and specific interpretation of the indefinite article, rather than the more complex interpretation in terms of relative purpose or the scope of *busco* (see 5.2.3).

The best argument for this interpretation is that the specific/non-specific distinction is relevant even where there is no subordinate clause, as in:

I'm looking for a unicorn
John wants to marry a girl with green eyes

These are both ambiguous in that they may either refer to a particular unicorn or girl, or to any unicorn or any girl with green eyes.

There is at least one language in which a non-specific reading of a complement noun is marked by a modal particle that is also used for 'irrealis', with many functions similar to that of the subjunctive. This is Jacaltec (Guatemala – Craig 1977: 70–3, 93, 96; see 1.5.3 for further examples):

x-'oc   heb ix   say-a'   hun-uj munlabal   (93)
ASP-start PL woman look for-FUT a-IRR pot
'The women started looking for a pot'

compare:

chiwa-oj   ab s-c'ul   anma tu'   (72)
get angry-IRR EXH ERG3-stomach people that
'Let them get angry!'

More dubious is the distinction suggested in 5.3.3 between:

El que asasinó   a Smith, esta loco
he who kill+3SG+PAST+INDIC to Smith is   mad

El que asasinara   a Smith, esta loco
he who kill+3SG+PAST+SUBJ to Smith is   mad

'The man that/Whoever killed Smith is mad'

This could be interpreted in terms of the referential and attributive distinction made by Donnellan (1966: 285 [1971: 102]), which is closely related to, but not identical with, that of specific and non-specific (see Palmer 1981: 192–3). However, the facts are not wholly clear.

Secondly, the distinction made in terms of negative and positive quantifiers in section 6.2 clearly relates to the noun phrase – negative quantifiers requiring the subjunctive.

These two features can be explained in a similar way – that where the subjunctive is used the speaker does not guarantee the existence of any persons (or objects) of which the relevant proposition is true. In this sense they exist not in the 'real world' which is normally described with the indicative, but in some imaginary, desired or potential 'world' which is a matter of the speaker's invention, and therefore described with the subjunctive.

6.5 Final observations

A question that must be asked is whether this study has shown that a typological grammatical category of modality has been demonstrated.

If a category as clearly demonstrable as tense, aspect, gender, person or number is expected, the answer must be 'No'. Yet even these categories vary considerably in their demonstrability and their applicability to different languages. Instead it would seem that a somewhat fragmented picture emerges, with the main distinctions being those between Epistemic and Deontic and, within epistemic, between Judgments and Evidentials.

Nevertheless it is significant that epistemic and deontic modality are found in so many languages that this study would still be well worth while if it had concluded that these were two quite different categories. In fact, as is clear from 3.5, the links between the two are very strong and justify their treatment as a single category.

Similarly, although judgments and evidentials may seem to be very different and the latter possibly not to be strictly modal at all, if the speaker's attitudes and opinions are part of the definition, it is clear that in most, if not all, epistemic systems (even in English) both are involved to some degree. Languages differ in the extent of their use of the two sub-systems, and often, as with English MUST, both are involved in the meaning of a single form.

There is less to be said about deontic modality. Directives are clearly the most important type; indeed they may be, in strict terms, the only type of deontic. But the most peripheral categories of Volitives, Commissives and Evaluatives are treated, in many languages, within the same formal system.

REFERENCES AND CITATION INDEX

Akmajian, A. and Anderson, S. 1970. On the use of the fourth person in Navajo, or Navajo made harder. *International Journal of American Linguistics* 36: 1–8. *164*

Akmajian, A., Steele, S. M. and Wasow, T. 1979. The category of AUX in universal grammar. *Linguistic Inquiry* 10: 1–64. *16, 44, 81*

Anderson, J. 1971. *The grammar of case: towards a localist theory.* Cambridge: Cambridge University Press. *124*

Arnott, D. W. 1970. *The nominal and verbal system of Fula.* Oxford: Clarendon Press. *42, 107, 109, 118, 132, 175, 179, 187, 205*

Asher, R. E. 1982. *Tamil.* Lingua Descriptive Series, 7. Amsterdam: North Holland. *61, 100, 121*

Ashton, E. O. 1947. *Swahili grammar (including intonation).* 2nd edn. London: Longman. *208*

Austin, J. L. 1956. Ifs and cans. *Proceedings of the British Academy* 42: 109–32. Reprinted in Austin (1961: 153–80). *196*

 1961. *Philosophical papers.* Oxford: Clarendon Press. *196*

 1962. *How to do things with words.* London: Oxford University Press. *13, 14, 27, 167*

Bach, E. and Harms, R. T. (eds.). 1968. *Universals in linguistic theory.* New York: Holt, Rinehart.

Barnes, J. 1984. Evidentials in the Tuyuca verb. *International Journal of American Linguistics* 50: 255–71. *27, 67, 74, 214, 222*

Bliese, L. F. 1981. *A generative grammar of Afar.* Summer Institute of Linguistics and University of Texas at Arlington. *96, 107, 109, 207*

Bloomfield, L. 1933. *Language.* New York: Holt; (1935) London: Allen and Unwin. *85, 145*

Bolinger, D. 1978. Yes–No questions are not alternative questions. In Hiz (1978: 87–105). *81*

Bouma, L. 1975. On contrasting the semantics of the modal auxiliaries of German and English. *Lingua* 37: 313–39. *59, 99*

Brown, G. and Yule, G. 1983. *Discourse analysis.* Cambridge: Cambridge

University Press. *94*

Bynon, T. 1983. Syntactic reconstruction: a case study. *Proceedings of the XIIIth International Congress of Linguistics, Tokyo*, 244–58. *161*

Cardona, G. 1965: *A Gujerati reference grammar.* Philadelphia: University of Pennsylvania Press. *8*

Coates, J. 1980. Review of Palmer 1979. *Lingua* 51: 337–46. *6*

1983. *The semantics of the modal auxiliaries.* London and Canberra: Croom Helm. *6, 37, 59, 63, 64, 100, 141, 211*

Cohen, M. 1936. *Traité de langue amharique.* Paris: Institut d'ethnologie. *110, 111, 113, 135, 138, 151, 194*

Cole, P. 1982. *Imbabura Quechua.* Lingua Descriptive Series, 5. Amsterdam: North Holland. *60, 69*

Cole, P. and Morgan, J. L. (eds.). 1975. *Syntax and semantics 3. Speech acts.* New York and London: Academic Press, 41–58.

Comrie, B. 1976. *Aspect.* Cambridge: Cambridge University Press. *1*

1981. *Language universals and linguistic typology: syntax and morphology.* Oxford: Blackwell. *3, 159, 174*

1983. On the validity of typological studies: a reply to Smith. *Australian Journal of Linguistics* 3: 93–6. *3*

Cowan, M. M. and Merrifield, W. R. 1968. The verb in Huixtec Tzotzil. *Language* 44: 284–305. *129*

Cowell, M. W. 1964. *A reference grammar of Syrian Arabic.* Washington, DC: Georgetown University Press. *112, 113, 132, 136, 139, 150, 151, 175, 179, 185, 200*

Craig, C. G. 1977: *The structure of Jacaltec.* Austin and London: University of Texas Press. *44, 149, 160, 207, 223*

Curme, G. O. 1905. *A grammar of the German language.* London: Macmillan; (1960 rev. edn) New York: Frederick Ungar. *45*

Davidsen-Nielsen, N. 1986. Modal verbs in English and Danish. In Kastovsky and Szwedek (1986). *72*

Davies, J. 1981. *Kobon.* Lingua Descriptive Series, 3. Amsterdam: North Holland. *104, 123, 135, 138, 150, 165*

Derbyshire, D. C. 1979. *Hixkaryana.* Lingua Descriptive Series, 1. Amsterdam: North Holland. *54, 65, 71, 74, 85, 119, 135, 146, 159, 164, 165*

Dixon, R. M. W. 1972. *The Dyirbal language of North Queensland.* Cambridge: Cambridge University Press. *105, 135, 174, 180*

1976. *Grammatical categories in Australian languages.* Australian Institute of Aboriginal Studies. Lingusitic Series no. 22. New Jersey: Humanities Press Inc.

1977. *A grammar of Yidiɲ.* Cambridge: Cambridge University Press. *105, 135, 138, 150, 174, 180, 181*

Donaldson, T. 1980. *Ngiyambaa: the language of the Wangaaybuwan.*

Cambridge: Cambridge University Press. *31, 44, 46, 65, 71, 72, 75, 80, 83, 92, 93, 105, 116, 120, 122, 135, 150, 177, 204*

Donnellan, K. 1966. Reference and definite description. *Philosophical Review* 75: 281–304. Reprinted in Steinberg and Jakobovits (1971: 100–14). *224*

Dudman, V. H. 1983. On interpreting conditionals. *Australian Journal of Linguistics* 3: 25–44. *190, 212*

Ehrman, M. 1966. *The meaning of the modals in present-day American English*. The Hague: Mouton. *124*

Fillmore, C. J. 1968. The case for case. In Bach and Harms (1968: 1–88). *15*

Fillmore, C. J. and Langendoen, D. T. 1971. *Studies in linguistic semantics*. New York: Holt, Rinehart.

Fries, C. C. 1927. The expression of the future. *Language* 3: 87–95. *216*

Gary, J. O. and Gamel-Eldin, S. 1982. *Egyptian colloquial Arabic*. Lingua Descriptive Series, 6. Amsterdam: North Holland. *60, 123*

George, I. 1975. A grammar of Kwa-type verb serialization: its nature and significance in current generative theory. Unpublished dissertation, University of California, Los Angeles. *205*

Givón, T. 1980. The binding hierarchy and the typology of complement. *Studies in Language* 4: 333–77. *162*

1982. Evidentiality and epistemic space. *Studies in Language* 6: 23–49. *53, 74, 85, 148*

Givón, T. and Kimenyi, A. 1974. Truth, belief and doubt in Kinya Rwanda. *Papers from the fifth annual conference on African Linguistics. (Studies in African Linguistics*, Supplement 5, 95–113). *148*

Grice, H. P. 1975. Logic and conversation. In Cole and Morgan (1975: 41–58). *84*

Grimes, J. 1964. *Huichol syntax* (Janua Linguarium, Series Practica, 11). The Hague: Mouton. *33, 46, 79, 118*

Haiman, J. 1980: *Hua: A Papuan language of the Eastern Highlands of New Guinea*. Amsterdam: Benjamins. *206*

Hale, K. 1969. Papago/či-m. Cambridge, Mass.: MIT (mimeo). *212*

1976. The adjoined relative clause in Austrialia. In Dixon (1976). *105*

Hall, R. A. 1964. *Introductory linguistics*. Philadelphia and New York: Chilton Books. *146*

Halliday, M. A. K. 1970. Functional diversity in language as seen from a consideration of mood and modality in English. *Foundations of Language* 4: 225–42. *63*

Hammer, A. E. 1983. *German grammar and usage*. Reprinted 1971 publication with corrections and Supplement. London: Edward Arnold. *20, 34, 35, 52, 63, 71, 99, 104, 138, 139, 147, 183, 192, 220*

Hamp, E. P. 1982. Latin ut/nē and ut (... nōn). *Glotta* 60: 115–20. *180, 182*

Handford, S. A. 1947. *The Latin subjunctive: its usage and development from Plautus to Tacitus*. London: Methuen. *196, 197, 200, 218*

References and citation index

Hardy, H. K. and Gordon, L. 1980. Types of adverbial and modal constructions in Tolkapaya. *International Journal of American Linguistics* 46: 183–96. *214*

Haugen, E. 1976. *The Scandinavian languages: an introduction to their history.* London: Faber and Faber. *35*

Hansarling, G. 1984. Evidentials in Kogi. MS. *76*

Heny, F. and Richards, B. (eds.). 1983. *Linguistic categories: auxiliaries and related puzzles.* Dordrecht: Reidel

Hewitt, B. G. 1979. *Abkhaz.* Lingua Descriptive Series, 2. Amsterdam: North Holland. *56, 217*

Hill, K. C. 1967. A grammar of the Serrano language. Unpublished dissertation, University of California, Los Angeles. *31, 55, 56, 71, 78, 84, 118, 218*

Hiz, H. (ed.) 1978. *Questions.* Dordrecht: Reidel.

Hockett, C. F. 1958. *A course in modern linguistics.* New York: Macmillan. *2, 78, 120*

1968. *The state of the art.* The Hague: Mouton. *39*

Hofmann, T. R. 1976. Past tense replacement and the modal system. In McCawley (1976: 85–100). *103*

Hooper, J. B. 1975. On assertive predicates. In Kimball (1975: 91–124). *4, 141, 142, 143, 144, 145*

Hopper, P. J. and Thompson, S. A. 1980. Transitivity in grammar and discourse. *Language* 56: 251–99. *178*

1984. The discourse basis for lexical categories in a universal grammar. *Language* 60: 703–52. *3, 205, 206*

Huddleston, R. D. 1971. *The sentence in written English: a syntactic study based on the analysis of scientific texts.* Cambridge: Cambridge University Press. *11*

1976. Some theoretical issues in the description of the English verb. *Lingua* 40: 331–83. *25, 33, 90*

1977. Past tense transportation in English. *Journal of Linguistics* 13: 43–52. *199*

1984. *Introduction to the grammar of English.* Cambridge: Cambridge University Press. *22*

Huot, H. 1974. *Le verbe devoir.* Paris: Éditions Klincksieck. *35*

James, D. 1982. Past tense and the hypothetical: a cross-linguistic study. *Studies in Language* 6: 375–403. *210, 211, 212, 215*

Jarvella, R. J. and Klein, W. (eds.). 1982. *Speech, place and action: studies in deixis and related topics.* New York: Wiley.

Jespersen, O. 1909–49. *A modern English grammar I–VII.* Heidelberg: Karl Winter; Copenhagen: Einar Munksgaard. *160, 167*

1924. *The philosophy of grammar.* London: Allen and Unwin. *9, 10, 11, 14, 16, 18, 21, 22, 96, 116, 117, 118, 131, 178*

Joos. M. 1964. *The English verb: form and meanings.* Madison and Milwaukee,

Wisc.: The University of Wisconsin Press. *123, 211, 212*

Joseph, B. D. 1983. *The synchrony and diachrony of the Balkan infinitive*. Cambridge: Cambridge University Press. *162*

Kastovsky, D. and Szwedek, A. (eds.) 1986. Linguistics across historical and geographical boundaries: in honour of Jaček Fisiak. The Hague: Mouton, de Greute.

Kayne, R. S. 1975. *French syntax: the transformational cycle*. Cambridge, Mass. and London: MIT Press. *36*

Kimball, P. (ed.) 1975. *Syntax and semantics 4*. New York: Academic Press.

Kiparsky, P. and Kiparsky, C. 1971. *Fact*. In Steinberg and Jakobovits (1971: 345–69). *17, 140, 141, 142*

Klein, F. 1975. Pragmatic constraints in distribution: the Spanish subjunctive. *Papers from the 11th Regional Meeting, Chicago Linguistic Society*, 353–65. *4, 120, 125, 141, 143, 144, 145, 153*

Klein-Andrew, F. (ed.). 1983. *Discourse perspectives on syntax*. New York: Academic Press.

Kuno, S. 1973. *The Structure of the Japanese language*. Cambridge, Mass. and London: MIT Press *45, 148, 167*

Lakoff, R. T. 1968. *Abstract syntax and Latin complementation*. Cambridge, Mass.: MIT Press *39, 40, 170, 171*

1971. If's, and's and but's about conjunction. In Fillmore and Langendoen (1971: 114–49). *182*

Langacker, R. W. 1974. Movement rules in functional perspective. *Language* 50: 630–64. *15*

1978. The form and meaning of the English auxiliary. *Language* 54: 853–82. *211*

Lavandera, B. R. 1978. Analysis of semantic variation: the Spanish moods. (Mimeo). *183, 184*

1983. Shifting moods in Spanish discourse. In Klein-Andrew (1983: 209–36). *17*

Leech, G. N. 1969. *Towards a semantic description of English*. London: Longman. *11*

Lepschy, A. L. and Lepschy, G. 1977. *The Italian language today*. London: Hutchison. *62, 146, 153, 178*

Leslau, W. 1941. *Documents Tigrinya*. Paris: Klincksieck. *210*

Levinsohn, S. H. 1975. Functional perspective in Inga. *Journal of Linguistics* 11: 1–37. *44, 52, 60, 93*

Lewis, C. I. 1946. *An analysis of knowledge and evaluation*, La Salle, Ill.: The Open·Court Publishing Co. *14*

Lewis, G. L. 1967. *Turkish grammar*. Oxford: Clarendon Press. *43, 56, 110, 218*

Li, C. N. (ed.) 1976. *Subject and object*. New York: Academic Press.

Li, C. N. and Thompson, S. A. 1981. *Mandarin Chinese: a functional reference grammar*. Berkeley, Los Angeles and London: University of California Press. *38*, *88*

Lightfoot, D. 1975. *Natural logic and the Greek moods. The nature of subjunctive and optative in Classical Greek*. The Hague: Mouton. *170*

  1979. *Principles of diachronic syntax*. Cambridge: Cambridge University Press. *5*

Lowe, I. 1972. On the relation of the formal and sememic matrices with illustrations from Nambiquara. *Foundations of Language* 8: 360–90. *68*, *73*, *77*, *221*

Lyons, J. 1968. *Introduction to theoretical linguistics*. Cambridge: Cambridge University Press. *217*

  1977. *Semantics*. 2 vols. Cambridge: Cambridge University Press. *2*, *12*, *13*, *14*, *15*, *16*, *17*, *18*, *20*, *21*, *23*, *26*, *28*, *53*, *58*, *81*, *84*, *87*, *88*, *94*, *99*, *109*, *140*, *169*, *209*, *211*, *216*, *221*

  1982. Deixis and subjectivity: *loquor ergo sum?* In Jarvella and Klein (1982: 101–24). *27*, *82*, *83*

Malinowski, B. 1923. The problem of meaning in primitive languages. Supplement to Ogden and Richards (1923). *20*

Matthews, G. H. 1965. *Hidatsa syntax*. The Hague: Mouton. *31*, *70*, *72*, *78*, *83*

McCawley, J. D. 1968. The role of semantics in a grammar. In Bach and Harms (1968: 125–69). *170*

  (ed.). 1976. *Syntax and semantics 7. Notes from the linguistic underground*. New York: Academic Press.

Merlan, F. 1982. *Mangarayi*. Lingua Descriptive Series, 4. Amsterdam: North Holland. *105*, *133*

Moore, R. W. 1934. *Comparative Greek and Latin syntax*. London: Bell. *42*, *108*, *175*, *180*, *202*, *203*

Ogden, C. K. and Richards, I. A. 1923 (10th edn 1949). *The meaning of meaning*. London: Kegan Paul.

Olson, M. 1982. Barai clause junctures: towards a functional theory of interclausal relations. Unpublished dissertation, Australian National University. *206*

Palmer, F. R. 1957. The verb in Bilin. *Bulletin of the School of Oriental and African Studies* 19: 131–59. *52*, *210*

  1962. Relative clauses in Tigrinya. *Journal of Semantic Studies* 7: 36–43. *179*

  1974. *The English verb*. London: Longman. *25*, *90*

  1977. Modals and actuality. *Journal of Linguistics* 13: 1–23. *104*, *198*

  1978. Past tense transportation: a reply. *Journal of Linguistics* 14: 77–81. *199*

  1979a. Why auxiliaries are not main verbs. *Lingua* 47: 1–25. *16*

  1979b. *Modality and the English modals*. London: Longman. *1*, *16*, *20*, *35*, *37*, *39*, *57*, *63*, *64*, *84*, *98*, *101*, *102*, *113*, *216*, *217*

1981. *Semantics*. 2nd edn. Cambridge: Cambridge University Press. *224*

1983a. Semantic explanations for the syntax of English modals. In Heny and Richards (1983: 205–17). *91, 125*

1983b. Review of Coates 1983. *Australia Journal of Linguistics* 3: 287–93. *6, 37*

1984. *Grammar*. Harmondsworth: Penguin. *5*

Plank, F. 1984. The modals story retold. *Studies in Language* 8: 305–64. *5*

Prince, F. 1976. The syntax and semantics of Neg-raising with evidence from French. *Language* 52: 404–26. *145*

Rastorgueva, V. S. 1963. A short sketch of Tajik. *International Journal of American Linguistics* 28. *56*

Rescher, N. 1968. *Topics in philosophical logic*. Dordrecht: Reidel. *12, 13, 14, 15, 50, 87, 115, 119, 128, 129, 209*

Rivero, M.-L. 1970. A surface structure constraint on negation in Spanish. *Language* 46: 640–66. *219*

1975. Referential properties of Spanish noun phrases. *Language* 51: 32–48. *198*

1977. Specificity and existence: a reply. *Language* 53: 70–85. *198*

Robins, R. H. 1952. Noun and verb in universal grammar. *Language* 28: 289–98. *3*

Rojas, N. 1977. Referentiality in Spanish noun phrases. *Language* 53: 61–9. *198*

Rosenbaum, P. S. 1967. *The grammar of English predicate complement constructions*. Cambridge, Mass.: MIT Press. *127, 129*

Ruwet, N. 1967. *Introduction à la grammaire générative*. Paris: Plon. *36*

Salone, S. 1979. Typology of conditionals and conditionals in Haya. *Studies in African Linguistics* 10: 65–80. *215*

Sapir, E. 1929. The status of linguistics as a science. *Language* 5: 207–14. Reprinted in Sapir (1949: 160–6). *3*

1949. *Selected writings of Edward Sapir in language, culture and personality*, ed. G. Mandelbaum. Berkeley and Los Angeles: University of California Press. *3*

Schachter, P. 1976. The subject in Philippine languages. In Li (1976: 491–518). *157*

Schogt, H. G. 1968. Les auxiliaires en français. *La Linguistique* 2: 5–19. *36*

Schubiger, M. 1965. English intonation and German modal particles: a comparative study. *Phonetica* 12: 65–84. Reprinted in Bolinger (1972: 175–93). *6, 88*

Searle, J. R. 1979. *Expression and meaning: studies in the theory of speech acts*. Cambridge: Cambridge University Press. *13, 14, 27, 28, 97, 154*

1983. *Intentionality*. Cambridge: Cambridge University Press. *13, 97, 115*

Semeonoff, A. H. 1958. *A new Russian grammar*. 12th (rev.) edn. London: Dent. *194, 206*

Shell, O. A. 1975. Cashibo modals and the performative analysis. *Foundations of Language* 13: 177–99. *39, 73, 89, 94, 140*

Smith, N. V. 1981. Review of Comrie 1981. *Australian Journal of Linguistics* 2: 255–61. *3*

1983. A rejoinder to Comrie. *Australian Journal of Linguistics* 3: 97–8. *3*

Steele, S. 1975. Past and irrealis: just what does it all mean? *International Journal of American Linguistics* 41: 200–17. *56, 105, 122, 210, 211, 212*

Steele, S., Akmajian, A., Demers, R., Jelinek, E., Kitagawa, C., Oerle, R. and Wasow, T. 1981. *An encyclopedia of AUX: a study in cross-linguistic equivalence*. Cambridge, Mass. and London: MIT Press. *7, 8, 19, 20, 44, 124*

Steinberg, D. D. and Jakobovits, L. A. (eds.). 1971. *Semantics*. Cambridge: Cambridge University Press.

Strawson, P. F. 1964. Identifying reference and truth-values. *Theoria* 30: 96–118. Reprinted in Steinberg and Jakobovits (1971: 86–99). *164*

Sweet, H. 1903. *A new English grammar* vol. III. Oxford: Clarendon. *160*

Sweetser, E. E. 1982. Root and epistemic modals: causality in two worlds. *Berkeley Linguistic Society Papers* 8: 484–507. *124, 125*

Thiagarayan, K. 1981. Modal systems of English and Tamil. Unpublished dissertation, University of Madras. *61*

Thrane, T. 1983. On the universality of AUX. *Acta Linguistica Hafniensia* 18: 154–200. *3*

Tucker, A. N. and Mpaayei, J. T. O. 1955. *A Maasai grammar*. London: Longman. *110, 113, 129, 133, 152, 157, 205*

Ultan, R. 1972. The nature of future tenses. *Working Papers in Language Universals* (Stanford University) 8: 55–100. *216*

Van Ek, J. A. 1966. *Four complementary structures of predication in contemporary British English*. Gröningen: Wolters. *130*

Veloudis, I. 1982. Negation in Modern Greek. Unpublished dissertation, University of Reading. *169*

Voegelin, C. F. and Voegelin, C. M. 1975. Hopi /qa/. *International Journal of Linguistics* 41: 381–98. *163*

Watanabe, Y. 1984. Transitivity and evidentiality in Japanese. *Studies in Language* 8: 235–51. *86*

Welmers, W. E. 1973. *African language structures*. Los Angeles and London: University of California Press. *208*

Whorf, B. L. 1940. Science and linguistics. *Technological Review* 42: 229–31, 247–8. Reprinted in Whorf (1956: 207–19). *3*

1956. *Language, thought and reality; selected writings of Benjamin Lee Whorf*, ed. J. B. Carroll. Cambridge, Mass.: MIT Press. *3*

von Wright, E. H. 1951. *An essay in modal logic*. Amsterdam: North Holland. *10, 12, 16, 18, 58, 62, 102*

Zayed, S. H. 1984. A pragmatic approach to modality and the modals: with application to literary Arabic. Unpublished Ph.D thesis, University of Edinburgh. *61*, *123*

LANGUAGE INDEX

GENERAL INDEX

238